MW01241978

THE DEAD TALKS,

&

ENLIGHTENED IMAGINATION

CONVERSING WITH THE BEYOND

MEG MCKEON

GMCP

The Dead Talks

Enlightened Imagination & Conversing with The Beyond

Published and distributed in the United States by Global Mentoring Coaching Publishing Center & Trust in Vero, Florida.

Editor - Snehal R. Singh

Ebook - ASIN: B09F5C89Z5

Print - ISBN: 978-0-9996791-9-7

Hardcover - ISBN: 9798753260413

My enormous soul moved toward me, inching its way, like a search light through the dark reddish tissue of the womb, still soft with yielding pliability. I was watching myself become, a consciousness in the small body to be born, and a vibrant, ancient spirit, meeting itself, watching its own entrancement of consciousness.

Tendrils of lucidity, brilliance, moving through the closing body, inhabiting cells held in suspense before the collapse of a failed system. My mother's consciousness already gone yet not quite departed. My mother slowly fell back into herself, lightly like a feather, coming back into a prison that would keep her safely locked up for the rest of her breathing days. I saw, with every cell in my infant body, the rays of a sun spreading into the confined space of the womb, I was consciously experiencing the light of spirit, as it traveled into the narrow birth canal and breathed life into my dead mother as I lay within.

She never fully recovered, never fully ventured out from her self-made turtle shell. Never knew the miracle we experienced in this lifetime. It is this experience that I know to be truly me.

DEDICATION

I dedicate this book to all of you who have walked through pain and suffering and lived to tell. You are my hero's.

To those of you who journey the path of recovery. I applaud you! It is a way of courage that is second to none and you are giants in your spirit for walking through this life lucid.

To those dearest members of Narcotics Anonymous, you saved me. I could not have done this alone. You are my heart, and you will always have my heart. For recovering addicts all over the world. You have given this world a freedom we would have never known. I bow to you.

To Lola. You awakened the world.

To my siblings. You are the light of my life. We are the box car children. We survived. Kudos!!

To my beloved parents, grandparents, Ian my son, and especially my fiancé and my boyfriend. I wrote this book for you. You tell this story. A story about how we do evolve and recover and thrive in the beyond. You are especially loved.

Finally, to the God of my understanding and my guides. You saved my soul. I breath you in and out to give you to the rest of the world. You are my truest loves. We dance at the edge of the universe and laugh.

Ultimately: To Jason, my son. This book is for you. I adore you.

Tu eres mi vida, mi amor, y mi hijo.

CONTENTS

1.

SWEET MAMA

"Babe you just went through a red light!" He was next to me in the car, this man I had been talking to for months after Zumba. I was attracted to him. The first attraction I had after years of celibacy. It had progressed and I invited him to a salsa party. He came. We danced. We decided to join friends at a dance bar downtown. He kissed me before we left the party. The first kiss I had in years. We picked up my son Jason, we were taking him to my friend's house to hang with her kids. He was in the backseat and couldn't stop talking. He hadn't seen me with a man since his father at least six years ago.

I stopped at the light coming off the freeway. There was so much distraction in the car. Jason talking, my friend talking. My feelings of discomfort and sexual energy. I looked at the red light above me and thought it had been red for too long. I slowly drove forward, through the red light into a very busy intersection. I could not take my foot off the gas. It was surreal. Jason was screaming, my friend was talking. I was in a trance, knowing I was proceeding through a red light. I was aware and unconscious at the same time. All the cars slowed down, except one. That car was going super-fast. He did not see me; it was too far out of the scope of his awareness. I shouldn't have been there; I was invisible to this seventeen-year-old driver.

He came straight at Jason in the back seat, speeding. At the last minute he saw this ten-year-old kid with the wisdom of death in his eyes. The driver swerved into my door. He hit hard. No time to slow down. I wasn't there. Our car was hit so hard it spun out three times and hit a streetlight on the street catacorner to us. I couldn't get out of the door. We were dazed. We got out through the passenger side. I checked on the other car. A lady screamed at me, accused me of being a horrible person. Never forgot that. Never forgot that everyone is harmed in an accident. It took hours for us to get back to my house. My friend left after a 'come to Jesus' conversation. I was eight months into my 50th year on this planet at the time of this accident.

I was tranced and awake. I knew. I could not live with this awareness. I knew so much was still left to be discovered inside, even after years of knowing the most brutal parts. How could I act in a trance? This was stage 3 for me. This is when it got real. The trance was in my bones and buried deep in my stomach and heart.

 A few months later, I was getting physical therapy after the accident, the therapists asked when I had first injured my shoulder. It seemed like there had always been injury on my left shoulder and neck. I tried a trauma therapy technique, I asked the question, *"When was the first time I injured my shoulder."* I immediately went past the collar bone break in my visual memory and found myself, quite literally, in my mother's womb. I did not 'remember' that birth experience till now.

I experienced my sister leaving the womb, like a vacuum pulled her out. Almost immediately, I felt my mother's womb and the rest of her body contract around me. I was suffocating and I could feel this dreadful fear around me. My head was under my mother's ribs and her stomach juices were present somehow in my cocoon of a uterus. I could feel us both dying.

The contraction of my mother's stomach and ribs pushed my neck away from my shoulder. I believe this was the first time I broke my collar bone. My own terror was mixing with the closing down of my mother's womb.

I am a soul as big and strong as an enormous angel. I saw, with every cell in my infant body, the rays of a sun spreading into the confined space of the womb, I was consciously experiencing the light of spirit, as it traveled into the narrow birth canal and breathed life into my dead mother as I lay within.

My enormous soul moved toward me, inching its way, like a search light through the dark reddish tissue of the womb, still soft with yielding. I was watching myself become, a consciousness in the small body to be born, and a vibrant, ancient spirit, meeting itself, watching its own entrancement of consciousness.

Tendrils of lucidity, brilliance, moving through the closing body, inhabiting cells held in suspense before the collapse of a failed system. My mother's consciousness already gone yet not quite departed. My mother slowly fell back into herself, lightly like a feather, coming back into a prison that would keep her safely locked up for the rest of her breathing days. She never fully recovered, never fully ventured out from her self-made turtle shell. Never knew the miracle we experienced in this lifetime. It is this experience that I know to be truly me.

Then I literally saw light. It was like the rays of sunlight entering the womb as it was closing itself off. I experienced an awakening as if this energy were opening my mother's body. I felt bathed in light and awake. Shortly thereafter I was born. I was totally aware when I was pulled out of the womb. I am lying on a therapy table and having the most 'in body' experience I ever had.

This completely changed my whole concept of my birth and birth in general. Before I remembered what happened in utero, I was always afraid of my mother. I thought she didn't care for me, and she only wanted my sister. I now know she had the same fear of me. She was afraid I would kill her. My being in her while she was dying would have killed us both. Sue, my mother's friend and nurse, helped me to understand how ill my mother was at my birth. My mother did not reject me, she was dying.

Up to that time I thought Mama was trying to kill me. I didn't know how abusive my father was to her. How he would verbalize the meanest, cruelest, demoralizing statements to her as well. He had spat his cult conditioned spewing of dehumanizing, disempowering hateful crap to her. My father has repeatedly said he was very abusive to Mama, since we started our '*dead talks*.'

So, my mother was afraid of me like I was afraid of her. We both felt our lives threatened each other. This was what we were left with, that each was a deathly threat to the other. My mother said she truly understood what happened in our death experience after she died. It made much more sense. Still, I don't think she saw the rays of energy engulfing her body and the womb.

Mama was in the ICU for about two weeks after giving birth to my twin and I.

Mama hid from difficult situations.

I never experienced that death; not like I was gone or dark or out of the womb. Mama did. She died. I repeat that because I didn't know till today my mother died. Then she came back. She didn't experience this massive light, this sun traveling down a cavern into her womb. A sun that lit up the space with atomic rays and filled me with lightness. Mama knew she came back. She knows that her baby was there. She didn't really describe what she experienced when she came back. Her greatest experience was dying while she was giving birth. My greatest experience was being filled with light when born in the middle of our dying.

THE BEGINNING OF ABUSE & FREEDOM

For three years my parents tried to conceive, amidst new conception drugs released on the market in the late fifties. To no avail. My mother went back to New York for the summer and saw her old doctor. After many tests, the doctor confirmed she was indeed pregnant. My mother was elated. Shortly after she started to bleed and went into a total collapse and her doctor sent her back to New Mexico by train. A plane would have been too dangerous.

Mama, being the good Catholic girl she was, followed directions very carefully and arrived in Albuquerque safely. She spent the last two months of her pregnancy in bed. After three days of labor, my mother was wheeled in to have a cesarean, she was asked which one she wanted out first. "The kicker", she replied, and very soon after my sister was born. She was bloody, black, and blue at her efforts to be born. My mother looked at her and fell in love. Then she proceeded to die. I along with her. In her dying was my rebirth and resurrection. She died giving birth and was brought back to the living.

Upon delivery, I came out bright, aware, eyes open and engaged. My father looked at me and claimed me. I was chosen. Again, and again, I was chosen. To what mal intent my choosing brought for me, I was claimed, brutalized, tortured, and still I lived. This is a story of a miracle birth, and a miracle life.

There was the mundane. We were twins. My mother slowly healed her broken body after the near death at the birth of her twins. I could see my sisters' crib within our room. We would coo at each other. The other half of the whole.

I am only conscious of a shadow over me in my crib. Perhaps smelling it was my father. Sometimes hearing voices murmuring from beyond the ceiling, otherworldly. I never knew if I was still communing with those I had recently left. In a plane of existence, I still carried within me. Or if I was already dissociating from events very present. Ghost memories of fingers within my small vagina. No concept of betrayal, just penetration into internal tissue from a shadow being, not quite real to me. So much still is not quite real to me.

This is how it started the ritual abuse in cult families. Parents starting with their infants. Training them in this hideous fashion. Babies learn to dissociate to stop the pain. Always there are ghost memories formed. The pain goes somewhere. Usually deep within the body into the sacs of amnesic fluid which will hold that pain and that tiny consciousness of the baby.

Often these held experiences can be cleared by finding them and experiencing the emotional frequency they hold. Bringing our awareness into this area and allowing ourselves to experience the emotions that reside there. We do not know what caused the weight in the cells. Nor is it necessary to know. Our consciousness is strong enough to explore and surround the emotional experience with compassion. It can even be done with curiosity and acceptance. We stay next to the expression in need and breathe. We feel our own breath become loving, accepting, acknowledging.

Perhaps we will feel the emotion. More often we are there to allow the emotion and let it be there. When there is such a state of recognition and freedom then this held consciousness will feel the larger stream of compassion that our awareness brings in and the held preciousness. This burdened part of our psyche will meld with the larger stream of consciousness. The deepest animated part of us, the inner knowing that flows through us. This can often happen in 30 seconds or less, it is our presence and its state of elevation that brings the hidden to the level of the divine consciousness within us.

2.

SHE'LL BE COMING ROUND THE MOUNTAIN WHEN SHE COMES...

"Shell be coming round the mountain when she comes, she'll be comin round the mountain when she comes, she'll be comin' round the mountain......

I had a recurring dream when we still lived in Albuquerque, in my first childhood home. I was asleep in my bed, and I would hear the folk song, "She'll be coming round the mountain when she comes," I was no older than 5 and already waiting to be rescued. I would see her in my dreams. She looks a lot like I do now. Long hair whipping in the wind, while 'she' egged the horse on with a whip that never touched them. In my dream 'I' as 'she' would be coming around the Sandia Mountains. The mountain chain I loved all my life. It sits just east of Albuquerque.

"She'll be ridin' six white horses when she comes, she'll be ridin' six white horses when she comes: she'll be ridin' six white horses......

I would see the lady riding six white horses around the mountains. On her way to me. I would see her getting closer. I knew she was coming. Then she'd come to a hole in the mesa, dismount from her perch, walk to the hole in the ground and jump into it.

I would wake up. Still five years old. Yet I knew she was here. I was her. Even then she was with me. Years later, when I was lucidly dreaming my inner champion into existence and rescuing the 'energetic signatures' of the scarred children within me, that held memories of stuck trauma, it was me, the lady riding six white horses, me as a champion. I came around the mountain.

I always knew I would come. Like I wrote the script. Perhaps my soul truly considered all the things that could happen in the environment I was born into. That there was a strong chance I would not live past five or seven. I am willing to believe that I chose death as a possibility. That one act of sacrifice of deep love for another being, changed existences. I do believe we decide certain things prior to entering our lives. We listen ourselves into existence. We evolve. We may even at times, truly do what we have set out to do, prior to our births. Is it so hard to grasp that we may die, but we never perish?

At times, I felt as if this life was a mistake. I was meant to be somewhere else. This was not the life I had chosen. Why would I choose such misery? Now I own every experience I've ever had. Perhaps acceptance comes with age. My experiences led to a great peace within myself, yet it's not just me that's been rescued. I was a ragamuffin in a diamond mine. When I started picking up the diamond pieces, and seeing eternity, I created a soul's journey that's shown through every diamond shard. I came around the mountain and jumped back into my five-year-old body. Now I'm the woman riding six white horses, I fully embrace each venture. I am a beacon of becoming, a bright diamond shining, pointing out a fulfillment we can all experience.

TRYING TO MAKE SENSE OF THE LIFE I WAS LIVING

Angst! This overrides my days. There is no transparency. I emailed Shay. Giving him time to decide if he wanted to contribute or leave. I can't hear him most of the time. He either mutters or screams. There is no in between. Still, he has not given a penny. He moves and cleans like a tweaker. Ian is sure he is. He is right. This feigned character that he took on a few years ago still seems to linger.

Does he add to the general malaise? Does it create fodder to deepen the pit of memories? Does it bring up the ghost life, the dark events that were so much a part of my first eleven years that they are hard to discover as separate. It's like going into a tunnel, or a dream, it happens in spurts. I get to see a memory like I am walking towards it, or the shutter opens and reveals. I am so familiar with this mind. Still, I balk at it because it is the life and love I live now that is the result of the constant nightmares of a looming presence of invasive darkness.

I cannot help but see it as a dive into murky waters. Suddenly back to then. I'm immersed in constraint. I cannot move on my own volition. I am smothered and conquered and trapped. Then I go again, leaving a little body to endure the violations, the impenetrable suffocation. A body over mine, harsh words of discouragement. Attempts to destroy what I naturally carry, a light, a consciousness in a light body that records all of it. That can enter into the act of betrayal in spurts to guarantee engagement of a body that is all too willing to stop, shut down. My body usually does, and I come to the next day.

Hurt and imbalanced in my head. Dizzy and unable to piece together thoughts or sensations. I sit and experience the fog and the physical pain. My mind shifting like I am on a sandy tectonic plate, and it tilts in various directions, like a surfboard in a rough sea. I follow the tilt. I can see myself surfing the waves, engaging in them so I do not fall into the pain in my body, the aloneness after invasion where its not safe but its over. I fantasize about my family leaving me behind. I'm not sure if thats a blessing or a curse. I look out the second story windows and imagine them gone for longer that I imagine surfing on the sandy tectonic surfboards and just feel the sensations move through me.

The now is what is the puzzle. The man that I am with. The men I choose. It's as if I have a litany of wounded men which tie me into the puzzle of who I became from the darkness of scattered shutter shots. Who are they provides me with the fodder of who I became. Never financially contributing. This certainty cements in a childhood of no financial support from Daddy.

Over twenty years my parents were married, Daddy was enraged, extreme, abusive, and more there than my mother, who hid so well within herself. Yet why is it this aspect is most prevalent in my relationships. Shay is taciturn and struggles, very seldom is his struggle about me, yet it affects me. I watch, as I have all my life, men who struggle through their own self-centered, self-obsessed strife. Usually starting the same way, mine did, early trauma. Are they microscopic examples for me of my father? Always. In some way they mirror him.

I feel for him a deep empathy of an ongoing loss. His unwillingness to leave the house. The torture he goes through. I see him naked in my mind, his beautiful body hard. His voice hard, commanding, engaged in an argument with me. Withholding himself, his body, his love, his money. Always withholding. Perhaps that has been the realist part of my messed-up love life. The withholding, the desires never filled. The angst of not having a loving, capable partner. Yearning for care and protection and getting uncertainty.

3.

THE BARN

My younger sister remembers the other kids that would play in the house when rituals were going on. I don't remember that. I believe her though. She carries a lot of memories and still struggles with them and with sharing them. I just remember the barn. I don't know how many rituals were performed on Diane's property. I know she wasn't the grand poohbah. I believe my father when he says she was evil. I 'met' Diane many times, she came back into his life many times. I remember listening to an audio tape of an acting scene she did. It was a scene from WWII and she was the girlfriend of a navy boy. The monologue was quite good. She kept reiterated that 'lose lips sink ships' and all that.

What happened to the kids? Why can't I remember playing with kids at Diane's? My reaction to her is visceral. I remember she came into store I was working at. I felt my lips snarl. All I remember is her voice in the barn.

She was influential in the cult. I don't know exactly how. I remember her barn; how big it was. I also remember, in bits and spurts, being raped by Daddy and Diane in that barn. I just know Daddy left us for her. I'm not sure why he came back truthfully. Except that I do know why. We'll get to that.

Daddy had a bookstore in Corrales, NM. It seemed like it was a half-finished building. I remember it well enough to try to find it again the many times I drove through Corrales. Especially when Maureen and her husband Mike built their adobe house there. I never could find the bookstore again.

I didn't really remember the ritual abuse. I just had this strange ghost memory of being put in a coffin. I could never believe it. I then worked with my sponsor in California. She kind of scared me. She was very honest about her childhood trauma and eventually about being subject to ritual abuse. Our 'sponsor' family was comprised of several women with severe childhood abuse and more than one ritual survivor. I admired them.

I was taking care of my sponsee's mother's apartment in San Diego for a month. It was right above the ocean in Encinitas and lovely. It gave me the opportunity to visit my sponsor and do step work with her. We were doing the 9th step, making amends. I told her about my ghost memory of being buried. She stopped and looked at me. She said that ritual happens. It is often the first ritual that children experience between four and six years old. My world tilted. I never imagined this could be true.

She gave me a ritual abuse survival manual. I went back to San Diego and called a good friend of mine. I was devastated. I knew this had happened to me. I knew I had been put into a coffin with the bones of the dead below me. I remember the coffin closing and the feeling that I couldn't get to God anymore. I had a tantrum.

I had accepted death but the idea that I couldn't leave my body and be held by that consciousness that was always there, felt like I was being damned to eternal hell, and I wouldn't ever know the God consciousness again. I spent weeks going within, while I was in California, surrounded by those nonphysical beings that had been loving to me all my life. It was the hardest truth to face. I spoke to few people.

When I returned to Arizona, I was still very vulnerable. I agreed to speak at the NA convention. I had just celebrated 28 years clean a few months before. I decided to share about my newly acknowledged awareness of the ritual abuse at the convention. I was slotted for 9 in the morning. I just knew that I was about to break the deepest secret I knew publicly. I was speaking of situations that people are killed for speaking out about. My sponsors' cousin was killed for telling what he saw in a ritual.

I was speaking on the eleventh step. Which states, "We sought through prayer and meditation to improve our conscious contact with God as we understood him, praying only for knowledge of his will for us and the power to carry it out."

I told the group about being buried in a coffin. I felt like I had broken a cardinal rule, "don't talk, don't trust, don't feel" goes much deeper than I had known. I violated a ritual code. I spoke my experience. I spoke eloquently on the eleventh step and the ritual abuse I spoke of was accepted by my peers. One of the women listening spoke to me afterwards. She remembered her own horrible experience when hearing my story. I know this started her on the amazing journey of becoming whole. Only I felt anything but whole.

I spent the afternoon hanging out with a group of men, which included several of my friends. I really couldn't speak. One friend had heard me speak that morning and turned to me and said I was very brave for speaking my truth. Only I didn't feel brave. I needed the men around the table. I had broken a taboo by speaking about being buried. I felt catatonic as if at any time I could be killed. If only this was just a fear. Many children never survive ritual abuse. My fear had merit. I was here. I was brave. Every ounce of my champion was almost not enough to overcome what I had experienced and what I had spoken. These men gave me solace. It took me over a year to really come to terms with the ritual abuse.

I read much of the abuse manual and heard the stories of extreme abuse and death. I didn't relate to any other experience addressed there. Yet it wasn't until my father told me the full extent of the rituals

I was subjected to, that I knew what I had lived through, and what my ability to be a champion had actually done for me.

I don't know what happened to the kids my sister saw. Many may have died. Ritual abuse is an addiction to death. Whether it's real or acted out, children don't know the difference. Ritual participants are often raised in satanic cults and are systematically disempowered. They become zombies but also get off on death. My brush with the world my father was raised in and how he rose through the ranks was eventually revealed to me. I am alive, truthfully and wholly, and I am grateful, but just barely.

4.

THEY KNEW

They go for the soul. But souls are so resilient. People can do the most horrible things imaginable. But we can also overcome just about anything and still be striving for health and wholeness and spirituality.

"Safe Passage to Healing: A Guide for Survivors of Ritual Abuse"

They Knew. Born from a prince of darkness, one prince of darkness among many, in a society as large as the Catholic church. Hidden, dark, powerful. Filled with members wealthy beyond compare. Long standing, with generations of worshippers.

Each one of them once a child overwhelmed with pain. Raised in dissociation. Programmed to dissociate with torture.

Experiments of overstimulation resulting in more dissociation. How much pain could be withstood before killing the infant. How much stimulation at predetermined intervals? How many stimulants or scary faces, loud noises, bad tastes, and suffocation was necessary to induce the child's conscious awareness to be encapsulated in a barrier of amnesia. How much electric current could a baby withstand before succumbing to the psychological dissociation.

But they saw me. Immediately. Brought into the 'circle of power and brutality' after birth. They saw what he saw. The prince of darkness. They saw the light. My light. My gift of birth. My resurrection. My conscious unwinding of my ancient soul, tall as the Eiffel tower, glorious, as it wrapped itself around my infant body. Intertwining the light of innocence with the breathing, pulsating tendrils of the essence of my eternal soul, a being so present. I was shrouded in light and understanding, the ethereal waves of bounty moved my newly molded body. Dancing gently in the constant intimate play of light, touching lightly, and leaving golden sparkles encapsulated in my viscera. Like a thousand stars alight within this newborn body.

They recognized my resurrected spirit within this newly emergent body. And I was chosen. From the beginning. It was always to be so. I was chosen, a most desirous sacrifice, sublime. Delicious. Filled with breath of the divine. The power to be had by sacrificing this child, to be tasted, given to the highest beast of Satan. This was truly glorious. It was spoken by those who reigned, yet not to the prince of darkness, not yet. He was high enough, in his generations of relatives who participated in this worship, for his daughter to be among the highest, the exalted.

I was groomed to be wed. Programmed with enough fear to lose all to the amnesic encapsulation of each painful memory of forced trauma. The sophisticated indoctrination of torture designed to create malleable creatures and split them from their consciousness. The dissociation worked. For many, many years I did not know the many ceremonies I was involved in. According to the prince of darkness there were at least 10 -15 ceremonies. Many where I was buried in a coffin. That ritual seems to be quite effective for children. Horrifically, engineered to build doubt of one's place in the world and in self.

Yet I was alive. In my consciousness. Delighted in moving within the life enfolding me. I felt the quality of the moving stream of cells cascading in my body. I knew the ineffable and experienced the air against my skin. The dissociations started infrequently, never dissipating my young delight of life. Each episode remaining unique and unknown yet having the desired effect of holding painful experiences deeply buried, to be called up at will. No burial, no painful abuse unremembered could separate the light that surrounded me. I could not be undone. I could not 'unshine'.

A delectable innocence, ripe with light, magnificent in the brilliance of spirit. The sacrificial delicacy. After seven years of rituals, of 'celebrations of life and death'. I lived through the intended sacrifice, the proposed marriage to the beast Satan. I survived the satanic cult. I was whisked away by the same prince of darkness, in the middle of the ceremony, a spark of his own humanity, took me into his arms, and out of the ceremony of sacrifice of his living princess, the highly prized sacrificial lamb.

To the roar of the calamitous reaction of the Priest and high council. A visceral growling of the crowd. The reaction of jackals denied their kill, their addictive delight of destroying a young girl, dismembering her body. They climbed the walls to tear into his skin. The erotic feeling of total lustful, slaying power denied. The hatred was palpable, as was the demonic desire to tear us both limb from limb,

I do not know what it felt like to leave. Yet I do know, in my gut I can feel their hatred. My father was banished for his actions. He who participated in the planning and production of this high ceremony, was cast out, torn asunder. He was barred from the sect for his intrusion into the ultimate sacrifice to the devil.

Later I was cursed. At eight years old I was cursed. A curse to punish my father, the betrayer, the ostracized, the prince who stole the crown jewel from his master. He would suffer as I suffered, and as I would for years to come, at his hand, the humiliation, the internal crumbling of my beautiful heaven. The cult couldn't do it, though, not quite, they could not drown me in pain or evil. They could never separate me from the heavens. I could not be conquered.

Yet the curse was heavy on my soul, and it ate away at my young being. Ate at me from the inside out. I heard voices of shame, of pity and slander of a self, spoken by my father in the dark dank basement as he too punished me for his banishment. I was burned, rejected, hurt and hated. He took it upon himself to try to destroy me for his moment of fatherhood.

Those within me, carrying their painful experiences of what we had seen, what we had experienced, they too were plunged into a darkness. Not the accepted darkness, rich in its promise of protection within the cult, the celebration at thirteen of becoming a full member, now one of the strong, the powerful, the protected. Part of a society, ancient and strong, 100-fold or more societies that make up the Satanist community. No, this darkness consisted of standing alone or lying buried underneath a man who hated me for his one redeeming act of protection.

I was folding into a self-obsession, finally believing all of the horrid voices and painful torture that plagued my mind and body. From eight to perhaps fourteen, the curse ate at me. Ate the beauty of the resurrection, the knowing bond of light, flowing freely from the eternal to my heart. I was crushed by the continuing incest, the words spoken to break my spirit, while my body was ravaged, and my spirit hung above me.

My leg breaking at my hip, was the beginning of being saved from this ongoing hell. At eleven, I tripped over a campsite while we picnicked. My father, white as a ghost, drove the family home and was turned away at the local hospital. It took a two-hour drive to Santa Fe, listening to deeply painful moans from me at every turn and twist in the road, to receive help. I could feel his thoughts, his fear, his terror at what he had done to the daughter he loved and yet wanted to tear apart for the light in her eyes. He took me to the hospital and saw me cared for and left.

He never came into the hospital again. He stood below my second story window when my family would visit. Banning himself for his satanic torture. I was hospitalized for six weeks, in a trance of pain and plagued by roommates tortured by the attempts to save their lives. In the middle of the night, machines sucked out mucus from their lungs and throat, while the inebriated patients screamed into the mouthpiece, the injustice of the attempts to take away their slow descent into a liquid death. Other patients, screaming the names of narcotics that would surely cure the delirious pain they found themselves in.

While I was recovering from a life of preparation into the descent of hell, my roommates rotated in and out of the nunnery turned hospital and were bound to bedposts until their rational minds drew them back to the streets, where they could die in peace, the liquid death and the narcotic OD, to be found with eyes dilated and bowls empty. I never saw one roommate. Just heard their treatments in the middle of the night. Followed by the sounds of screams in various parts of the hospital. Truly a macabre experience, so befitting my cursed state.

Then came the nurses. They surrounded my small tv set on my bedside table and gathered to watch General Hospital and Days of Our Lives. These souls, seeking time to share another story not of their making, became my blanket of love. Never over demonstrative. They would just gather around me, protective, without the lack of obsessive focus, but nevertheless they were the angels that gathered while my spirit moaned and mewed its way back to life.

Each night a coke followed the Pepto Bismol meant to assist bowel movements, which were only successful with enemas. The hip break made it too painful for my small arms to lift me up on the bar. This only served to further the spasms of my shattered femur. The scenario was straight out of American Horror Story.

Yet this was sanctuary for me as a child, dissociated and indoctrinated into the deadliest of societies, unaware truly of the fate that was meant for my demise, not knowing of the patient plodding and obsessive delight of those that dwelled upon how they would send me to my Satan husband, as a prize for the beast of hell. I was brilliant at seven years old, the age I was to be sacrificed, still encased in the golden light of spirit, a chosen one. By eleven the curse had run its toll.

Now safe in a horrid hospital, amid the screams of the undead or soon to be. Nurses surrounding my small body, leg raised in a sling, vulnerable to those that would seek me out if they hadn't had already cursed me. This is the me that I truly adore. My sweet girl. My survivor, my sweet angel, trapped in an internal hell, damned by those that would be pleasured eating her dismembered body, tasting the sweetness of the marinated soul now imprisoned in a cult's idea of hell. She is my beautiful baby and I bask in her glorious ability to survive. The curse broken sometime between my internment in the hospital, before beginning middle school at sixth grade, and the start of high school.

The curse was broken. I did not lose the deep anxiety of the years of abuse. Only drugs kept that at bay. For all time, though, I was free from the family abusers. I would in turn find others. A history like mine, sought out that which it did not know, until the time I came to see how deeply flawed my ability to relate was, and how I only knew betrayal bonds, relationships mired in stress, pain, and betrayal. Never though, could it be compared to the evil unknown, kept hidden through painful dissociation until only now am I learning of my life before seven. Now when I know deeply who I am and still immerse myself in the richness of my spirit. I realize I was never broken. Sometimes anger alone, kept me whole.

5.

BROKEN MORNINGS

In therapy I remembered the mornings after. I walked into therapy session with a headache, feeling woozy. I thought, this is how I felt so many mornings. I felt broken. I was dizzy. My body hurt badly. I had headaches. For years I thought I might have an aneurysm. I wanted to have scans done in case I had something wrong. I believe I did have something wrong. I was hurt, raped, tortured by my father and the cult. Yet the next day it was as if nothing had happened. No one acknowledged any wrongdoing. My mother still lived in a bell jar. I was afraid of her trying to kill me so I wouldn't mention anything to her. I do believe my father enhanced that fear.

At the very least he must have told me no one else cared for me, no one would come for me. I still don't believe words. They have no meaning to me. I rely on what I see, and what I sense and feel. I also rely more on tone, which conveys the emotional content of the discussion.

So, in the morning I was broken, dazed. My memory was of being alone when I felt like that. I fantasized a lot about my parents being gone and me taking care of the other children. Eventually that happened several years later. Still at this time, I often woke up with dizzy brain, which continued till I was eleven, I also often woke up broken. Unable to utilize my brain. Unable to remember and feeling numb, experiencing dizziness like I was desperately trying to integrate what was going on with my body and brain and I couldn't process it. I do believe this creates neural mapping that is wired differently. It's a wiring more like a battle zone. I am sure I tensed up during the abuse. I know now that this can cause tension in the brain and wrinkles in the fascia that impairs the brain functions.

6.

WHERE DID YOU GO?

M y mother told me a story once about my father. It was shortly after they separated. We stayed with my mother in Las Vegas. It wasn't the first time they separated. The first time I remember daddy was staying in the country. We would visit him and wade in the river. There was an outhouse right outside the house he was staying in. I remember dancing the jitterbug with him. He would throw me over his back. It was thrilling.

After my father left, when they separated, my mother told me that my father would leave for work every day when they lived in Albuquerque. She thought he still worked at St. Joseph College. One day one of us kids got sick, it was snowing outside, and she couldn't leave. She needed him to come home. She called St Joseph's and asked to speak to my father. She waited for several minutes for someone to come back online. When they did, a woman told my mother that my father had not worked at St. Joseph's for over a year. I believe that was the beginning of the unraveling.

I also believe that for much of that time my father was having an affair with Diane. My father stated that in a recent reading. We speak often through a marvelous medium. Diane lived in Corrales; she had a barn. I believe my father was introduced to the Satanists in Albuquerque through Diane. I think several rituals were done on her property. It must have been close to a graveyard. That seems to be a rather essential part of the rituals. I have ghost memories of being abused in her barn by both Diane and my father. My father was raised in Ohio. In a cult, that both his parents participated in. My father was destroyed before his teenage years. He returned the favor by destroying the lives of his children and stepchildren, he most likely destroyed other cult children as well. Of course, the life span of cult children can be rather short.

When my mother was nine months pregnant, my father left her to be with Diane. He told me recently he couldn't believe he had left his wife to be with Diane. My mother took a taxi to Diane's house and banged on the door. No one answered. Shortly afterward my youngest sister was born. Perhaps this is when my mother disappeared completely into her bell jar. She wouldn't name my sister. My father didn't want her either. My sisters' birth was a tragedy that my sister still feels in her bones. It took some time for my mother to name my sister.

This was the environment that caused my father to look for another job and end up in Las Vegas, New Mexico. We moved into the rickety cold beautiful Victorian brick house. My youngest sister had a crib in a small room behind my parents' bathroom. I imagine her ignored and neglected. When she was five, she set the room on fire. She was moved upstairs with the rest of us. The move to Las Vegas opened a whole new ritual community for my father. This time he did not involve us children in the rituals. The damage had already been done. That's another story. This one is about the neglect we lived with. As well as the confusion as to who loved us, if any adult within our lives was capable of that.

My father played the piano beautifully. He would play the blues. He had long fingers. I loved hearing him play the piano. He also played classical and Spanish music. He smoked a pipe with cherry tobacco. I loved that smell. He seemed, in so many ways, so peaceful. He read a lot. He always had a drink. I didn't realize he spent most of his time stoned with that drink in his hand. This was the daytime reality. Mama hired a housekeeper, Mrs. Gallegos. She also became the babysitter. She would talk to herself and was mean to us.

Daddy found a job working in the library at Highlands University. He was gone for several weeks finding a job. He would come home and bring us candy. We moved into a three-story brick Victorian house, which had no insulation. Maureen and I were six at the time, we were going into second grade. Mama was hired as the head librarian of the public library, a block from our house. In so many ways Las Vegas was a peaceful mountain town. The nightmare remained hidden for many years.

The worse thing Mrs. Gallegos did was to hang my baby brother out of my second story window. He must have been about four years old. I came in when she was holding him by his ankles and shaking him upside down. He liked to open my screen window and look out. When I came in and found him being shaken upside down, I froze. I also felt like I went into her body to try to stop her. One thing about persistent sexual abuse, I always left my body. It seemed relatively easy to enter other bodies. I liked entering trees and birds too. Anyway, she scared me. I may have screamed; I was so scared that she would drop him.

It is still the worst memory I have. No matter what happened to me. I could take it. The thought of her dropping my brother out of my second story window was terrifying. She was hateful. We ran away from her and voyaged to my father's job, at Highlands library. I don't think he was there. My father always seemed more affectionate than my mother. She would come home and bury her head in a book.

When my sons were born, I was afraid that I would drop them from a large height. We lived in Portland and would bike on the Hawthorne Bridge. I was afraid I would push them over the bridge. It was like I retained a portion of Mrs. Gallegos' desire to drop and hurt my brother. I was terrified of boys around heights. I would imagine throwing them off a height and scare myself. I avoided heights for this reason. I scared myself just thinking about harming them in this way. I never wanted to harm my boys. In a way it taught me how children grow up to do horrid things to children.

It's like the child jumps into the body of the perpetrator, feels the overpowering power to subdue and subjugate the child. It was a horrible feeling, to feel the anger and hatred Mrs. Gallegos felt for this young boy, my brother. Abuse is always a shameless act which is an attempt to reduce the shame within the perpetrator. I felt that fear of hurting others, terrified I could possibly do shameless acts to my children. They tell me I screamed too much. Thank God they don't know how scared I was about perpetuating abuse.

Thank God screaming was as bad as I got although I did fight with my siblings. My sister and brother still think of me as very loving and very mean. The fear of hurting others was always present. My tongue can be a wicked tool that slashes those not deserving of the judgement I hold. Especially of companies I still depend on for services. I can get very irate at their inability to meet my needs. I realized a long time ago that my needs were never met. This anger, when they are not met now, is displaced. Now I have a voice and will use it. It is often stronger than it needs to be. A sponsor once told me when our reactions are stronger than the situation calls for, it is based in the past.

Since my neuro mapping was quite warped it can often be difficult to modulate my reactions. I am all too aware of the difficulty of being right sized for the right occasion. Compassion helps.

After she died, my mother told me she felt like she lived in a jar in this lifetime. Perhaps it was a bell jar, like Silvia Plath. My mother went away. She was never present. She still grieves this now. She is learning to be a mother. I thought my mother and Mrs. Gallegos were trying to kill me. We sought out our father. My father drew two naked women on the wall in the basement. Mama and Mrs. Gallegos. How does one reconcile a murderous father and a ghostlike mother? One leaves, too bad I couldn't take my body with me. That would come later when I became a champion.

In that six-month period of nightly 'alcohol driven honest' talks my mother and I had, she also told me that my father raped her repeatedly for six years. The timeline fit well to our living in Las Vegas. I never told her about the incest. I hid that reality from even myself until I got clean.

I thought my mother was trying to turn me against my father. Consciously he was still the rescuer even though he would organize us to 'thumbs down' our food and do other childish acts to offend her. He often acted like the spiteful oldest child. His spite and rage were much more malicious than childish games at the dinner table. That is what my mother was trying to tell me.

When we started contacting my loved ones in the medium readings, it was still hard for my mother to be present even in her nonphysical form. She hovered. Yet I know she accepted the bell jar she created for herself during the abuse she too suffered. Now though, my mother has come full circle. It was only after her death that she grieved her greatest loss. It was her intense desire to be a loving mother. I was privileged to see my mother become a glorious mother in the beyond. I watched her blossom into the sweetest, most loving, attentive mother.

It took her forgiving herself for locking her heart away. She now takes care of the babies in the meadow, the ones who are killed or die soon after birth. She is phenomenal. The greatest awakening came when our family did a medium reading to heal the family. It was clear that our lungs, which are tied to grief, and our stomachs, which is tied to anxiety, were still so injured within our genealogy. It felt like my mothers' lungs had not healed after she died at our birth. When we meditated as a full family, my mother, father, son, and fiancé on the other side; and all of us siblings present physically, my younger sister felt intense pain in her stomach. My mother was so present and loving with her. At our next reading my mother was beaming. She had given love to her daughter, a daughter she had abandoned in this life. The metamorphosis was astounding. We do amazing healing when we work across the veil, for both sides.

My father has stated several times he was horribly abusive to mama. My father's willingness to accept who he was in this life has helped him to raise his frequency and be willing to address what he did. I am truly now blessed with a tremendous love for my parents, and their willingness to be a part of my healing in this life in their nonphysical forms.

7.

"THE SACRIFICE"

L osing Thorne was painful in so many ways yet finding him, in spirit, and journeying with him to see who he is now has completely changed my life. The first impact was learning that my dead, Satanist father, was waiting for him when he passed. When he 'came to', my father was there waiting for him. When I learned that, my heart melted for my father. This man that was so evil and destructive to me and so many others, was present for the man I loved, when he transitioned into a different consciousness.

The gift of their relationship is that I now have a relationship with both my father and mother. In many ways I am coming to know them deeper than I ever have. I now know two 'spirits' unbound by their own foibles, those strangling acts, deeds and thoughts about ourselves and others, that strangle us and often lead directly to our deaths. It can be a little unnerving how much the dead are with us. My father and Thorne love to ride in the car with me. They are here, around me a lot. Still, it is their choice to be here and to me, it gives a much deeper meaning of love.

My mother, on the other hand, struggled to accept how she lived her life. She shows up fainter than the gentlemen. It is harder to be present for her. She told me how she cut herself off. According to her, she's had many lifetimes of pain, yet this one of hiding, not seeing, not acknowledging, and not facing the sins of herself and others, this life gives her pain. In our last conversation, she said "even these two have a higher frequency than I do." Referring to Thorne and my father.

There is humor in heaven. Still, I cherish when my mother is willing to show up. This is the gift of death. I've learned there truly is a life review. My father told me when he experienced his review, he realized, only then, who he had been and what he had done.

Since there is an absence of self-flagellation in heaven (my choice of words), there is so much more acceptance of ourselves possible.

Now I ask questions. After a lifetime of struggling to remember what happened, I am given the gift of finding out. My parents and Thorne are willing to be a part of this book. They are giving themselves an opportunity to heal, and they advised me that it is much easier to face life issues on earth than in heaven. One must be committed to accept who they are, and having the opportunity to speak to loved ones here allows them a deep growth. Our loved ones still feel on that side, which is amazing to know that what doesn't leave us is our emotions or sensory experiences.

The first question I asked my father was about the satanic rituals he was involved in and why had he allowed me to be buried in a coffin. This was his story:

The Sacrifice:

Daddy grew up in a household of Satanists. Both his father and his mother were ritual participants. My grandmother had a rare blood type and lost three of the six babies she carried. My father had a complete blood transfusion at birth. My Aunt was born with retardation and cerebral palsy. This may not have had anything to do with their participation in Satanism, yet crucifying babies seems to be a common ritual. Certainly, makes me wonder. My grandparents were extremely abusive to my father, and most likely my aunt as well. Ritualistic societies are extremely effective at de-humanizing children. My father never told me about the abuse he endured. Of course, that would break the code of silence. However, when came out and I read it, I knew that my father had experienced similar horrors to the book "Sybil." The abuse of tying a child to the piano for hours was one that my father experienced.

Daddy's family was high up in the cult. He was groomed to lead. This played a large part in the event that my father told me about. This telling changed my life in many ways:

Daddy became an active part of a ritualistic cult in Albuquerque. There is a network of cults across the country, or he just had some ability to find what he has always known and lived. However, it happened, Daddy became a member of a cult in the village of Corrales, on the outskirts of Albuquerque. There he began his affair with Diane, a woman who appears to influence in this group greatly.

I know that I was abused by both Daddy and Diane in the barn. I remember the smells and the hay, things that would catch my attention in my dissociation. Daddy was a part of this group since we were born. Daddy was rising in the ritual status. It seems that the acts he needed to perform became more macabre as he rose. Sometime right before or after my 5th birthday I broke my collarbone when Sheila accidentally overturned the wooden swing and my year-old brother and I fell out.

I was hurt badly; I broke my left collarbone. I still have problems in my neck from my head being pushed to the side so violently when we fell. I wore a cast for my collar bone. At one point the cast cracked when we were jumping on my parents' bed. My babysitter gasped and told me to look in the mirror. It was like her fear and my fear jumped into the healing bone.

It became an area of fear and numbness for me for most of my life. I know that incest and ritual abuse survivors are often preyed upon since birth. I remember being molested in my crib. I remember his body standing over me. I've known that the abuse started that early and was systematic. By the time I broke my collar bone I was very fragile and very adept at dissociation and being programmed.

I asked daddy about my memory of being put in the coffin during a ritual and how I had a tantrum and was taken out. From that experience I never trusted people, especially groups of people. I felt deeply that their intent was to kill me. Daddy then told me much more than that happened. Daddy said Diane was evil and she had been pushing Daddy for some time to involve me in a ritual. I was seen by the cult as a 'wounded lamb' that had been the outcome of the rituals and manipulative dissociations.

However, I was also considered to be very "God-like, or angelic". In some ways I believe I never truly entered my body fully. As it turns out I was a prime example of what they sought. To capture the spirit of innocence in a ritual. The more innocent the victim, the more power they gained, as if one could ever truly 'eat' the innocence of another being.

My father, in his rise to become a 'priest' in this group, was part of this decision. He was actively planning my sacrifice. Perhaps that is the worst thought of the whole experience, that my father would plan to kill me. This event was regarded as a lofty event because of both my brokenness and my angelic innocence. I also think there was a sense of the spiritual being I am and have been on the other side. Now I remind you. I am learning this from my disembodied father, who has proven time and again how much he adores me. I know this information is not only to heal me but for him to accept perhaps the single most evil and vile act he attempted. He was willing to sacrifice his daughter.

What has helped him to grow and accept who he was is his willingness to own what he has done, who he really was. What he attempted to do. My gift is sight. I see the meadow that I created in heaven. I see the children there. While any recollection of this in my five-year-old mind is hidden away, I saw the event as my father said it, just as I saw the event of me being put in a coffin. I remember screaming and kicking to get out of the coffin.

I was there in my larger consciousness and as the broken, angelic little girl. I was wearing a white nightgown. I wonder if I had been aware of other children in white as the rest of us played inside. I can see myself led down a path towards the gathering. My father is not with me, I am led by adults, perhaps Diane is there.

I am terrified and yet more out of my body than in, the energy of the group is somber, and the feeling of an elevated event is strong. I do not know if there is a leader however, I believe there is. I believe that he is the one that put me in the coffin. I do know my reaction is the same. Abject terror, incomprehensible fear that God couldn't find me in a coffin if I was alive. I can imagine walking towards the group, fires in candelabras and eyes on me. I know there was a central area. I think I was placed there briefly and perhaps this coffin was one built for sacrifice.

I was in a coffin when my father entered the scene. I can imagine him opening the coffin and me pleading with him to get me out. This juncture was crucial for my father. This was his moment to prove his commitment to the cult, or his daughter. A daughter he had groomed for the cult since birth. I begged him and pleaded with him, so terrified. He picked me up and all hell broke loose. The priest forbade him to rescue me, the cultists coming out of the trance of death addiction and realizing the break of ritual they were seeing. I almost can't imagine myself living through this, but I know it's a pivotal point in both of our lives and greater existence.

My father carries me out. I believe they did everything to stop him. He came alive. He stopped me from being murdered. I paid for that act for another seven years, in the basement at home with his sadistic torture and rape. Partly because he lost his standing, his opportunity to advance in a society with ties around the world. With members of the highest society killing off both worthy sacrifices and those easily found, the homeless, prostitutes, young pregnant cult members, those who told and died for breaking the code.

My father took me home. He was ostracized by this cult. Banned from ever returning. His royalty no longer mattered. His given rise from his respected lineage no longer mattered, whatever leadership or priesthood he was groomed for stopped for the rest of his life. My father resisted his own rise to power to save and keep me alive. In so doing he created a shift in his future. He saved his soul and lost his stature. Only after death could he see how he changed his soul's trajectory. He opened a window to another possibility. My father continued to participate in rituals for many years, as he slowly drank himself into prostate cancer. His metastasis of addictions to alcohol and the ritual of killing. He continued to sexually abuse me till I broke my leg at eleven.

My father told me this. What I love about the dead the most is that they don't lie. My father told me his hand is on mine while I'm writing. He wants to blow this wide open. He feels it's time that this abuse stops. He is doing this with me. Hearing this was a bittersweet pill. It was easier to take knowing that my connection to spirit has always been whole in this life. Therefore, I've been given beautiful visions to help me find every part that was 'encompassed in a barrier of amnesia'.

I was given the strength to save myself and provide a map for others, whether alive or dead to return to self. To grow. Finally, I asked my father and Thorne why I would be willing to participate in a barbaric life, in a family ran by a power obsessed father, who saved me and then continued the abuse. What could motivate me to participate in a life like this? I truly believe we make agreements before we are born. I wanted to know why I would willingly agree to this. Both my father and Thorne looked at me and stated that I did this for them. I was on a level higher than they had evolved too and I am a part of their spirit tribe. I did this for their evolution. Yet we are all healers.

This answer brought me to an understanding of myself which completely changed how I saw myself. I know who I am. I know that I make decisions, sometimes based on previous agreements. Now I am willing to accept a commitment even if I may question why I am doing it, if I feel a strong pull to participate, I may have agreed to do this long ago. I trust my soul. This is the greatest gift of my life. I trust my soul. I learned to love myself, because of the decisions I made in response to my deadly childhood. I am eternally grateful for the visions I have been freely given. Now, more than ever, I trust my soul. I just don't always go willingly.

The fear of betrayal is still very real to me, especially with men. Can you blame me? However, this life has been beautifully played out to create even more of who I am. I am a healer and a teacher beyond a shadow of a doubt. I am willing to lose a life to assist a beloved being to find their soul. To awaken from a misery of contrast, to move further into exquisite evolution. Yes, it took me sixty years to write this story. To be able to help many to realize who they truly are. This is so much greater than me. I evolve with each word, and still walk through my earthly mistakes and sloppy efforts. I am eternally grateful to glimpse my largest self on this earth and know who I really am.

To those who struggle to regain themselves after similar experiences. I wish to tell you that the strength and fortitude you build within, is the single most important gift you will give yourselves. However, I could not have even stayed the course without a stronghold of family members, good friends, lovers, therapists, and fellow recovering travelers. At times I had to build my inner strength by watching brave men and women face their own demons. Sometimes it was their deaths that motivated me to continue.

Addiction recovery opened a door to a deeper, inner recovery and a place that I could talk about the realest, rawest, parts of my story. Many thanks to my sponsors who have literally been there when I realized the most horrible parts of my story. The greatest thanks to those angels and guides and dead loved ones that have carried me through my life and stand at awe of what I have managed to do. Most of all I thank the Beloved! God as many would say, for being a true living being within me and in every molecule I breathe. May I do thy will always! Allow me to bring back those souls that ache so badly to our meadow. Allow us to one day see their healing flowing over a thousand meadows in your Garden of Eden. May we bring them peace and raise them on their journey. Allow this story to heal souls.

> "I want clinicians, therapists, mental health workers, and survivors to understand that for ritual abuse survivors breaking the silence constitutes breaking the bonds of mind

control and programmed messages. The ritual torture, cannibalism, the dismemberment, were all used specifically, repeatedly, systematically over a period of time to indoctrinate me to the sick and harmful worldview of someone else."

Adam, "Safe Passage to Healing: A Guide for Survivors Of Ritual Abuse": *Chrystine Oksana*

8.

NIBUS

Perhaps it was a dream. I don't remember this happening in real life. Not even sure I ever saw the dilapidated house I remember being in. This might be a dream. As I have realized, important events in life may not always be based in this reality.

I was in the dilapidated house. In the bedroom. It seemed to me that the event was more detailed than that. There was a coming to the bedroom. However, that is not the moment that stands out. Nor is it the livingness that continues to be an essential part of now.

There was an old-fashioned mirror in the bedroom. One that had legs attached to the middle of the frame. The mirror was long and thin. I could see myself in the mirror. I am young, as I was young when I had this experience. There was fear. As if I were in a haunted house and was frightened at what could happen, or perhaps the trepidation of what I was about to experience.

While I looked in the mirror, what I saw changed. I was now in an attic. Still looking at the mirror. A woman was looking back at me. The change caught my breath. Yet I was also in the bedroom. To this day I do not know exactly what she looks like. I know it was me in another life. I called her Nibus. She has dark hair. The fear feels like I am crossing a boundary, as if her being here is not common.

She was, uncommon. There was also a feeling of others being there. She was the one that was important. I wanted to run. The fear was still there. The feeling of the house being haunted. Nibus still feels otherworldly, a little scary. As if I don't know what she lived. She is still me. It was strange knowing this so young.

Nibus came to the meadow. She is essential in the meadow. She is of now and then and her continuity is important. She was my distant past and is still a mystery. So is the visit to the haunted house. A place I have never been.

Except that she is me, and the mystery of me. Where I found her, a place that still feels unreal, as if I never experienced it in the world, yet it is, was and will be always real.

Nibus is a strong part of the family we built in the meadow. I do not know what role she takes. She is there when I go there, almost as if she is a pillar. Like one of stones in an Indiana Jones adventure film, that keeps the grounding between what I imagine within a body and what is created in the non-virtual. Nibus lives. She is another tie to who I am now, and what I have always been, and will continue to be.

9.

OVERARCHING RESPONSIBILITY FOR IRRESPONSIBLE ACTS

C hildren raised with trauma are groomed to take responsibility for shameless acts. We can thank John Bradshaw, counselor, and one of the most influential writers on emotional health, for speaking that truth. It may have been him that stated, "Children will take on the shame of shameless acts."

I'm going further. I have taken on the responsibility for irresponsible acts since birth. By irresponsible I also mean shameless and acts of torment, violence, abuse perpetrated on others, usually harmless others. Young babies and children who have no capability to care for themselves, who then 'take in' the shame of a shameless act. They carry that shame, or the essence of the shame. The experience of being violated, often by those in a position to protect us, to care for us.

The experience is humiliating. That humiliation has an emotional frequency, a note, a tone, and a feeling, attached. It is an act committed with impunity. The perpetrator carries out an act with malice, or vice or hatred. An act often intended to lift that exact feeling from their own being. Yet it seems to perpetuate the feeling more. Each act of harm, of violation, often stokes the feeling of malice in the perpetrator.

There is a release and a sense of power in overpowering others. Often it is done with the intention of hurting, and/or overpowering the child.

Many times, there are a slew of seeming perpetrators involved in the act, for turning one's cheek can end with the result of cruelty, and sometimes even the death of a child. Is the one that turned the cheek any less culpable. So, we have made clear that perpetration, abuse, abandonment, sadism is a shameless act. An act then that is 'taken on' by the victim. A shameless act states that the shame must reside elsewhere. The message then is a shameless act is carried by the victim, the one that was shamed.

This is how it starts. Mine started at birth, as is common in ritual abuse households. My father was extremely abused and had scars to prove it. The parent(s) reenacted the torture done to them thus transferring that feeling of shame and sense of unworthiness. The heaviness of shame, the density of powerlessness and a lack of control. The deep unworthiness that seeps into the bones of a child. That creates a layer of muck, of curving in on oneself. An inability to address the perpetration. An inability to fully have autonomy over one's life.

There is an inability to stop both the abuse, and the deep dense emotions, which are passed on during the despicable acts themselves. One becomes the receiver of that bowl of slush, the poison which filled the perpetrators heart. This becomes a betrayal bond. The perpetrator never fully able to be truly powerful and controlling, and the victim never having needs met. So on for generations.

These acts become the deepest emotional state. Long after any memory of the abuse and the torture, especially for babies and children before the development of sensory memories. It is just a part of the soup, the liquid mess we feed on, so few may know why they wish to harm themselves, or why the grief is so overwhelming.

The shame carries along with it, a weakness. A deep weakness which creeps into the bones. A weakness that aids the powerlessness experienced during the harmful acts. A weakness that then becomes the key to an inability to stop the perpetration, to gain the strength to fight back, or gain the strength to say No! It is the weakness which may impact an abused child for the rest of their lives. Are they victims? Certainly, they were, they may overcome a tremendous amount of trauma, or they may live a life of desperation and degradation.

Often, they can overcome and rise, feel happiness within their lives, find relationships and careers. Many may find relief in the sweet slumber of drugs or the excitement of other drugs that give them the adrenaline they so desperately need.

Yet it is the weakness that sustains past the trauma. The inability to stop taking on the torment. Each tormentor has their own unique way of perpetuating the torment. Those that lived the torment find themselves allowing the very thing that threatened to take their lives. This is the essence of a betrayal bond. A perpetration so deep, so stunning that the one's perpetrated keep reliving it repeatedly.

I have relived my powerlessness and weakness in intimate relations in just this way. Dear God and all Angels and my sweet guides; please help me stop this. If not for me, then for the others that I can show a sense of sweet responsibility for self. I am worth so much more. We are all worth so much more.

10.

"THE BEGINNING"

I'm cold and it's dark. I had to get out. I don't know how late it is. Maybe past midnight. I'm walking. Don't know where to go. It's so cold. I'm alone. I can walk. It hasn't been that long since I was in a cast, on crutches.

I don't even know if they know I'm gone. I could go and not be missed. I pass the big Victorian houses. The only place left to go is my school. Middle school. It seems so far and I'm so cold. I walk forever. I get there. It still feels like a converted ranch. Memorial Middle school with all its mods. Everything is open, classes are in glass areas. Except now all the doors are locked.

I walk around the grounds trying to find comfort and shelter. I don't have a jacket. I find a place, an embankment of the dry ditch. The leaves almost keep me warm. I feel alone and unloved. I close my eyes and see. In the dark and cold. I close my eyes and build my house. I find my imagination.

The first thing I create in my house is a swimming pool. There are glass walls all around it. I can swim anytime. It's a long swimming pool with lots of sunlight. I can feel the sunlight warm on my face. I don't think I swam there that night. Yet I created warmth. Then I create see-through walls in the rest of the house.

No secrets, no basements, just light and trees all around, and warmth. It was so warm. Comforting. I brought my brother and sisters there. We would run and play. We were safe. I don't think there was even furniture in my sanctuary. There was eternity. And then there was a meadow, a long green meadow.

A lion was running in the meadow. A handsome lion with a large mane. The lion would open its big mouth and roar like it owned everything. I ran to the lion and hugged him with his beautiful mane. Then I jumped on his back and rode on this majestic lion and roared with him. I had found my higher power at 11 years old. Later I would crawl into his mouth and be in the universe. Surrounded by galaxies and traveling through the Milky Way. I would close my eyes and see the stars I created; glittering, being born.

Still today the Lion runs through the meadow, between the children's sanctuary, that part of the meadow where they find such joy, and Daddy's castle, that Daddy created when he was dying. I still ride the Lion as do the children. So many populate the meadow now.

That night on the ditch bank, a freezing, abandoned child created a universe, a home, and a God that would never leave her. They all still exist, as she called herself into existence, in the most sustainable way possible. With her imagination, where many stars were born, and many children have been saved. I was no longer cold or alone.

11.

WHAT DREAMS MAY COME

The dreams became bigger. The meadow that started as the place where the lion roared and I jumped on his back, when I was 11, became greater. By riding on the lion, I saw more of the meadow, and I found a place, a hill covered with grass. The grass was beautiful, soft, and green, not prickly like some grasses, soft like a kitten's fur. The hill was little more than a mound, surrounded by trees. Some trees were tall with fluffy branches and leaves and provided shade from a sun that never burned. A sun which was dazzling and golden. We could look up at the sun as we lay on the soft grass. The sun on our skin held us in a soft ball of glowing warmth and sparkled around us. The trees were a cover of safety and a place to play. Some of the trees having footholds we could climb up and low hanging branches we could jump from.

As I looked around, I could see my past-self there, Nibus. Her beautiful long dark hair flowing in a light breeze and a smile on her face. She was happy to be there. She loved to walk on the hill and create gardens at the base of the hill with beautiful flowers that would grow quickly and sometimes take on other shapes or turn into different flowers. She loved to feel her hands in the ground. Slowly the children came. The babies came first. I was there with them and Nibus. Very soon after a beautiful man and woman came into the garden. They wanted to be there, to greet the children, and to love and play with them. They are still there, so loving and giving, there to hold the babies and children. To give them the feeling of nurturing, and speak to them softly, wrap them in warmth. Swim with them in the little lake at the end of the hill. Close to where the lion runs and roars. The children roar back.

The children, of all ages see the lion coming and hear his roar and they run down the hill, or roll, and greet the lion with bear hugs and jump on his back. Sometimes he'll roll on his belly and the children will crawl on him. I brought many of my inner children here as I rescued them. I would take them from the trauma they were experiencing and carry them to this paradise. They rejoiced with the children gathered here. They cared for each other and enjoyed holding the babies and running on the hill and meadow. There was a lot of laughter and sometimes tears and always loving arms. The loving guides would come as well as more children. My older children came later. Depressed or depleted, they too were loved, often by the little ones and always there were guides and angels there to hold them.

The animals came soon after. The Doe with her soft eyes that spoke into our minds in her singsong voice. We could get lost in her beautiful big, melting eyes. When we looked at her eyes, it felt like being carried away on the galaxies. She would come out of the trees and be there as long as I wanted to be with her. Such a feeling of lightness, like floating on a cloud. She would listen to my troubles, and they would be transformed in front of me, into stars and colors. First came the Doe and then came the giant birds. I flew on the giant bird and felt so free. Once my sister and I flew on the birds. My sister choosing her own bird. We flew over the meadow and saw the lion below us. The birds would trill and caw and call to the lion who would roar. Thorne flies all the time on the birds. He first came to the meadow as an adolescent. He came to the meadow as a spirit when he died. Sweet Thorne I told him about the meadow before he died and when I attended grief camp he was there, so strongly with me. We were in the meadow together, loving each other. We still dance there.

Many children have found the meadow. It is known as a place of healing and safety and family. A place each person will see differently yet always with love. They know they can be free there and be loved. They can tell their life story and be adored. Many children came when they were awakened from the dead-like state of the cult. God did that he brought them back. That tale is next.

Thorne is deeply loved at the meadow as is Daddy, who lives in his castle close to the meadow. Each can see the meadow in its own special way and with its deep healing. Now I see many, many hills with many spirits, many who have come home, some still in their human bodies that dream themselves there. They are called to this place. They serve and are healed and know this as a respite into joy and playfulness. Still, each will have their separate dream and dream with others and all dreams add to the meadow where children are sung to sleep and held, loved, adored. I started this meadow when I was eleven as a safe place for me to be. Now many find safety and love and family. The family is now large, yet you may only see those that you call to yourself as you venture there. Those that love you, those you deeply love.

12.

LOVE, MEN, MONEY & DEATH

Perhaps the most wounded area of my life is relationships. I've spent most of my life out of intimate relationships. Incest doesn't leave one with warm and fuzzy feelings of love and sexuality. I remember being terrified of my friends' parents. Authority figures left me speechless. No matter how nice the parents were, whether mother or father. I became mute when passing them. It wasn't only an inability to speak. I was so scared that I would squeak involuntarily. It was humiliating. I wanted to faint. I remember this happening in grade school and junior high. It was exhausting. I wouldn't look at them, but I would try to show deference.

This was also a big clue of how the satanic rituals I was involved in were my kryptonite. Being buried in a coffin was a death sentence, perpetrated not only by a leader but by the cult followers which seemed to experience a state of satisfaction or compulsive eroticism. It was a painful message of what little value my life had. I had been sentenced to death by a crowd, the deepest ostracism imaginable. Then brought out again to walk a path of shame. Parents were the ritual remnants of adults hovering over an unspeakable act of cruelty.

Intimacy was warped. I didn't speak to boys for many years. I feared the abuse they may have been capable of. Love was being possessed sometimes quite literally, sometimes with the malicious spite during an incestual rape. The best I could do was leave my body. Until my sister was brought in one night to the horrid little room my father used for his cruelties. Successfully bringing me back into the room. I was furious to be in my body and terrified of her being hurt yet also resentful of her presence and the need to keep her alive. This set up a dynamic of fear and hatred between us. Fear of her experiencing what was common during the incest and hatred that she saw me there. That she was a witness to my humiliation, and a victim of her own humiliation.

To interact with a man was to lose autonomy and possibly be under kryptonite powerlessness again. Incest wasn't only perpetrated within the belly of the intimate family unit but was also practiced amongst cousins.

When my parents separated, all five of us were sent to live with my father. It was my mother's attempt to teach him parenting skills. We five kids traveled around Albuquerque like vagabonds, begging for money. My youngest sister was five at the time and she was a master manipulator at the bus stops. We often made enough for a McDonald's meal. Daddy went back to Diana, the evil lover still participating in the cult he was banned from. We were basically orphans.

Diane's daughter, MaryAnn, and her two very young children, lived with us, we cared for the babies more than she did. My sister remembers coming home from school and the baby still being in the highchair. MaryAnn was in her early 20's and was a practicing Buddhist. She got me stoned the first time I tried pot. I remember thinking that I felt the same as I always felt since I was connected to a universe that wrapped me in satin. Later though, pot would be the satin lining that would make the words go away and my body feel mellow.

Since Maureen and I took care of the kids most of the time, my mother sent me off to my aunts and Maureen came home to live with Mama. We were on the cusp of our 13th birthday. The three youngest stayed with Daddy. Later I heard horror stories of my middle sister trying to protect the younger two.

My parents were going through a divorce. We were split up and I went to my aunts. I landed squarely in the middle of her divorce. My uncle had the most piercing, cold eyes. A man whose eyes shot daggers through them. He was rich, powerful, and very scary. He was not there long in my six months stay. It was long enough to experience the dynamics in the household.

My aunt lived in Houston Texas. I walked into a household which included my femme fetal aunt, who was always slighting and cutting in her put downs, my cold uncle that moved out, my oldest cousin, who was graduating from high school, arrogant with a pretty girlfriend, Bill the middle child, rejected by his dad, and already struggling with drugs, loss and his own abuse, and then the youngest son, spoiled and bratty and jealous of me.

I bonded with my older cousin, Bill, and the incest took on a whole other dynamic, one of mutual pain and protection. Bill and I had an 'affair'. He was sixteen, I was thirteen. We clung to each other. I loved him even then. My oldest cousin also molested me. It was the two of them but Bill was special. He went on to be a heroin addict and got clean for a while. He was the first person to make amends to me. Later he got sick, really from working on his abuse issues. He went back to the soft velvet underbelly of heroin. Supported by his spiteful dad who hated his weakness.

He and his girlfriend set their apartment on fire, in their drugged comas. She died in the fire. Bill survived in a burn unit for several weeks in terrible pain. He died in the unit. My uncle threw him away. He had him buried and never told the extended family. I doubt if anyone came to the funeral. I found out sometime afterwards, probably over a year. It broke my heart that my beloved cousin, was thrown out like garbage. I grieved Bill's passing, as much for how he was thrown away as I did for the closeness that kept us alive. I still think it is one of the most tragic losses. Another addict dying from this addiction in the worst way. I love you, Bill.

13.

MENAUL

Maureen and I were sent to a boarding high school for the 'bad children in northern New Mexico'. We had been hanging out with a group of kids, and young adults, that were under surveillance for being a drug ring. We knew they were watching us because the narcs would drive by. The town thought, perhaps rightly so, that most of the drugs entering the town, were coming from our gang. My mother was still the head librarian in Las Vegas and was informed of our gang by other city leaders. She was warned to get us out. She found a boarding school in Albuquerque; we were sent to school there. To Menaul which housed us 'nortenos'. The bad kids in northern New Mexico.

Menaul was a place where healing came in at twilight and the age-old buildings softly carried the cry of mothers, seeking to soothe the many children taken from their homes. It was the original 'Indian School'. Used for years to tear away native children all over New Mexico, from their homes and pueblos, often they were kept there and were not allowed to go home. Generations of native children were taken away to 'whiten' them. Native ceremonies still wail at the loss of their children.

Yet for me this was a magical place. An even greater sanctuary. I was restored. We lived in dorms condemned shortly after we left. We could hear the rats in the walls and each spring would bring an infestation of moths. The room mothers, in all their spitefulness, could never come close to the evil of my father and the absence of my mother. I thrived in a place of peers.

I did not like our dorm mother much, she said I had a chip on my shoulder. I am sure I did. I did like living on campus. I was homesick for a while but got better when I shared a room with Maureen, my twin. Menaul had a beautiful campus. The classes were small, but the teachers were good. Menaul was a life saver. I liked living with kids my age. Even if the dorms were condemned a few years after I lived there. The campus was graced with new dorms.

The campus had a whole grove of trees that were beautiful. It was fun exploring the campus and having the sports games so close in the gym. I did better there in school than I would have at my regular high school. Everyone had a job. Mine was feeding the pigs at the farm that was a part of the campus. I loved being there alone. The pigs were a little scary though, they were huge, and they would hear the wheels on the wheelbarrow, that was filled with milk and bread and would charge the fence. It was always a competition of who got to the fence first. I had to get there and get the slop over the wheelbarrow before the pigs got to the fence or they would spill the slop, or I would miss their feeding trough altogether.

That was scary. I also got to sneak a smoke at the farm before I went back to the main campus. The food in the kitchen was so-so. Later as juniors and seniors we could get off campus easier and enjoy Wendy's or McDonalds. Being on campus didn't stop us from partying, but it limited a lot more craziness than my hometown.

I loved being in the choir. We would go on tour every year and sing at different churches across the southwest states. This is where I would see my father once a year when he attended one of our choir tours. It did give me a sense of working on the road and was my start of being in the arts. In my senior year I started dancing in the one modern dance class we had on campus.

I wanted to dance for most of my childhood. They did not have dance classes in middle school or high school in Las Vegas, New Mexico.

After Maureen was kicked out of Menaul for smoking pot, I went underground and chilled out. We didn't party on campus, but we did sneak out and party in the graveyard across the street. It was thrilling sneaking into the graveyard.

Yet once I was in there, I had a sense of peace. It reminded me of one of the books I read as a girl in my mother's library. "Are you there, God? it's me Margaret" Margaret loved graveyards. She saw several of the ghosts and they became her community. I loved that. She eventually gained love and confidence. I remember the spirits that Margaret would talk to in the graveyard.

14.

OUR BICENTENNIAL TRIP

The year I turned sixteen was also the 200th anniversary of our country. From the founding of America in 1776 to 1976, the founding of my freedom, for I now had a driver's license. All the time I spent in math class, staring out the window, yearning to drive away across the meadows and out of Las Vegas and now I could. That summer we started out from Las Vegas and traveled all around the south, starting with Texas for a stop at our aunt's house in Houston, then down to San Antonio, and the river walk, as part of the bicentennial tours then off to New Orleans for Mardi Gras.

We stayed very close to the action and our little family of six got plenty of taste of the raw, sometimes sexual festivities of Mardi Gras. My sister got a tongue down her throat. The younger two had eyes filled with wonder with a few peeing drunks thrown in. We all got a lot of necklaces, and my mother and aunt were in horror and glee alternately for the attractions. Besides the festivities and the pulse of Mardi Gras, that drew me despite its lewdness, I loved New Orleans.

I drove from New Orleans to Florida into a huge red sun as it dawned on the horizon in front of me. All night I kept up with the truckers we could hear on our two-wave radio. Sometimes we would hear them talk about our white van as they attempted to flush us out of their convoys. I remember being the only one awake. Driving into the red sun, as if I were on Dune, a world other than our own. The highway shimmered in the waves of heat as this great sun rose before me. There are moments of awe in life, despite what our internal emotional state is. This was one for me. An enormity, a coming of age. A passage back to the east coast.

We visited the newly opened Walt Disney World in Orlando, Florida and St Augustine, the nation's oldest city. We stayed in Florida for a few days and continued our trip up the coast. We visited Charleston and Virginia Beach following the bicentennial tour. Next was Williamsburg, and Washington DC. This really was exciting for our little family. We rarely traveled and now found ourselves in Washington at museums and national monuments. We had never ventured out to the east coast. We took a tour of the White House and ate saltwater taffy and visited Atlantic City, where my great grandmother, Teresa McVey, matriarch, and bitch extreme, lived out the rest of her days.

Then to New York City, now that was exciting, and my mother turned into a New Yorker! She was a totally different persona. She obviously enjoyed living in New York in the fifties and left New York to move to New Mexico to raise a family. New York was exhilarating. It was also hot and full of people everywhere. For a sixteen-year-old raised in the big sky country of New Mexico it was a panorama of delights.

We stayed with my grandmothers' best friend from college, Mable. She lived in a small, well-appointed apartment right off 5th avenue and Central Park. She could barely contain five children, certainly a first in her lovely apartment. That night we went to the ballet. I had a lifelong desire to be a dancer. When I resumed school in Albuquerque, I joined the sacred dance class and still dance to this day. I see dance as an art and a discipline. I left college with a double minor in theatre and dance and consider it one of my best choices. That night the ballet inspired me to live my dream.

We went sightseeing in New York and visited the statue of liberty and climbed up to the tower. I could not imagine how anyone could navigate the streets of New York but obviously many did. New York was my favorite city. Mable still stands out to me as a grand dame of New York. Very glamorous and educated. A true New Yorker.

From there we went to Pennsylvania where my mother was born and raised in Lansdown. We had never seen my mother's home. I grew up seeing pictures and hearing stories about my grandparents and how they met at the Army/Navy football game in 1922. Both were reporters. My grandmother reporting for the Army, in all her 4ft 2'in glory. My 6'2 grandfather for the Navy. It took five years for them to marry. My grandfather, being considered 'shanty lace' Irish, was not the best fit for the daughter of a dirt, poor Irishman that came to the US and became rich buying hovels and becoming a slum landlord.

The first night we stayed in a motel in an industrial area, and I woke up thinking this was nothing like the stories of my grandmother's youth or even my mother's youth with all her cousins. We did visit Lansdown and saw the home my mother grew up in. It was a quick drive by of row houses and I missed the familiarity of the celebrations back in New Mexico with my grandmother signing songs about Pennsylvania. My mother was a graduate of Penn State, we did not see the campus.

However, we enjoyed Philadelphia and the liberty bell. We also enjoyed the Quaker farm houses we visited, and the home cooked meals served for many. We were birth right Quakers and attended Quaker meetings but had never seen the Quakers that still lived in the old ways and dressed in the old ways. It was eye opening to see how communal they were. I still believe in communal living and sharing resources however probably not to the extent of the Amish or Quaker homesteads.

By this time, we had been on the road for over five weeks, and we were spent. It was time to go home. We did so by following the Santa Fe trail back to New Mexico. It was not one of the more scenic routes. The heartland of America is filled with wheat and other grains, and it is not interesting to look at. While we understood the travails of the pioneers, it was not very pleasant to stop at many of the stops. In fact, by the time, we reached Kansas I was so sick of seeing nothing but grass and wheat fields that I was running a fever of over 100. We stopped for a few days just to rest our eyes, literally.

All told we spent eight weeks on the road visiting towns to commemorate the bicentennial anniversary. It is still the biggest trip around this country that I have taken. It is an amazing and large continent, and I would still love to travel to many of the parks I have not seen. Our trip gave us all a taste of America. My mother gave of herself in the way she knew how, and we all benefitted from seeing parts of this country we may never see again. I am truly grateful to her for giving us a sweeping vision of America. I have since filled in my knowledge of America by traveling and living in different parts of the country. Yet I am a southwestern girl, and this will always be my home.

WITHERING HEIGHTS

We had done our big bicentennial trip in the summer before my junior year. We went all over the country and looked miserable in every picture we took. My mother came home and promptly went to bed where she stayed for almost a year. Withering away with a cell depleting depression that drew the life out of her. She told me that every cell of her body hurt. I came home one night, and the police greeted me at the door. Mama tried to slit her wrist with a knife and my younger brother called the police. Mama was being escorted out when I walked in. She ended up in the mental hospital just outside of town. I was at rehearsal for the first play I had done. I never could go back. I needed to take care of the family. That is what I did.

In my junior year I stayed in Las Vegas. I was running our paper distribution. I would wake up at five in the morning and get all the newspapers for the town at the post office. We would distribute them to all the paperboys and girls and fill up the paper machines. This was back when people read the papers. We would also do the out-of-town routes, which is where I learned to drive a stick shift. I continued doing the paper distribution and took over all other parts of the business. Maureen was the mom. Caring for our siblings. I was the mean one that got the kids out of bed to do their paper routes.

We continued going to school but it was not easy. Sheila came home and did not get a warm reception. Poor Sheila in so many ways she was so rejected. I did not want her there because it was enough to take care of everyone else. It was unfair to her. She stayed. We made do. One of my teachers told me I had to choose between work and school, I could not do both. FU! Watch me!! I did both.

Mama was only allowed one person to visit with her. That was me. The first few times I visited; she was almost comatose. She didn't talk much. She was still so lost within herself. After a month or so, she started coming out of it. She found new friends in the confines with her. They were hippies. She asked me to find pot for them. I did. I was happy that she had found a community no matter where it was. She kept getting better and returned home. She was changed, perhaps less naïve, certainly more realistic. She lived through hell. I don't think she ever had another relationship, but she found her place.

While I was in Las Vegas, I took a mechanics class at the junior college. The instructor was so angry that a girl would take a mechanics class, that he would not let me in the classroom. I learned how to do overhauls and minor repairs in the shop with the mechanics. I never got the book learning, but I learned a lot about auto mechanics.

In my senior year, I was back at Menaul and took classes at the newly built career enrichment center (CEC). I walked through the same graveyard we partied in to get there. I realized I was very happy walking through the graveyard to CEC. I loved the sunshine, and I could take the graveyard almost the whole way.

Funerals were rather tedious, and boring but the grounds themselves the gravestones, grass and trees were soothing. The same peace surrounded me in any open spaces. Sitting on my mother's porch and watching the clouds move over Albuquerque. Looking at the lights twinkling in the city at night. Seeing the sunrise come up behind the mountains. I realized early that I was at peace a great deal in my life, underneath the trauma was a deep peace. Particularly when in nature, just looking at the sky is awakening. The southwest is a deep jewel of moving clouds and muted colors of the high desert. There is peace, there has always been peace.

Since I had extra credit for the auto mechanics class, I was able to graduate high school after half a semester. I had a great last semester taking mainly art classes, dance, and choir. We moved the family to Albuquerque. My family was staying at my mother's parents' house. That wonderful property was at its breaking point. It was an older house and our family of five outdid the plumbing. The toilets were backed up constantly. The sewer system backed up and was nasty as hell. The house was not meant to sustain that many people after being a home for two. When I left school and joined my family it was too much to take with the house falling apart.

I ran away from my grandparents' home when I was seventeen. I took a bus to California to see my father and ended up in a small town just outside of Santa Barbara called Capitola. I was there until my mother called me to come home. My aunt Julie came to see me graduate from high school. By the time I graduated Maureen and I had an apartment. Mama was so upset that I invited my father to my graduation that she almost didn't attend.

15.

LOVE & PERIL

Daddy knows how badly he was tortured as a child. He says he loved us, his children, more than his parents did. It did not sound like there was any love for him. I knew his parents, not well, only through the eyes of a frightened child. They were scary. Jules, my grandfather was never kind or attentive. Sheila says she remembers being molested by him when she was about three. In our house in Paradise Hills. That's what kids were for? To overpower, to hurt, to exert. I can see Jules doing that. I don't remember any eye contact with him.

Our visits to my grandparents weren't that long and not very pleasant. I remember an eeriness about the estate. This beautiful estate in Los Altos Hills that we visited maybe once a year for less than a week. Julie, my aunt, was the largest component. She was retarded and had cerebral palsy. She was scary. Her body was deformed, and she could not speak well.

She chewed with her mouth open, spoke loud with an open mouth. Moved with great difficulty. At Christmas, she would get jealous and take our toys. That was scary to have this big lumbering, angry kid come at us. Julie loved daddy. I'm not sure if it was returned to her. I think he went from gentle to disgust with her.

The ranch style house was, at best, somber. I don't remember ever spending much time with my grandparents. The house seemed empty, devoid of love and laughter. People would gather in the kitchen and there were always helpers, gardeners, pool cleaners, housekeepers, care takers for Julie. She had a caretaker for many years that cared for her, even when the estate was decimated and there was very little money coming in. I remember looking at scrapbook pictures of daddy. He looked so much like my brother, such a handsome boy.

So unhappy. My brother was unhappy too. Not always, but he carries the weight of our family. Such pain there's been underneath the surface. We were so unhappy as kids. In a way clinging to each other, surrounded by adults, that at best were unable to demonstrate the love they felt, at worst, my father was affectionate in the day and a rapist at night. There were some heavy vibes in our house. It was like my parents' demeanors, their state of being was so burdened and depressed, such heaviness. I don't even remember talking to my paternal grandmother much. I remember brushing her long white hair. She was a big woman. Both of daddy's parents abused him viciously.

I loved my mother's parents. My grandmother, Grammy, was the life blood of our family. She was the life of the party at holidays. Grammy would lead us in singing all these songs, old songs about Pennsylvania, "Any ice today ladies…NO!, Pennsyl, pennsyl, Pennsylvaaania".

We would have our Champaign and hor d'oeurves, and her stories would hold the melancholy at bay. Sometimes my cousins would join us at Christmas. Three boys from Texas. But that was years earlier, time keeps morphing for me. I never really knew linear time except as one long, often miserable, sequence of events. Most of them occurring below the surface and acknowledged by a conscious mind that rarely worked well.

My father was living with his second wife, who at this point looked more like my retarded aunt. Her alcoholism had progressed to a point that she was a zombie most of the time and shuffled through the house dazed. She looked like she was nine months pregnant and smoked constantly. She would remain in that state until she left my father and stopped drinking. I think she died sober, thank God.

My father was in one of the weirdest, scariest places I ever knew him to be. When he picked me up at the bus stop, I could feel his inarticulate simmering. I do not remember so much about the satanic period since I was so young and buried those memories, just as I was buried over and over. Here his demeanor and interactions were very strange. He had the bookstore in his house, which no one was going into. The house was creepy. He barely spoke but what he emanated spoke volumes.

Later, in my early recovery, I worked as a crisis counselor. We responded to calls regarding low functioning men whose affect was the like Daddy's back then. It was almost like they were stalking, the look in their eyes and their movements were predatory. They were waiting for an opportunity. We crisis counselors were often accompanied by the police during those incidents.

It was usually the mothers that would call in for help. The prowling and silence and preparedness to recoil and attack was palpable. These were the most intimidating and terrifying calls.

This is how I encountered Daddy in Capitola. Waiting to attack, prowling. This was not a sophisticated, calculating mind. It was much deeper. An unconscious ruling from the lizard brain, perhaps even deeper than that. What was in control was old, ancient. A presence waiting, almost evil. Too deep to respond to with words. This was shadows of darkness, in control; stalking, slinking, watching.

The pervasive feeling of impending doom filled the quiet lovely house, and the moroseness was thick. Daddy was deep in a depression. His cognitive functioning severely stunted. He would forget words in the middle of his sentences frequently. I had seen this in the infrequent visits I had with him during the high school choir tours I was on, that allowed a visit with him once or twice a year.

Linda, his wife, was quickly digressing into her nonconscious alcoholic state as well. A state that would worsen and appeared almost more impaired than my severely retarded aunt. I didn't feel entirely welcome in their home. Even then, they were two shuffling zombies, barely speaking. He was circumspect. She was drowning in her drink.

I was back in the muddy thickness of emotional powerlessness, again feeling that deep feeling of unsafety. I remember we went to dinner. The conversation was null. Perhaps by the time he was in Capitola he had succumbed to what was eating him alive since he was a child. This beautiful, sweet boy was overwhelmed by a darkness with few words. How terrifying it was for him to be eaten up by this dark void.

Capitola itself was quant. A last vestige of a hippie culture that hung out in coffee houses, listening to mood music, and playing board or card games. It was jovial and welcoming, and my father would cheer up somewhat on entering the cafe. I think my father always had pig pen cloud over him, an ambiance that would repel and avert eyes. He still wore his patchwork sleeved coats and still looked grungy. I would see some remaining life and camaraderie from my father in those scenarios. When he was away from others, he was back in his dark misery. I could feel an internal rage.

It did not take long for me to meet a few stoners and find a place to hang out. The sky was winter grey, and the sea mirrored the greyness. The beach still offered solitude as it always does, amidst the clutter of branches, bark, and washed-up reefs. The grey beaches were a haven for my malcontent that I easily slipped into around my father's depression. I felt full, free and a lot safer outside, watching the surf and seagulls. The ocean was an infinity that soothed.

I did not stay long after that, maybe a week or so. Then we were on our way to the grandparents' estate. My grandfather dead of a heart attack a few years before. My grandmother, in a coma, after a stroke she suffered a few years before my grandfather died. Daddy drove me up to his parents' estate in Los Altos Hills. This was a beautiful ranch house with several cottages. When purchased it was 40 acres of prime real estate overlooking San Francisco Bay. Eventually it was sold off and was now only 17 acres. The estate was overcast with a degree of sinister even back then.

My father barely spoke on the trip up Los Altos hills in the dark. His feeling state was pervasive. It emanated in waves from his body, alternating between morose introspection and outward hostility. I felt the energy like a death threat, as if his being wanted to drive over a cliff or stop and stab a knife in my heart.

When I hear my father say he was in intense pain all his life in our 'dead talks', I feel the energy of that night. Driving up the hill surrounded by death, and the desire to perpetuate it. I feared for my life in the dankness of that morbid, pervasive feeling state.

When I got to my grandparents that night, I strolled around the grounds and smoked a joint looking up at the stars. As I was looking, I asked, "Where should I be?" I saw a plane flying towards New Mexico. I knew I had to go back.

My grandmother's internment room was my first stop in the house. Her door was open and her still, white robed body lay on its side facing the wall. Perhaps she was coming back to the truest part of her life. Encapsulated in the amnesic silence of the coma. Living out the rest of her days before she slipped out of her skin, already hanging lifelessly to a dying form. The house was still somber. My aunt the only lively being on the property, yet I have few memories of her on that trip.

I stayed in the cottage closest to the house. It was perfect size with a living room with dark beams running across the ceiling and a nice fireplace. There was one bedroom and a good-sized kitchen. The cottage allowed me some distance from the somber mode of the main house. My grandmother setting the stage for a drama long played out. Julie, still cared for by her lovely elder caretaker would make her appearances. I think it was me that wanted small chunks of time at the house. I was still trying to shake the feeling of death and dome from the ride with my father.

I couldn't light the fire in the cottage. It was my first line of business, and I couldn't get it started. I finally gave up and went to bed. In the middle of the night, I awoke and heard noises in the living room. I walked out to find a roaring fire.

Even in the glow of the fire and its heat, there was the sinister feeling I felt in the ranch house, not as strong, but still there. It was almost as if my grandmother was roaming the property, angry and grieving that her life now destined her to walk in shadows while in a body she couldn't fathom, reliving her extensive harshness toward her children and satanic husband with a glee that she had survived him. Such a low-lying malevolence.

I stayed a few days and enrolled in a community college. I was excited about school. I enrolled in a photography class and was very excited to see through the eyes of the lens. I met an Asian groundskeeper on my grandparents' property. I told him that I felt the estate was haunted and he confirmed that was his suspicions and he had seen what appeared to be ghosts. He told me a great deal about the property. There had been another caretaker/groundkeeper who had absconded with a great deal of money. There was no one really looking out for the wellbeing of the family and staff. I received a call from my mother stating I had to come back to New Mexico, or my leg was going to fall off. She was rather dramatic. However, I love her for getting me out of that solemn estate and back home.

That household always had a pall over it. No one seemed to be present other than Julie. I do not remember my grandmother being with us much. Now I know she was a member of the cult and her abuse of Daddy was mind numbing, Sybil like, if you remember the book, Sybil. Sybil had multiple personalities and the abuse she suffered was unbelievable. My grandfather was a satanic cultist and arrogant. He played with other people's money and, most likely, was a shyster lawyer.

He had a heart attack on the golf course and died after Nana had her stroke. The estate was left in limbo with barely enough to care for my grandmother and aunt.

The only one not walking in unseen silt in that household was my father's sister, Julie. She was born with cerebral palsy and retardation. My grandmother bore six children, two survived. One of the other four children may have been sacrificed. I believe that is when my father succumbed to the dark shadow that haunted him the rest of his life.

Julie remained childlike. She would come toward us, lumbering in her big body, her legs were different lengths and she always seemed to have her mouth open. She would make weird sounds. Julie was virtually deaf as well, so the sounds she made were scary. We could always see her chew. I was terrified of her but also aware that this was her body and her experience of life.

As I got older, I was more able to accept Julie's condition and she was better at communicating. I still feared the physical maladies but respected her a great deal more. She raised miniature Collies that I thought were beautiful and I admired her for that. In a way Julie was happier than anyone else in that family. I don't think she was spared from the abuse but lived in the present. That is a gift far greater than intelligence.

It was Julie who left us grandchildren the only monies we would see from a multi-million-dollar estate. She hand-wrote a will that was clearer than the twenty-one-page monstrosity my grandfather wrote which appeared to leave everything to the Bank of California. The money was actually my grandmothers and Aunt Julie's. My great grandfather, Nana's father, left the estate for the two of them.

Years later I would visit the estate. It was even in more disrepair. My aunt and caretaker living in poverty. My grandmother dead long since but the estate still in probate and mangled at the hands of my grandfather. My aunt had almost been kicked off the estate and she ran next door to the neighbors for help. They basically took over, moved into the house, and siphoned whatever funds were there.

They were in the process of remodeling and taking out loans when a representative from the children's hospital, who was listed in Julie's will, acted, and filed a lawsuit. It took years to restore the original will that was over the estate, written by my great grandfather who had bought over forty acres in Los Altos Hills. The property was to go to my grandmother and to Julie. Jules had taken the property when he had Margaret declared incompetent. Finally, my aunt was able to enjoy her home. The neighbor that took advantage was disbarred for his actions on the estate. Julie enjoyed a few years of newfound freedom before her death a few years after my father had died.

16.

SUNNY SUNDAYS

I t seems all my life, or most of it, Sundays have been sunny. I love this. It may be a statement I make after my death. How awesome my life was because Sundays were sunny? I looked forward to sunny Sundays. Maybe its Gods way of saying it truly is an awesome day. It's becoming abundantly clear that the act of remembering, and what we choose to remember, maybe the most impactful aspect of our lives.

I've wondered if humans may be predetermined to remember pain. Certainly, it would help us avoid situations that would place us in positions to be hurt. However, utilizing our beautiful frontal cortex, filled with cells uniquely human, for the act of remembering pain, may create a feedback loop which naturally focuses us, even more, on painful situations.

Is it more natural to be focused on pain? If so, does it take a higher order of functioning to focus on what brings us happiness? I practiced focusing on finding the good, the beauty, the interest, and the happiness. Divine Openings has a saying, we can rant about what's wrong or rave about what's right. I learned to wake up in the morning and look at the most mundane things around me and describe aspects I liked about them. The blues in a picture, the curve of the woman's arm in that same picture, or the way my curtains hung. I spoke those things out loud to hear myself rave about my environment. Finding what interested me for five minutes in the morning created new neurons and pathways of fascination and interest in the life around me.

Recovery also teaches us similar practices, to enjoy our lives and seek out what we want. More than anything we learn that we are responsible for our experiences. As the Big Book of Alcoholics Anonymous states; "Driven by a thousand forms of fear, we step on the toes of our fellows, and they retaliate. Seemingly without provocation, but invariably we find that somewhere in the past we made a decision that placed us in a position to be hurt." In other words, we create our own reality.

So, what do we choose to see? I experienced ritual abuse as a child as well as sexual abuse. I found that my world was very small, scary and distrustful. I had no place of safety until I found drugs and they became my solution for the pain within my mind, body and soul. When I got 'clean' and learned how to live life without the use of drugs, I found love and acceptance within a 12-step fellowship. I also 'worked the 12 steps' and faced the demons of my past and rescued those aspects of self still stuck in a loop of trauma.

What gave me life was recognizing that it was entirely up to me what I chose to focus on. Shall I be a drama queen and focus on everything that is wrong. I have days like that. Yet even amid the pain of betrayal, I was ecstatic to walk down the road and watch the clouds move past the sun. I love being alive. What depth I've experienced. To come back from the brink of death and go back in to find any part of myself that still lived there. Now that is glory. The ability to find, soothe, and create a place of solace and acceptance inside myself is truly the greatest act of self-love. Pain may be inevitable, but suffering is optional.

I create my own reality as soon as I utter the words 'I create my reality'. I dive into a pool naked and adore the blue sky as I swim the three or four strokes that it takes to get to the other side. Then enjoy the garden that give me hours of pleasure and looking at my garden around me while I swim is always heavenly. Perhaps the key to happiness is the ratio of how much time we think of what's wrong with our self and others and how much time we choose to see beauty and wonder in our own lives as well as others.

So, we are back to remembering and recognizing we create what we see and think and feel. Remembering the pain can also bring the deepest compassion. 'Embracing what is' may truly be a higher order functioning. Perhaps it's a ratio of how much we love ourselves vs how much we obsess on things outside ourselves. I truly think it very much depends on how we talk to and treat ourselves and how quickly we can let go of the difficulty with others. Again, it's a choice to rant about what's wrong or rave about what's right.

I love enjoying life and laughing. I went through hell to get here so I do not need to go back and remember what hell felt like. Trauma happens, pain happens, discomfort and betrayal happen. It's what we do with the trauma, pain and discomfort that will determine if we smile or become fixated on our difficulties.

For me it's always sunny on Sundays. Graveyards are peaceful and I am happiest when I am happy inside. May I laugh a thousand times a day and when I get to the world of the nonphysical, I want to laugh twice as much as I do here, until my friends, focused on the latest issue in their lives, can look up and feel the sunshine on their faces all the way down to their toes. Only we can change the most basic elements of our beingness and gain satisfaction from that change. Then we can go out and watch the leaves shimmer in the trees in the slightest breeze and wonder at true grace. Live in the highest order, my dear friends, and know life is the greatest gift we receive. Look for the love, the joy, and the laughter. Enjoy sunny Sundays.

17.

LIFE AT UNM

I had major surgery on my upper femur and had the semester to heal.

I started college at the University of New Mexico (UNM) in a wheelchair. I had a boyfriend that would carry me up the stairs to my apartment and then get the wheelchair up, that lasted a few months. Later I used crutches for the rest of the semester. I worked for the campus police as a dispatcher on the midnight shift, with the Sargent sleeping through half the night next to me. I was grateful to have him there. By the end of the semester, I was walking well enough to start exercising again.

I stayed at UNM and eventually got a degree in business communications. I loved being on campus and college life. I loved the classes I took, even if I didn't do well in all of them. My first semester I took Latin and French.

My classes started at 8:00 am, after I finished my midnight shift and wheeled my wheelchair over to the classes. I flunked Latin and got a D in French. Way too much language in the morning. I eventually took Latin over again. It was the only A I ever achieved in my bachelor program.

I loved the communications program. Students in the 1980's were engaged. We were involved and the classes were interesting and exciting. By my second year I was taking dance classes, costuming, and theatre. I loved being in the arts and in the communication program. While my grades may not have been stellar, I thoroughly enjoyed school. We lived close to campus in apartments. There was one apartment complex with murphy beds. I loved that place. My sister lived in another apartment and a good friend in another one. The apartment complex looked like a pueblo.

I worked for the university police till I graduated with my bachelor's degree. My mother graduated from law school the same day we graduated from college. I was so proud of her. We would attend the law school functions with her. Later when I became an auditor for the Department of Defense, the law training, I picked up from her helped me to be an effective contract auditor. I learned a lot from you mama. You are amazing with what you did with your life. You had a wonderful law practice that you loved for years, and a great group of friends. I am so glad that you had that second career you were an inspiration to me.

A few decades later I received my master's degree in accountancy and worked for many years as a DoD Defense Contract Auditor. I was able to do well because of Mama and her brilliance and, in many ways, how she taught me to learn. Mama saw all her children graduate with master's degrees or an equivalent standard. My two boys saw me complete my education and were inspired by that. My darling Ian made a lot more money in his sales career even though he left college in his junior year. He was a gifted salesman. I desperately wish he was still on this earth. I speak to him all the time and yet still miss his face, miss his loving hugs and his support.

Jason is an amazing musician and model. He has talent coming out of his pores. He is my baby. I love him beyond life. He is everything to me. He is my only surviving son and I want everything for him. Ian is so happy now since he passed. I know that beyond a shadow of a doubt. Still in my heart I wanted him to live a long and fruitful life.

Just like I wanted that for Thorne. They have taught me that it is not over. There is life beyond, whether we are incarnate. My heart has broken open, more than ever before. I am so grateful that they are still here. They make themselves available and I would have never known the life I have now if it was not for the loves and relatives that died and then showed themselves as still so present. I love you all. We continue to thrive, and the forgiveness keeps unraveling the pain and torture that we all knew. I am forever grateful.

18.

AFTER COLLEGE, TRAGER & PERFORMING

I finished college in New Mexico and received a bachelor's degree in business communications and a double minor in theatre and dance. I am an artist and a performer. Since my mother graduated from law school the same day my twin sister and I graduated with our bachelor's degrees, we have a picture of all three of us and I am very proud of our accomplishments. We had a big party at our house. It was one of the highlights of our lives.

Maureen and I went to Mexico to celebrate our college graduation. We had been to Mazatlán before, partying for spring break with some girlfriends. When we went back there after we graduated, I met two gentlemen who had ultralights, the small gliders equipped with engines. I was enthralled so I went with these gentlemen, which they truly were gentlemen, to Guaymas, Mexico. There was a mountain chain there very close to the ocean, where they planned to fly.

We rigged up a second seat on the ultralight and we went over the mountain at sunset. It was beautiful and scary as hell. I had been afraid of heights since I saw our babysitter hung my four-year-old brother out my second story window by his feet. I was much more worried about his death than mine.

When we were flying over the Guaymas mountains I thought, well if I am going to die of falling down a large height it might as well be here. I was literally on a very small piece of fabric, and we were flowing over mountains at sunset and the wind was changing directions like crazy as the sun went down. A drop like that into the mountain top would kill me instantly. I did lose a great deal of my fear of heights flying on that ultralight over the mountains that day.

When we got back to Mazatlán, my sister had a roommate. She met this woman after I took off and was sharing our room with her. She was lovely, very tall, and lanky with the longest neck I had ever seen. I was dancing around on the beach a little later and I did a leap, and my leg went out on me. I literally could not remember how to walk. This was the hip that I broke at eleven which stopped the incest and had surgery on my leg in my first semester in college. I started college in a wheelchair.

It took almost two years for my leg to heal and then I was back to being active, although it can still be troublesome. I graduated with a degree in dance. My emphasis was in Flamenco. Today I still love the fire and emotional expression of flamenco. It is a challenging and beautifully expressive art form.

After the leap on the beach, I hobbled back to the funky little hotel my sister had found for us. She kept switching hotels in Mazatlán and each one was skankier than the last one. I was lying down on the bed when the 'roommate' came in, Sarah. I told her what happened, and she had me lay down on her bed and started wiggling my leg and applying traction. In a few minutes I could feel my leg connect in my brain. That was exactly what it felt like. I could not find the mechanism to move my leg and then suddenly, with this passive joint movement, my leg reconnected. I knew whatever she had done was something phenomenal. I learned all about the therapy she was using. It was called Trager and it was invented by a doctor who started working with people who had polio and were severely crippled. Dr.

Trager would just ask in his mind, 'how could this be a little lighter, how can this be freer'.

I was so taken by this technique that I went back to New Mexico and was fortunate enough to get enrolled in a training for Trager that was hosted by the Massage Institute in Albuquerque. Trager changed my life. It was the first time I felt free in my body. On the last day of the training, Cathy, the instructor had us move as if we were flying. I could not remember a time before that when I had such freedom in my shoulder. It had been bound since I broke my collar bone at five. I always felt like I had a frozen shoulder till I found Trager. Trager is considered sensory integration. I did another training in Trager later that year then moved to San Diego to be closer to the Trager Institute.

Moving to San Diego was scary. I had not lived away from my family before. I was twenty-four, loved dancing Flamenco and I loved the feeling of Trager. San Diego was beautiful. I first stayed with a friends' Aunt, one of my Flamenco sisters. I would steal Diane's weed and smoke it. It became an unspoken game of seek, find, and smoke. She eventually got angry enough about it to kick me out, but she did get quite a few Trager sessions out of the deal, which she loved.

Trager introduced me to a sensory vocabulary which went way beyond the emotional feeling state. Trager is like having every part of your body rocked and lovingly mobilized. Every movement had a little name. Hello leg, wiggle, wiggle, wiggle. Trager was amazing. I learned to question the mind, 'how can this be freer, how can it be lighter' and move the body as much as it would allow me too. I became aware of so many different sensations. Each practitioner had their own qualities. I found such freedom in my neck and head with the gentle holds and the rocking done in Trager. I remember realizing that the body was responding to the questions of how it could be different. I got a little freaked out by that. I realized I was truly having a conversation with the body and mind. To me it was like I was dancing with a body and exploring how much movement it was capable of in such a gentle way.

I remember getting sessions and getting off the table and not even feel like I was walking. I was so light. It had a tremendous impact on healing my body. That time of my life was truly memorable. I had finally found something that made me feel better than pot. Smoking dope helped me not hear my obsessive thoughts or feel the pain in my body. Trager transformed my pain into awareness. It was the first time I really questioned getting stoned. I had found something even deeper to restore the goodness to my body. I was certified in Trager in 1984. I stayed in San Diego for a year and a half before finding a boyfriend and moving to the San Francisco Bay area. I was there for longer than a year and danced in the bay area and still did Trager and lived with a handsome Algerian alcoholic in a studio apartment until I moved in with a dance friend.

She was one of the most beautiful dancers I had ever seen. The way she played with extending and releasing or quick movements was phenomenal. I was a part of a Flamenco/Persian dance ensemble in Berkeley till I left. That time in my life was so fulfilling with the amazing music and dance I was a part of, and the Trager practice. I was never able to duplicate the music and dance scene I was a part of in Berkeley and San Diego and I will never forget how much it filled my soul. I miss the sounds of Flamenco and the Oud, most of all I miss the mystical Santur. An instrument that captures the depth of modal music. It is a Dulcimer keyed to the modal scale. We would get stoned and listen to Dariush play the Santur and be transported to the depths of the universe. My artist soul was never filled as much as it was then.

19.

IMMOBILE RIBS AND THE CANCEROUS BREAK

D addy was in town. I had recently returned to Albuquerque and was engaged in musical theatre in one of the most gorgeous old theatres in Albuquerque. I don't remember if we were in the middle of Guys n Dolls or the next musical production. It didn't matter, except as a frame of reference to my life at the time, and the fact that I was once a triple threat.

Of course, I was one of the dolls. Anyway, after sitting on my mother's porch and weeding for a few months, and subsequently recovering my sanity after believing that the world was a very scary, dangerous place; I 'came to' enough to realize I never wanted to experience that soul crushing type of belief system and became the artist again I had been for many years.

That's when Daddy showed up. For most of my adult life, Daddy showed up looking like a Vagabond. Always looking unkempt, as if within this handsome man there was a monstrous capacity to destroy himself. No matter how he tried to appear, this visible devastation followed him. This time he was taut, fragile. The permanent brooding presented itself in the shallow breathing. I smelled death on him. It was traumatically frightening.

He couldn't breathe. I offered to give him a Trager session. A gentle, rocking massage approach which frees up joints, muscles and ligaments. Only I couldn't move his ribs. They were so fragile; I was afraid they would shatter if I applied pressure. This is not the freedom the ribs usually move with. Something was terribly wrong. He hurt all over. I knew he was dying. It took months to consciously accept his unraveling. This realization affected my depression and recognition of my addiction more than any other event.

Daddy was diagnosed shortly after that with metastasized Prostate cancer. Already it was in his spine and most of his bones. He'd visited around November. He was diagnosed in January and sought treatment in Germany for a month before his young girlfriend had a fit and demanded to come back to the states.

20.

NOT WITHOUT YOU GOD

I had my last drink a week and a day after my 28th birthday. I took one sip of wine and decided I was done feeling altered and out of control. I was out to dinner with my boyfriend, in a very nice restaurant, and I knew I was done. To be fair, especially to Alex, my birthday had been a whopper.

I got drunk, I don't remember where we were, except that it was a party, or a bar. Like I said, it was a party. I stopped smoking pot a few months before my birthday. After we had come back from Mexico. Mexico was the last hoorah. We went into Mexico on New Years' Eve. Easy enough to do, only there is a border station fifteen miles into Mexico. That's where my boyfriend realized he didn't have his passport, or birth certificate...sigh. We were turned around and came back into the United States, from Mexico, in a VW van, with curtains on the windows, after smoking a dooby (joint for you straight folks). Oh yeah, and the driver, said boyfriend, had no passport. We came in through El Paso, on New Year's Eve, around 10:30pm. It was cold as hell.

The Mexican border patrolman came to my passenger window, and knocked on it, mimicking for me to roll down the window. I did, you can image what smells escaped in that process. He was smart, he sniffed, and reached in and opened the glove compartment. Several smoking devices rolled out. We were asked to exit the caravan. It was classic. We were separated, and searched, as was the vehicle, thoroughly!

"We know it's his" she said," Just tell us where it is". "We smoked it all!" Nothing else needed to be said. I was 'released' to the parking lot after a feeble strip search, yeah it was a small border crossing. To pace back and forth and look anywhere but at the van being torn apart. "Please God! Please don't let me get clean in a Mexican jail! Please God....and nausea. What a drama queen. Truth was I was scared shitless. We had enough to be escorted back to Mexico, most likely to jail. We weren't carrying much money. The pacing continued. Everything was out of the van. Thank God there were no guard dogs!! They let us go at 11:45pm. We put everything back in the van. Including the cooler, which was inside a packing box, with the box sleeves pushed inside the box under the cooler. Yeah, don't try it, by this time the patrolmen are wise to that one. If you don't know what I'm talking about, have fun in Mexico!

It stopped working after that. We got into Mexico, smoked a ton and I never got high. This was my final hoorah, my last splurge, and it sucked. Soo depressing. I stopped after I got back. I only smoked one time after that. I was drunk and belligerent and I got stoned. I realized that it seemed to temper the emotion tirades I tended to have drinking. Until the night of my birthday. Nothing tempered that tirade. I was pissed as hell that my boyfriend didn't give me a present. You familiar with the term 'self will run riot'? Yup that was me. We got home and he had flowers and chocolates and a card...God I was such a bitch! A week later it wasn't just the alcohol weighing on me. It was the truism of 'instant a@$hole, just add alcohol'. I was humbled. That last sip at dinner was enough. I was done. I didn't like who I'd become.

Three days later I was absolutely nuts. There was a reason I had a 'head full of zombie' for so many years. 12-step recovery taught me that drugs are just a symptom of the disease. In my chosen 12 step program of Narcotics Anonymous (NA) (and yes, it's my anonymity to blow) the disease of addiction is three-fold: physical compulsion, mental obsession, and spiritual self-centeredness. I was truly experiencing the disease of addiction. My head wouldn't shut up, I missed the 'zombieness'...my emotions were worse than La Jolla waves in a California sunset. I was anxious as hell, then furious, I couldn't stop crying, then crazy horny, all in five minutes. Then it would start again. Talk about a rude awakening. I had been numbed out for years. Welcome to reality. See, this is why addicts go to meetings. It was the only place that I felt somewhat normalized.

Meetings were amazing. Someone would share what they were going through, then someone else would share what was happening with them. After hearing half the room share, I realized no one was 'cross talking'. That means no one was giving anyone else suggestions or judgements or telling them what was wrong with them, or rudely carrying on conversations with the person next to them while someone else was sharing. I still hate cross talk.

I suddenly felt safe. After the noise in my head calmed down a bit, I was able to relate to what these people were saying. It was, is and always will be, one of the most intimate environments I have ever been in. I was struck by the authenticity shared.

That didn't happen in my first meeting though. No before my first meeting, I wanted to die, literally. I wanted to drive my car off Sandia Mountains. They are over a mile high. I hated being so out of control and felt miserable. My counselor 'Told me' I had to go a 12-step meeting or be put in a treatment center. All I knew about were mental hospitals and regular hospitals. After my mother's stint in a mental hospital, there was no way in hell I was going there! I'd had a massage, which included at least 45 minutes of deep stomach kneading, and I couldn't stop cramping. It felt like all the drug toxins in my body were purging. I was in deep pain and decided my 'will' chakra had been burned out. I found an NA meeting.

I walked in late with my boyfriend, I couldn't walk by myself. We sat in the 'gallery', rows of seats away from the main table most people were sitting on. I literally couldn't sit still; the pain was so bad.

Someone was talking at the table. Impulsively I shouted; "Help me, I need help, I'm dying," ...... There was complete silence, and Everyone turned to look at me. (Oh hell...). The guy who seemed to be leading the meeting said, "Stay there and after the meeting people will talk to you." (WHAT!) Supreme humiliation rained down. "Let's go!" I said to Alex, "No, he said to stay here." Alex wouldn't budge, dammit! I hid even deeper behind his shoulder, feeling my head spasm against his back. I couldn't have walked out if I wanted to, I really didn't want to stay there. In my imagination, I was back in my car driving off the mountain.

The meeting ended and I was surrounded by women reaching out to me. I did take their numbers and listen to their suggestions. One being to take salt and baking soda baths. I lived in the bathtub for two weeks. It helped immensely. I would call the women and say, 'well you told me to call!' However, this long vignette ends with what happened three days after that first meeting.

I lost my mind. I was in Safeway. I 'felt' my mind recede, literally. I heard a voice in my head which said, 'go get the salt and go to the checkout counter' (if it ain't practical, it ain't spiritual). I went to the check-out counter; I'm telling you there was nothing else going on in my head. After all the obsessive thoughts that bantered me about, it was eerily quiet.

Then the voice said, 'get in the car and drive home'. GOD is sometimes described as an acronym for 'Good Orderly Direction'. These directions were very specific, and easy to follow. Oh, if only it was always like that. Damn free will. I made it back to my mother's house. By that time my stoner boyfriend had heard enough about me driving my car off the cliff and had retreated into his own semi-coherent zombie space between his ears. Mama's house was my current sanctuary.

I sat on the back porch overlooking the Rio Grande River and the city of Albuquerque. As well as those grand Sandia mountains that I was so fond of 'zooming off the cliff' in my imagination. From the view on my mother's porch, the whole scene was peaceful and majestic.

I very clearly stated to the universe that I didn't want to be here without God. Oh, and by the way ...could you give me a reason to stay? And I waited. Then I had a vision. One that had been developing in my imagination for years.

It was like God plucked out a dream of great importance to me and I accepted the mission. For the first time in my 28 years of life I was truly serene. My head was quiet. My heart was settled. I agreed to stay if God was with me. I had a purpose. I would never go another day without the presence of God. Writing this many decades later, I know I have never been alone. Every cell in my body is infused with life. I know even more now. We may die, but we will never perish. Turning my will and life over to the care of God restored me to sanity. Best decision I ever made. Best care I ever had. I started to become.

21.

DESSERTS ROOTS GROW DEEPER

I t was suggested that I get a sponsor. I wasn't sure what that was, but I started paying attention to the women in the NA meetings. I knew a sponsor helped others to work the steps, but I wasn't quite clear what that was at first. I noticed one woman at the meetings that truly looked like she was listening. This intrigued me more than anything. I asked her if she would be my sponsor. She agreed. She truly did have an amazing gift of listening. She told me that her ex-boyfriend had held a meeting hostage at gunpoint with her in it, when she tried breaking up with him. The meeting was in the hospital. He held the meeting hostage for about three hours. Eventually the police got in and arrested him. Sometimes the best stories keep us here.

When I started to go to meetings regularly, I got crazy. My thoughts were insane, and my feelings were all over the place. One minute I was angry, then lonely, then horny, then sad. It was crazy. I couldn't feel stable. That is when I really understood the definition of addiction. It wasn't using drugs until your insane, it was much deeper than that. It was a recognition that the dis-ease is already in us. Drugs are just a symptom of the disease.

Narcotics Anonymous defines addiction as follows, physical, mental and spiritual. After the craziness in my head and the wild emotional ride, I truly understood what the definition of addiction meant. Drugs hid the wild thoughts in my head and the instability of my emotions. When I cleaned up, my real insanity became clear. Our malady is in our thoughts and feelings. We do not have a patent on obsessive thoughts and compulsive feelings. It appears to be a human trait. I do believe the more abuse or trauma we live through the more unstable we become with our two most dysfunctional ways of meeting and greeting the world, our thoughts, and feelings, and more importantly how and what we tell ourselves the world is.

I thought that if only everyone else could just get there shit together, I would be ok. Everything seemed to be wrong. From my personal relationships to politics, religion, education, corporations, boyfriends, jobs, friends. Etc. I was very sick and very uncomfortable in my own body. Mostly though everything was someone else's fault. I could barely accept the world I knew. It was toxic and I was in the middle of it. Don't get me wrong, I enjoyed my artistry I engaged in.

I came home and pulled weeds at my mothers. It was symbolic. I was pulling the weeds in my soul. I started doing theatre in a large dinner theatre complex. I was briefly wrapped up in a belief about good battling evil which brought me to therapy and to recovery. It scared me. It also showed me the deeper trouble in my soul that was so hard for me to see, which gave way to the recognition of the evil I experienced in the cult. This only really came to light when I went to Phoenix and took care of my father when he was dying.

Back to my sponsor and the NA meetings. I went to meetings every day before I left for Phoenix. It really helped to have my sponsor. She was supportive and taught me a lot. She gave me some very good writing assignments to start with that kept me sane. She also explained a lot about recovery and the 12 steps. She was loving and kept a job.

What affected me the most was when I ran into a little difficulty at work. I was doing singing telegrams. I enjoyed this immensely. We would get information about the person we were singing to and write it into a little ditty. Often, I was doing PG strip-o-grams that took place in homes, or offices or even restaurants. I had an incredible wit and could turn it on you in a second. It was comedy with an edge. I had some great characters, I was a widower, all in black with a wide brimmed veiled hat, a bag lady, who was obnoxious as hell, and often got kicked out of the places I went to perform in till I told them I was there to do a singing telegram. Yes, I was that good. I was also a professional dancer, or a myriad of other characters. It was a lot of fun.

The woman who owned 'Flim Flam Singing Telegrams' was sober. It was one of the reasons she gave me the job. She was a clown. She double booked herself on a gig and asked me to fill in. I did not have much 'clowning' experience, but I stepped in. My boss had a great following as a clown. I showed up at the child's birthday party and as soon as the birthday boy saw me, he got very upset that I was not my boss. I tried to be the clown but even the other kids were upset that my boss was not doing the show. I eventually left. I'm not even sure if the parents were happy that I was there.

That one event tore me apart. I kept thinking that no one should treat a child like that and disappoint them. I really went downhill on this one. I got suicidal again. I decided I did not want to stay in a world where children were treated badly and abused. My reaction was much larger than the situation called for. One thing I learned from a later sponsor is that when my reaction is much bigger than the situation calls for, then the trauma is in the past.

This event was what alerted me to the fact that I had some serious issues in my past. I could not stop thinking about kids that are mistreated and abused. I stopped working for the signing telegram company. This 'issue' was what really pulled the covers off a deep pain and a strong desire to die. Even the effort it took me to keep dreadful things in the past was an energy drain. An effort that was doomed to fail.

The cancer had eaten through Daddy's right femur, in the exact spot that I had broken my femur running down the hill to clean the marshmallow skewer at 11. I had a visceral reaction to his bone being eaten away. I knew then it just seemed too much like self-blame, even before I knew the details of the long years of hell, he perpetrated on me and others. The cancerous malice was the last call of the last dance of a deeply broken man.

I traveled to Phoenix. Armed with a broken-down car and two months of freedom from all mind- and mood-altering drugs and a sponsor chosen because of her uncanny ability to listen with compassion. My sponsor had me do a 'fear, anger and resentment' list and read it to her.

I did not really know what that meant but she walked me through how to write it in columns and get this stuff I had hidden, out. I did write a great deal on this exercise. Thank God for Sponsors. I read my list to my sponsor. She listened. That day I was listened in to existence. My sponsor really was wonderful. Stating all this stuff that I had held inside was incredibly freeing to me. I was lifted and felt like I had unburdened myself for the first time ever.

I am still very grateful to my first sponsor for all she did. I was able to go to Phoenix and take care of my father till he died. More was revealed in the time I took care of him. I stayed in Phoenix for two years. I didn't see my sponsor much when I went back to Albuquerque. She was doing more AA. I will never forget her. She started me on a path that saved my life.

The resulting freedom I gained sharing that information with her, gave me the peace to get to Phoenix and be there for my father

Shortly after the fall from grace with the clown fiasco and coming face to face with the pain I had been hiding, I got the call from my brother about my father's health. Daddy's cancer ate through his femur. He got out of bed and his leg buckled underneath him. He was in the hospital in Scottsdale. His girlfriend called my brother before she took off. She could not handle it anymore. Finding NA meetings while in Phoenix continued to save my life and kept me from killing his girlfriend.

Dan asked if I could go down to Phoenix and be with him. Daddy was pretty much held hostage to his girlfriend for months after his diagnoses. She would have fits and demand the money he promised her in the middle of whatever treatment he was receiving. Until the cancer shattered his femur bone and he ended up in the hospital. That's when she called my brother and said she couldn't take care of my father anymore and I was called out to care for him.

Unfortunately, she kept showing up after my father's hospital stay, I chased her away in not so sweet ways. She turned out to be a victimized piranha. Quite fitting for a man that had eaten souls for much of his physical existence. Nurturing my father through his dying, restored my being in more ways than I knew possible. It also gave me the strength to keep discovering who he had been and what he had done.

Years later another sponsor would save me, and subsequently my mother, by the same qualities of compassionate listening. She gifted me with a phrase I cherish. In recovery we 'listen souls into existence'. This is still one of the most beautiful spiritual principles we practice, given that at any meeting we will share no more than once, for usually no more than five minutes, then listen for the rest of at least an hour. We restore our own souls while listening other souls into existence.

I got to Phoenix after a seven-hour drive, and it was hot as hell. My father was in the hospital, so I stayed at his apartment, which was in Scottsdale off Hayden boulevard. I fell in love with Hayden. All the greenery on the sides of the road. I had the pleasure to live there a few months ago. I visited my father in the hospital for several days. I made a very common mistake in recovery, trying to make amends when I had not done any other steps. I had no idea of the history I had with my father.

It would take me twenty-five years to get an idea of what I lived through. I am still healing from what I've learned but I am very much on the other side of it.

The first day I stayed with him at the hospital my father told me of the romantic love he had for my mother and how they met in Europe. It was the first time ever I had really heard of their love and the romantic time they had together in Europe. My father was stationed in an Army office as a typist. I don't even know if he was ever in the army or if he was just a civilian employee. He was working in Paris and living in Spain. My mother was traveling with a girlfriend of hers. They both graduated from Penn State. My parents met in Lisbon Portugal. There was four of them that palled around together, my parents and my mother's friend and a pal of my father. They spent the summer in Europe. My young naïve, Catholic mother was devirginized. Now I know that had a lot to do with their eventual marriage, but I know now there was love between them.

They met both families at the wedding. Since my mother was not a virgin, they did not have a Catholic marriage. That was also because my father's family was not Catholic. Mama wore a blue silk 1950's dress. She looked beautiful. My grandparents looked sad. It was almost a foretelling. Their brilliant Catholic daughter not walking down the aisle in a church. This was bigger than anybody ever let on. Funny how none of my father's family was in the pictures. Shortly after the wedding my fathers' mother, my grandmother, told my mother that she would go to her church, and they would go to theirs. They rejected her almost as soon as she became a part of the family. The dismissal that went on for generations was alive on both sides of my family.

I loved my father for showing me that there was romance between my parents. It gave me hope. I have had bursts of romance in my relationships. Thorne truly was the love of my life and still is. Romance is hard to find. We cannot help but love, even despite ourselves but romance is an art. My parents knew romance. May we find more of it in our worlds. It is a truly novel practice.

Daddy was moved to another hospital to have surgery in Scottsdale AZ. His girlfriend showed up again. She had this victim demeanor. The day Daddy came home from the hospital I fixed him dinner. I stepped out for a minute and when I came back, she was sitting on his hospital bed eating his food. I'd had it with her sniveling tantrums and leaving him then showing up and eating his food. Enough! I grabbed the food then I grabbed her face and pushed her off the bed and out of the house. I officially became his caretaker. We found a wonderful healer for him, and Daddy's last days progressed with love. This was true of him too. He looked at me with so much love. Never had I seen him do this. As he wasted away in his last months, he gave love.

I started having dreams that he was molesting me. I would tell him that his leg was unable to walk, and he couldn't molest me. Still after the dreams started, I had no doubt. We moved to an apartment very close to the hospital and his doctor's office. He was getting targeted chemo every day. His oncologist was an asshole, so we fired him and worked with Jeff the healer.

Jeff put me on a cleanse as well to clean out my stomach and liver. I would make a tea out of white oak bark and another of dandelion root. I would drink a cup of each in a day. I still believe my physical recovery was phenomenal because of the tinctures I drank for the last two months of my father's life. I would read Daddy the Big Book of AA. I loved the stories. Daddy was never able to get sober until the end of his life.

There were times when I tried to talk to him about the dreams of being molested. When I did, he would freak out. I could see the fear in his eyes, and he would go into a panic attack. I would get angry that I wouldn't have a chance to address the abuse with him. He could not handle it. His cancer would literally grow when I mentioned abuse. I believe his cancer was his penance for the pain he caused others.

I told Daddy about the meadow in heaven where my loved ones were. At that time, I was visiting the meadow, but I had not started rescuing the children inside of me. Daddy wanted a place to go in heaven. So, we created a castle for him. It was right across the field from the meadow. Daddy kept saying that there was nothing else he had to do while he was alive. I heard him say this many times and I would get scared. Then I accepted it. I knew then that when we don't have any more dreams to live, we may be ready to die. This is not a bad thing. Daddy was done. He wanted to move on. We would walk to the chemo treatment and walk back. Then he had his gentle session with Jeff, and they would talk calmly. I think the end of his life was the best time he knew.

22.

DADDY'S DEATH

I t's hot as hell. I could see his shoulders slump. There wasn't much left, his clavicle caving in on itself in his hospital gown. His labored breathing, the ribs that I knew could break with the slightest touch months ago. His hair short, unkempt, thinning on parts of his scalp, while the turn of his head caught his skeletal cheek bones and dryness of his lips. Such a handsome man he had been, now he was barely there.

"Take him home, we could get a nurse to look in on him tonight,"

This oncologist motivated getting the apartment a block away. Saw him through the daily pinpointed radiation treatment.

"We could try morphine to ease him through the night".

That was it. Now he was struggling to breathe, to bear the heat bouncing off the sidewalk, baking his bare feet. He is fading, I am wilting, sweating, and struggling to hold onto the manual wheelchair. His last day here and it's a sauna, there is still a block to walk. Anxiety sets in with his imminent death.

He is done, his body continues to shrink, but we made it back into the living room, placed him in the hospital bed in the middle of the room. He knows, says nothing. A moment held in time for eternity. So hot.

The middle of July in Phoenix, an intense day to be out on a final walk. Two weeks before, his girlfriend Beth was there. She locked the front door and held the paper for his signature. Leaving the 'it', the minutia of his life, to her.

She already had a vibrant lover, but the drama was played out. She locked every window and door. Snide in the deserved remains that would be lost soon after. She disappeared in his wobbly car, lost in the Bisbee Mountains, showing up as his ashes scattered in the trees and he whispered away. Remnants of the quiet struggle to remain viable for years under a surgical evil and malice that menaced and sliced away the innocence of his soul. So disturbed was he, the pedophile barely lived that once filled his inebriated belly and damaged mind.

It started in his legs, the hardening of the flesh, the breath constrained and soon that pain can't be tolerated as the lungs filled with fluid. It took the night. He rang the little bell on the hospital tray. I was tranced, deeper and deeper, as the lack of oxygen moved up his legs. His body became a rock, so little movement of sweet cellular fluidity, it was just a hardened foot, then a hardened calf and knee. The pain and the panic showing in his skeletal face, and the trance gripped me more. I became the ghost that he had been in my dreams of him rising out of the hospital bed to molest me.

I'm aware. It's dark. Someone is coming towards me. It's foggy. I can't really tell what's going on. He's all white as he gets closer, he gets clearer. "You can't walk, your leg is broken", fear paralyzes me, "the cancer ate through your leg." My father keeps advancing. He is like a zombie, not conscious. He's touching me, he's harsh. He tries to take my blankets off. I'm terrified. I scream; "You can't walk!!" "You can't touch me". He can't move. The cancer ate through his bone, right where my femur was broken when I was eleven. Yet he is there trying to molest me.

I wake up. I can hear the oxygen machine. I hear him turn in his hospital bed. The dream is like a ghost vision. I see it in my head like two stick figures. Me sitting up in bed, him advancing on me. I can't deny it. This was real. For years I'd had vague memories. I hid them so well. I was broken. I was suicidal. The world was an unsafe place. I was miserable. Now I'm here, caring for his broken body and I can't deny what was going on in the dark. When the night became a separate thing, an unreal reality.

When my femur broke at eleven, the lower femur bone literally pushed past the splintered upper bone. I was in the hospital, in traction for six weeks, then in a cast and on crutches for a year. When I heard that the cancer had eaten through his bone when he was in the hospital...it felt like justice. Denial clears as cells reach safety.

I remember, after the accident, him driving me to the hospital in Las Vegas, New Mexico. They couldn't treat me there. We had to drive to Santa Fe. We had been picnicking in the country, close to the river, and I ran down to clean a marshmallow off the skewer. I tripped on the rocks of the campfire. Maybe I did a summersault and landed on my feet and snapped the bone, causing a spiral fracture.

My cousin whispered 'faker' all the way to my house. I passed in and out of consciousness the whole trip. I remember Daddy, being afraid. His skin pale, eyes wide. He knew, it was him, his actions, and his deathly intentions. His attempts to capture an innocent soul, his rage that he could never possess the innocence.

As my awareness dawns while I cared for him as he was dying, I would attempt to address the abuse with him. He shuddered and couldn't hear it. I could see the cancer growing in him. Like he was killing himself with the distorted cells for his horrific actions. He would panic. His life of hell killed him. He killed himself for what he inflicted on others.

"You can't hurt me; your guilt has eaten your bone right where my femur was torn away. This stopped you from invading me with your overpowering dominance, from filling a backhoe of betrayal, tearing into the tenderness that could never be stolen".

Now I was the walking zombie, his fear and suffocation, striking into my life, my pulse. Still the medusa snakes sucked the air out of the room as his pelvis turned to stone and his shining eyes turned to me, begging to be anything but what he had been, so honest in that interminable suffocation. Medusa was blessed to become stone within minutes, his hardening took hours.

"No more, I can't come out again"

This is all I could speak to him. I needed to be released from the zombie state. I allowed him to drain my energy to prolong his stay. Until I uttered those words to him. He did not speak again. It was shortly before dawn.

I called Billy, I could not walk out again, begged him, to be there, in that moment when the cells hung in the air, as if my father's body was everywhere, fascia pumping in thin air, the lack of blood and oxygen squeezed out in a scream, clawing to breathe in air that could not replace the stone of his organs. His eyes transfixed on his frozen blood cells. The consciousness of his hell released me, and I fell into a pulsing black sleep.

It was quiet, it hurt my ears, my breath mixed with grief and vulnerability. The oxygen machine was off. The sound of nothing was so loud. Now it was the fear of no sound, the air molecules oscillating as I ran out of my room. The silence unbearably terrifying. He was there, gone. His mouth in the shape of a scowl from the last breath which stopped when his viscera hardened hours ago. His lungs now quiet caverns, filled with solidified liquid. Still no sound of oxygen. I saw the machine in the corner, not moving.

There was nothing but his stone feet, cold on my lips as I kissed them. I wasn't there, as desired; desperate, since I had not stayed to see him leave, to hang in the balance, watch in the precipice as he slithered away. As if I had failed. I kissed his ankles, the silence deafening. The stone body there, where before was movement, coloration of liveness that fills our marrow. So quiet, screaming quiet. This was a body, nothing more. Who he had been, his adoring eyes in the hospital bed, more liquid and magnetic than I had ever known him when he could stand and hurt. His 'self' so abruptly missing.

He's dead.

My father died two months after I came to take care of him. His girlfriend did get all his stuff. It may not have been much of a blessing, but she did get his car. I relapsed on cigarettes the day he died. His death was the last day I ever felt suicide. It was not easy after that. I feel apart at Christmas and went into a treatment center in February. I celebrated my one-year clean anniversary in treatment. This grungy ghetto place kept me clean and alive.

23.

THE PHONE RINGS

The phone rings. It's late, very late. The darkness shreds my eyes. I'm in between. Daddy's been dead less than a week. I'm still in the apartment. I grope through the darkness and find the phone. I answer it. There's no response. Suddenly I'm being pulled into the veil, that misty line between me and death. I feel it pull me. I'm dizzy, I'm moving. The darkness moves past me. Soon I'll cross that line. If I touch it, will I disappear, will I see him? Will he still be grimacing? He's calling me. I know it's him. I can feel the pull. I can feel my heartbeat. How close do I need to be before my heartbeat stops? I hang up.

The phone rings. It's dark again. The pulling starts immediately. I answer the phone. I'm in a vortex. My heartbeat is choking me. It's in my throat. I can't scream. The darkness whirls around me. Maybe he's touching me with cold fingers. Maybe I'm just so close to that veil. I won't be able to stop being pulled in. I'll be sucked up by the darkness. I'm raw. I hang up.

The third night the phone rings. I can't move. My eyes are open but I'm frozen. If I move, I won't come out. I'll be swallowed. Finally, the ringing stops.

I answer the phone the next night. There's silence. The stillness on the other end changes and I speak, "I don't know what you're doing but you must be sick. Is this some kind of deranged game?" I hang up.

I awaken before it rings waiting. I vacillate between trepidation and preparedness. I may still be pulled in, there is still the swirling darkness somewhere in the room. I'm sure of it. I let it ring a few times, then answer. I listen to the changes of the stillness. "It's ok. No matter what you're doing. You are still loved. This seems psycho. I accept it. You'll be ok. I forgive you for this." Then I hang up. The dark isn't spinning as much.

Later, that night the phone rings again. I feel the fear, it's still in my throat. I answer silently. I hear him speak. "No one has ever said that to me, no one has loved me like that, has let this be ok." He sounds a little older than me. His words stop the vortex. The darkness, pulling me toward a precipice I wasn't ready to fall into, softens like a sound wave melting into the night. I hold onto his voice like it's a rope to a reality that stopped existing weeks ago. "Why are you calling me?" Silence. He hangs up.

The phone rings. The vortex raises slightly. I breathe. The darkness moves in molecules bumping into each other. I answer with no words. "It's part of the turn on", he says. "I call random people when I'm sucking my lover." There is a relief, this act, perverted as it was, is so human. The darkness levels. I breathe in. I can't speak about the brink, where I was being pulled over, it was a sexual prank. There is a lightness before I'm hit with irritation. "Why would you do that, call random people to get off?" He paused, "It heightens the experience, to suck him when strangers are listening." This man, in this perverse way, brought me back from the edge. I gave myself the gift of acceptance. I gave him love. I learned how to love what threatened to swallow me into death. I forgave the darkness, the death, the perversity.

He became a part of my life; I became a part of his sexual bottom. He called frequently and told me of his escapades. The strangers in the theatres, the midnight calls to heighten his acts of pleasure. Places he would meet strangers, how lonely he was. How torn he became. We talked about sexual addiction. I don't think I told him how he saved me from the dark. I was there for him for months as he bottomed out. His attempts at suicide, to stop the behaviors that were killing him. We talked about treatment. His calls became more desperate. Then he stopped calling.

I hope he is here, alive, healthy, in a loving relationship. We may have traded the darkness. I learned recovery, where nothing should be denied love, even death and addiction. This was one of my first healings. Yet addicts come to me always, in many ways. Some are the children of multiple personalities. They call needing a mama, needing someone who will not judge, who understands. I am a healer. I am a teacher.

24.

THE PERFECT WAKE

S ometimes an event creates such an aura of 'alrightness' that it is awash with perfection. There is a shimmering as if even the molecules align with the resonance of 'what is'.

It started with the funeral director, my brother and myself. Yes, a dangerous combo. My brother and I in the same room can ignite simply based on subtext and tone. Add in a snide funeral director with his soft, insulting, benignly irritating voice and cadence, and a perfect storm is born. At least in my supremely kinesthetic sensitivity, I was geared to seek out and react to the undertones insinuated from across the mahogany desk. He was guaranteed to sell the most expensive coffin, the only option a decent grieving family member should choose. We chose cremation...and a grand coffin for the viewing. Coffin $10,000, viewing hour $2,000, cremation $500. And off we go.

I walked out shuffling in barbed wire. Family dynamics were sufficiently ignited. My super saturated Spidey senses were interpreting data ten feet ahead of me and the hammer found every nail in the form of insults potentially stated, or thoughts, insinuated in facial muscles, and/or in the silence so heavily burdened by what 'That' meant.

Still came the day when we gathered. The family, the few friends my father had, my recovery friends, and most of all ...my mother. Amazing she showed up. Rarely escaping from her self-imposed glass jar of denial and safety, Mama was actually there, almost fully aware. Sweet, curious, perhaps feeling a safety she hadn't had known since Europe 34 years prior. When she met the man she fell in love with and lost any semblance of familial sanity she may have glimpsed in her younger years.

My siblings were there, all except for my youngest sister. She utterly lacked any sense that she belonged at the wake or had any consciousness that he would remember her or acknowledge her. Given that his current state was dead, it's highly likely he wasn't acknowledging any of us. We mingled, chatted, looked at his 'sleeping' form in the golden coffin and watched the kids run around the viewing room.

Amidst all this I experienced a sense of calmness. I was raised up while sitting down and what was happening glistened with an almost a theatrical filter. It was perfection. Everyone there was truly in the place they were meant to be in, the light, sound, my father's body, the chairs, the short eulogies, the full feelings of love for everything around me created a lightness and a completeness to the night. I became bigger than myself. All was right.

We spread his ashes in the Bisbee Mountains. His girlfriend showed up and I welcomed her. This was the woman who locked me out of the apartment long enough to get him to sign over all his worldly possessions to her. Which turned out to be a house with a balloon payment, and a bookstore in the middle of a liability suit since a woman had fallen down the stairs; and his personal items, poetry, books in the middle of Spanish translation, and other as sundries. I wanted his written work more than anything. Sometimes what we don't get turns out to be the biggest blessing.

Goodbye daddy. All your dreams were shared. How you've grown since then!

25.

ADDICTION

When I cared for Daddy, he would look at me with so much love in his eyes. I think it was the first time anyone had ever taken care of him. He was a monster in this life, not only a Satanist, and a rising priest at that, but he abused all of us and his stepchildren. Yet when I addressed the abuse, Daddy would panic. I think his cancer was metastasized alcoholism and guilt coupled with self-hatred. When he died, I was lost. I slowly sunk down in a morose grief.

So, I lived. I lived through daddy's death, hard as it was to accept the recurring visions of rape and incest, I experienced during his death. After leaving the apartment we shared, I moved in with a recovery friend. And quickly fell apart. Daddy died in July. The world gets turned around after death, I felt like the shade.

My life kept spiraling down. The sleeplessness got worse; I was paying less attention at work. My self-centeredness was becoming more of a problem. Let me define that. Self-centeredness, in recovery terms, is the obsessive focus on self. While at times it may be arrogance, most often it is defined as the harshest self-punishing thoughts. The disease of addiction, as defined in Narcotics Anonymous, is physical compulsion, mental obsession, and spiritual self-centeredness. I will say this again. It is important this is known. This is a killing disease.

It ends in jails, institutions, and death. If we don't find a new way to live.

The obsession is like playing a record over and over in our heads, only it is a thought that we cannot stop thinking. Almost always it is a thought that is disturbing and keeps playing out something that happened or how we interpreted the event that was disturbing to us. Maybe we play out what we wanted to say or thought we should have said. Most often we go over and over what happened in each experience or conversation and cannot stop replaying it. The compulsion is often the feelings we have about the thoughts we're thinking. Compulsion can also be with a substance and the physical need to feel the high or compulsively eating or compulsive sex.

Most often the obsessive thought, and the compulsive feeling generated by the thought, such as anger or fear or shame, form a closed loop that is extremely difficult to get out of. Think the thought, feel the feeling. Only it's more like think a disturbing thought, then feel a disturbing feeling that we ping and then it is back to the disturbing thought. The fact that we can't get out of the closed loop is what makes it self-centered. We literally need a catalyst to stop the self-centered obsession, and compulsion.

Recovery is an ongoing practice of finding more and more tools to stop the 'addictive' cycle of obsession, compulsion, self-centeredness. That is why I stayed in NA. The fact that we understood that addiction was a much deeper malady than picking up a drug is why I stayed in NA. That made sense to me. I knew I struggled from the constant negative thoughts and the feelings I felt from the negative thinking. The drugs just helped us stop all thinking and feeling. They were not long-term solutions. Addiction always worsens and the mental and physical maladies become more pronounced. Either we find a new way to live, or we go on to the bitter ends, jails, institutions, and death.

Alcoholics Anonymous Big Book passage, page 62:,

"If the rest of the world would only behave; the outlaw safe cracker who thinks society has wronged him; and the alcoholic who has lost all and is locked up. Whatever our protestations, are not most of us concerned with ourselves, our resentments, or our self-pity?

Selfishness - self-centeredness! That, we think, is the root of our troubles. Driven by a hundred forms of fear, self-delusion, self-seeking, and self-pity, we step on the toes of our fellows, and they retaliate. Sometimes they hurt us, seemingly without provocation, but we invariably find that at some time in the past we have made decisions based on self which later placed us in a position to be hurt.

So, our troubles, we think, are basically of our own making. They arise out of ourselves, and the 'alcoholic' is an extreme example of self-will run riot, though he usually doesn't think so. Above everything, we alcoholics must be rid of this selfishness. We must, or it kills us! God makes that possible. And there often seems no way of entirely getting rid of self without His aid.

Many of us had moral and philosophical convictions galore, but we could not live up to them even though we would have liked to. Neither could we reduce our self-centeredness much by wishing or trying on our own power. We had to have God's help.

This is the how and why of it. First of all, we had to quit playing God. It didn't work. Next, we decided that hereafter in this drama of life, God was going to be our Director. He is the Principal; we are His agents. Most good ideas are simple, and this concept was the keystone of the new and triumphant arch through which we passed to freedom."

26.

FROM LIFE COMES LIFE

I was hired at Bobby McGee's. All the waiters were characters, I was a gypsy. That was the funniest part of working there. I would give kids glass marbles and tell their fortune. I was hot for the cook; damn was he sexy. He was dating Raggedy Ann. Yeah trippy.

Bobby McGee's was the first full time job I had after taking care of Daddy. It was a hopping place in the bar after the dinner shift. I avoided that as much as possible. Being clean was still new at six months. In fact, I remember a man coming into Bobby McGee's and celebrating his nine-month anniversary sober with a beer. So much for his recovery. I knew that would not work. I was losing myself. I stayed up all night watching tv.

My performance as a waitress slowly went downhill. I was always a good gypsy. Bobby McGee's really started hopping around 10pm long after the 4pm early bird special and the 8pm birthday parties. The food was surprisingly good. I was losing my mind again and grief kept me up most nights. I was also stealing my roommates Jenny Craig's meals. She got tired of it eventually.

I was called in for a 'chat' at work and my lack of attention to detail was made painfully clear. I never went back after that meeting. I couldn't face the shame that part of my losing self to find the hell I lived, and hid in denial, was obvious in my work environment. I totally fell apart after I went home for Christmas. We often don't realize how toxic our families are until we return for the holidays. Armed with six months of incest group therapy and nine months of abstinence, returning to the family fold brought me face to face with the sick dynamics my family lived and practiced.

For me it was poison. I don't remember the visit being particularly bad or the events being horrid. I was filled with knowledge of abuse, which I was still coming to terms with. The family silence was deafening. After a lifetime of being split and shattered, of feeling broken in the morning, or enraged over apparently nothing; I was getting a glimpse of what was real. It was almost impossible for me to see it. The biggest truth was that I could not look at myself in the mirror. I gained weight. I had friends in the incest group which helped me live in that reality. Being at home was again like living in smoke and mirrors. I was fractured. Too many parts were not coming together. I didn't mention my newfound therapy at home. I just went back to Phoenix and feel apart. It took me till January to slowly lose my ability to care for myself.

It became obvious that I couldn't work. I didn't try much. I just watched movies all night and secretly ate Jenny Craig. I attended some incest anonymous groups. It was the only program I attended where I felt like my skin was burning off. People shared honestly about their abuses and it left me completely vulnerable. I didn't want to be alone after an incest meeting. I was scared, alone, and thoroughly shaken. I stopped going when I found out one of my friends had killed herself. She was very active in the incest group. It took them longer than a week to find her dead. I realized I needed my skin and the incest therapy group gave me a slight feeling of grounding.

My roommate put up with me longer than she should have. I had no money for rent in February. Another recovery friend offered me her place. She was one of the few strippers I knew in recovery that had no qualms about stripping. Had I but had her resolve. She was going out of town for a few weeks and asked me to bird sit. She had three birds.

One was her baby; I think it was a cockatiel. The bird was not happy that my friend left. The two weeks left me scarred from bird bites and a surety that I would never own a bird. Shortly after she returned, she stopped going to meetings. We lost touch.

I had nothing left and was accepted into a treatment center, Calvery, in a bad part of Phoenix. It was an established facility with meetings daily and Catholic overtones without too much preaching. I went into phase 2 and was able to skip the intensive treatment program with a year clean. I was humiliated to find myself in treatment and grateful to have a place to go that I didn't have to pay for.

Many of the participants came right off the street. I butted head with another 'patient'. She was black, hardened, street wise, and took no shit. We left respecting each other. I never saw her in twelve step meetings. I hope she's alive. I met friends in Calvary that I still know to this day, we still share recovery. Six months later I was able to work again and got a job as a crisis counselor on a mobile team. It seems like an oxymoron going from treatment to crisis counseling. I was surprisingly good at it. Except when dealing with using addicts. They were the hardest ones to help on the street, even with the ability to relate.

Early recovery was painful but also filled with discovery and developing close ties with good friends that are still in my life. We had a big meeting and dance every month and everyone in NA at the time would be there. Activities haven't been the same after those dances stopped. The dances created a closeness in the fellowship that lasted for years, even after we lost the space.

Crisis counseling helped me to assess a situation quickly and take action or get backup. It also taught me how to handle myself and others in dangerous and tragic situations. It is not against the law to be insane. It's only against the law if you are a danger to self or others. The grey area between the two leaves people very hurt.

I also waded through knee deep crap in houses to remove the kids from truly toxic environments and cried over the tragedy of mental illness when we responded to a football player in his senior year who tied himself to his workout bench when he was diagnosed with schizophrenia and was told he had to go to a mental health center after school instead of play football. His grief was palpable. To watch this very large boy devastated and hand cuffed to his workout bench was tragic.

I dated the smartest man I knew. He had been in recovery about a year longer than I was and he was sweet and brilliant. He also wasn't interested in having children. I was. I broke up with him when I was pregnant. I saw the life flow out of him, and it looked like a candle had been blown out. I hurt him and it took him many years before he was in a position to have a relationship with his son. I was incredibly lucky to have such an amazing boy. Ian Andrew. At two months Ian and I and my beloved cat moved back to New Mexico and in with my mother. I was back to the toxic environment that created the crazies. Back in the bell jar.

Even with all the personality conflicts I got into. I made it through gratefully and soon I was going to the monthly NA dances and had a little apartment in central Phoenix and worked as a crisis counselor for two years till my beloved baby boy was born. I was a part of the NA community and I felt connected. I even started incest therapy before I left for Albuquerque. This was when the hard part started, I could not even look myself in the mirror. I do thank God for the 12 steps of NA. I am grateful that I could be just as I was in NA and still be accepted. The 12 steps are a journey into us. We learn a tremendous amount. We become responsible for ourselves. Thirty-three years later I am still here.

27.

THE BODY, MY BODY, MY BELOVED SELF

I've learned to love my body and experience myself from the inside out. For most of my life I rejected my body. When I started sexual abuse therapy after Daddy died, I couldn't look in the mirror. A large part of the difficulty was a rejection of being in a physical body. It was almost like I was rejecting my body after the amount of abuse in early life.

I went through a period of being unable to dance. I had danced all the way through college and afterwards when I lived in San Diego until I got clean from drugs. I felt clumsy and not in my body. This was while I was addressing the abuse and active in NA. This is not easy. I did not remember my ability to dream and imagine a different reality.

I think also what kept me alive as a child was having almost a fantastical relationship with God and Jesus. It was not religiously based. I was a child of the 60's and Jesus was a friend, an imaginary being with me often. I think this was true, I was very much centered in a spiritual world. I also remember thinking I was not supposed to be on this planet, I was really from somewhere else. Nonbelonging a strong residue from the cult practice of burying children in coffins. Not much loving/embracing there.

I struggled with weight in early recovery. We have a saying. We put down the spoon and pick of the fork. I did gain weight after daddy died, sneaking the Jenny Craig food of my roommate. I kept that on and felt grosser than I really was. There was such a feeling of lack of control with my body. I got pregnant at 30 and went on the Bradley diet suggested for natural birth, it did not work well.

My pregnancy was very difficult, and I gained 60 pounds. I felt like my belly was going to burst open and the baby would fall out. At the time I was working as a crisis counselor on a mobile team. One of my partners, a father of four, was so good at soothing me and calming my pregnancy craziness. I admired that his wife may have that support.

I broke up with Michael, my baby's father, during the pregnancy. I needed to create stability. Michael was anything but stable. He is a brilliant man and he struggled for years after Ian was born.

My body shut down after two days of attempting a natural birth. Mama was kind enough to be with me when Ian was born. We had a lovely birthday dinner for me and I went into the hospital the next day. I was in labor for two days. Ian never engaged in my birth canal. Thank God. However, it took two days before the doctor decided to perform a caesarian. Mama read the whole time. She sat next to me in a chair and read her books. Only once did I finally ask Mama to be present for me. I really struggled after the caesarian birth of my son at 31.

Yet I had my amazing son. He was 10 pounds at birth and never engaged in the birth canal. I'm sure that saved us both. I remember the doctor trying to get his shoulders out, pulling them side to side. I named my son Ian Andrew Mallon (I AM) purposely.

The babies were in a nursery in the recovery ward. I could hear the babies crying, then I'd hear Ian wailing. He was head and shoulder over the other babies. So adorable. Mama loved Ian. He was her favorite grandchild.

The physical difficulties continued in my life. I struggled to nurse my son although I did gratefully. It was very painful but worth the closeness I had with him. Mama provided us her home for two years and Ian was a love light for her. For me, I learned to get up every day and wash the dishes. Soon it became the Tao of Dishwashing.

My mother and sister not speaking but together in their bubbles of non-participation. The lack of awareness and engagement was choking for me. So, I washed the dishes and was grateful that Ian had family who would sometimes engage with him. Mama wasn't easy to live with. Partly because she was so out of it.

Ian adored my mother and my sister. He taught my mother how to hug and love. This created a closeness between him and my sister and mother. He adored them and they thought the world of him.

28.

LOSING OURSELVES
OR BECOMING A CHAMPION

It was the first time I felt the physical experience of the abuse. I'd recently moved back to Albuquerque with my beautiful baby boy Ian and found a therapist specializing in trauma. I later learned the process she used is Reichian therapy. I was lucky enough to experience much more of this process later. This first time I was invited to lie on a mattress in a therapist's office and 'throw a tantrum'.

The result of the tantrum was an actual feeling of being invaded in my vagina. I felt aftereffects of having an unwanted body part in my body. I finally experienced a physical sensation. For the last year of incest therapy, it had only been a mental process. It took me that long to introduce the idea into my mind that I was sexually abused for years. I could not experience the physical act within my body until this day in therapy.

I had been present at the ghetto treatment center when women would go into natural regressions and involuntarily relive the abuse. Most often they would snap out of the experience and not remember what had just happened. Yet I witnessed it. It was very similar to what I often witnessed as a crisis counselor when we were called out to deescalate a situation and the individual appeared to be incoherent of their state of being. Instantaneous regressions were a lot like that.

I joined an incest group the above-mentioned therapist facilitated. I wasn't much interested in more 'talk therapy' although the therapy group in Phoenix had been very helpful and supportive. It's always a little awkward walking into any therapy group. This one was small, maybe six women. What I learned there, changed my life and my approach to me. From the first session I attended, what I learned from the other women was priceless.

At least two of the women spoke of having regressions with very little control of how or when the regressions would come. Regressions are reliving an experience of abuse simultaneously. It can be very frightening to the person experiencing it. One woman spoke of having regressions while she was at work and one while driving. They would take over and then she would 'wake up'. Another participant was extremely dependent on her therapist. She was incapable of calming herself and needed the therapist to respond to save her from herself and her inner demons.

This inability to control what was happening to their bodies and minds was deeply concerning to me. While it was difficult for me to come to terms with the incest that I knew was perpetuated upon me since I was a baby until I broke my leg at 11, I was very unwilling to be at the mercy of instantaneous regressions and/or deep dependency on outside therapists.

Another mind-blowing awareness I developed in the six months I attended this group, was that recovery from this deep turmoil was timeless and spaceless. I was acutely aware that the essence of time was not linear. These early experiences were still active within me and transcended time. The energetic eddy was still within me. The past is only in the past if it is addressed and transformed within the larger energetic field.

'I' still held the emotional brokenness within me. I made a decision. I would not be at the mercy of a regression I could not control or would hold me hostage. Nor would I be subject to heal only when I was in the care, literally in front of, a therapist. What had happened to me existed within me. This was my journey. I became my own champion. I chose to find those parts of me still struggling with the experiences that disempowered me. Where was I still held hostage? What kept me in a prison of memories so painful I could not even know them, much less walk through the trauma inflicted.

I decided to rescue myself. I was now an adult. There was no one that was still 'at fault' for my life. No matter who had harmed me, they were not capable of bringing me back to right relationship with myself. Only I could fully do that. I made a commitment to find the living memories of the trauma that still played out in my psyche. I did that through the one true tool I had available. My imagination.

I began to imagine the scenarios that plagued me and become a part of those storylines. Again and again, I rescued myself, my young self, often within the act of brutal abuse and rape. Incest is not a 'nice' experience. While it differs for all of us, at its base it is disempowering. It is a way for the abuser to attempt to take back the innocence they lost, often in the very same way they were abused. It becomes ritualistic.

It is always overpowering and hurtful and soul crushing. We hurt our most innocent children, inflict on them a bone crushing pain that disrupts the most basic functioning of our neurological systems. It creates a mapping completely different from one organically developed. I know this because I have walked and unwound that pathway within me. Starting with recognizing the vertigo created 'the morning after'. When there is absolutely nothing in the environment that reflects that the night before a rape took place in the household. Nothing to explain why my body felt broken and I could not move. It was denial at its finest.

So I went back in my imagination, to the point of abuse and rescued myself. I walked down the basement stairs and found the child being mutilated and became a giant in my imagination. I became bigger than my abuser. To rescue my child self, I became as big as the block I grew up on. Often, I destroyed the image of the house we lived in because I grew in stature to become the giant that could free the innocent girl held hostage in the basement. I would become whatever shape or being I needed to take the child out of harm's way. For years I rescued myself in whatever way I could. Venturing down into that basement again and again, or into the barn or the field or wherever the abuse took place.

I walked through the landscape of my own mind finding where I was hiding. Finding my younger selves in caves or by rivers or caught in bubbles they could not get out of. I became the champion, the rescuer, which sought them out and brought them into the meadow. The bright meadow where they were welcome, whole, loved by a host of selves there to receive them. So many children were brought to the beautiful meadow I created when I was eleven. This was the essence of my journey.

This journey went into my soul and the abuse went deeper than I ever imagined. This has been an ongoing journey of reawakening my spirit. The beauty of being both the traumatized and the rescuer has fortified my soul and has gone beyond rescuing only myself. It has become a mission that has taken many souls out of their imprisonment. It is the importance of this writing. To help those trapped within their trauma to become champions.

We are not superheroes. We dare to walk into the most depraved situations, still suffering, to find ourselves. Holding no one accountable but ourselves. For all the trauma, we are blessed with spirits many times greater than we can even fathom. We become the compassionate giants needed to find the ones still stuck in a prison of deep pain. We become whole. Our rescued children as much champions as the giants we make ourselves become.

29.

BETRAYED BY OUR BONDS

The best thing I learned when I got clean and participated in 'recovery', was that I did not have to know everything myself. I could develop a toolbox and the more tools I had, the better. I also found that the tools that helped me at one point may not be the tools I needed later. I get to keep finding new tools in my toolbox. It really is like we are peeling an onion, but each layer is a little different and it becomes more dynamic as we become more dynamic.

We have amazing literature in Narcotics Anonymous. It speaks to our 'condition' as we Quakers say. This reflects what we have gone through in our lives and why we chose drugs as a solution in the first place. I have also learned that I can adopt any tool that works for me. This is not a bad thing. Having more tools in our arsenal only gives us more options. There are brilliant people out there. They too address the malady of obsessive thoughts/compulsive feelings. So, I allowed myself to learn from whatever resonated with me. Recovery literature is amazing and my stability, my skeleton, is the 12-Step process of Narcotics Anonymous which begins with recognizing that drugs are just a symptom of our disease.

Our dis-ease resides within us. NA defines addiction as a three-fold disease, physical compulsion, mental obsession, and spiritual self-centeredness. It was this definition that attracted me in the first place. Ultimately it was this definition that kept me in recovery. I recognized that the malady I suffered with started way before I picked up a drug. I have found amazing tools by reading books that address our malady. One such book was 'Betrayal Bonds,' written by Patrick Carnes. He was the director of 'The Meadows Sexual Abuse' program. This book was one of the clearest descriptions of the relationships we have that never fulfill our needs. Instead, betrayal bonds are defined as relationships that will not fulfill either party need. Sexual abuse is a betrayal. The bond that is created may be even stronger than a loving bond because each party is trying to meet a need and neither party meets their unspoken needs.

The incest I experienced with my father was a betrayal bond. I desperately needed love, affection, protection, and recognition. I was overpowered, raped, and repeatedly demoralized by the verbal throw up of words which depicted what a worthless person I was or how no one would love me or care for me. My father was attempting to take my light, and my innocence, to regain his own. He wanted to overpower me to rekindle his spirit. Neither of us got what we wanted. Both were traumatized, each need only growing stronger and more desperate. At times, especially with the Satanic cult, the need seemed more like an attempt to murder me. There were many sacrifices acted out, many were not actual sacrifices, but kids do not know the difference between real and make believe and there were real sacrifices made.

Even then, the cultists could not get back the power they lost as babies and children. They relied on the rituals to give them the thrill of killing, of taking life, and the power and control of murder. Still, it did not give them satisfaction long term. It was a drug, a thrill, an ecstatic orgasm brought on by the murder or simulation of the murder. It left cultists waiting for the next fix. What it really showed was the lack of power. As we say in recovery literature, "Lack of power, that is our dilemma. Drive by a thousand forms of fear, we step on the toes of our fellows, seemingly without provocation, etc." This is one of my favorite passages from the Big Book of Alcoholics Anonymous.

Fear and the lack of power seem to be huge contributors to betrayal bonds. It all seems to be based in self-centered fear. That is why that passage from the big book captures so much truth. The problem with betrayal bonds is that what we want is so palatable, so thick, so very painful to be denied. That is why we try as hard as we do and keep going back again and again. Hoping it will be different, truly wanting what is being withheld. Be it love, or belonging, or money, or hope, or company.

It is very daunting and hurtful to be in a relationship that obviously has the potential to be different, and often is... until once again it is not, and the withholding starts again. It may be the use of drugs, or isolation, or filth, or unkindness and harsh words. Then you are dying inside again, unhappy that it is so impossible to continue and experience a healthy love.

So here is the real thing about betrayal bonds...we continue to perpetuate what we knew as children especially if our needs were not met. We will pick partners that have very similar traits to our parents or care providers that were abusive. The behaviors are not always a perfect match to what we experienced, but the emotional reaction we have to the behaviors are often very much the same as what we experienced as children. We find ourselves in the same trap that we knew before and feeling like we cannot get out of the cycle of betrayal. Every boyfriend or girlfriend is a painful reminder of an earlier time of pain.

My weight yoyoed in Portland as did my ability to be physical and active. I would often take several days to get my body to stop hurting after a dance or exercise class. I found certain foods like wheat and dairy contributed to weight gain. Portland is a wonderful city. It also rains a great deal in the winter and people disappear.

I was lucky enough to attend a video production certification program at a community college and worked with three other awesome women. I was still heavy and gained more in the humid climate.

I loved our life in Portland. After finishing the production program, I created a pilot for a television series on herbs. I never felt as alive as when I was writing and producing the pilot. It was a beautiful refreshing experience and I felt grounded in the many small and quant plant nurseries in Portland. We shot most of the scenes in one nursery run by a very sweet, humble woman.

The pilot was a variety show with sections on gardening, cooking, crafts, medicinal value, and folklore. We focused on Basil for the pilot and shot at the plant nursery as well as McMenamins' Edgefield Hotel. Our chef was the head Chef at McMenamins, and she prepared a meal where every dish had basil as an ingredient. It was an amazing dinner. We also created vignettes out of the folklore available. It was an incredible experience and the volunteer support of film artists and designers, and actors was unforgettably generous.

I never felt more alive. I also realized the activities involved in the production, the gardening, feeling my hands in the earth, the cooking, crafts and medicinal usage, were all life affirming. While I found the pilot was a great deal harder to market, and was never able to produce a television series, it changed my life and my health. I refocused my life on what created vibrancy in my life. It was a resurgence of a deep relationship with what I love on earth. The earth itself, its beauty, its abundance, my mother's garden, watching the sun come up behind the Sandia Mountains.

Driving past the green hills in Portland. The greenbelts and lake communities in Phoenix. How deeply I cherish life here. How incredible it is to be touched. Watching the leaves shimmer in the wind.

30.

MY BELOVED CUBANS

I met Lazaro in Portland through a friend of mine from the Quaker meeting, Patricia. We became good friends. She stopped by one day and introduced me to a friend of hers Angel. He was from Cuba. He was cute and I was intrigued, he asked me out and I accepted. His English was not all that good.

When he came over, we talked about what we wanted to do. He mentioned dancing and I said I love to dance. He mentioned his roommate was a Salsa dancer and I said we should go dancing sometime. He misinterpreted that statement and before I understood what we were doing we were picking up Lazaro and going dancing. Awkward!! Lazaro was very friendly, and it was a little embarrassing to be the object of his attention, to Angel's chagrin.

Angel and Lazaro and I went dancing. Lazaro swept me off my feet. Quite literally. He danced with me all night. He was rather overwhelming for me, a single parent that didn't venture out much. He was a great dancer. I was completely overwhelmed. I danced all through college and received a minor in theatre and dance. Lazaro was a street dancer, a rumbero. Cuban rhumba is a mixture of salsa and African dance. Its powerful and incredible. Angel was kind of left in the dust. I liked Angel, that wasn't my intention, yet it happened.

A few days later I asked Lazaro to teach me how to dance Cuban salsa. That's how we got together. We danced together. He was younger than I and his mother had just died. He was in mourning. He stopped drinking when we got together. He was having terrible delusions about people surrounding the house and being after him. I don't know how much the drinking created the delusions, but I know that some of it was the stories that were told by Castro about America. He really thought that people were out to get him. I think in Cuba they were. He was an artist and wanted something better. So sad he got here and was super paranoid about what would happen to him here. Course, this was another man that was paranoid and delusional. Bingo daddy all over again.

About two weeks after we started dating, he needed a place to stay. He was mean the night before and I really did not want to talk to him. He literally called me all day. I finally talked to him, and he wore me down. He did that a lot. He was incredibly persistent. So is his son. I said he could move in for a week. We would try it out. He did not leave. I was in love with this man.

He was also very scary. He could not hold a job at all. Lazaro was an 'hijo de Castro', otherwise known as Castro's children. This was a generation of Cubans who had no work ethic. They were raised under communism, which is really a theft economy, Lazaro worked in the hotels in Cuba. He stole a lot for his family. He had very low skills, I also think that Lazaro may have been a teenage sex worker. I am not sure but his whole demeanor points to this. Lazaro could not keep jobs.

I write that and again it is looking through the looking glass. Daddy all over again. At the time I was going to a lot of Al-Anon and I really saw for the first time how much every man I was with was like daddy. Lazaro was the first man that I made the connection between daddy and the man I was seeing. I saw so much of Daddy's incapacity. It was painful.

Lazaro had such a dependency on me. It was like I had three children. He could be mean. Yet again another trait of Daddy. I was determined to know what happened to me as a baby and a girl. In some way I kept choosing these men. Each loved me in their own way.

I may not have had the ability to attract men that were not like my father that betrayal bond was way too deep. I did have the ability to be aware in my relationships. Know what was going on around me and make sense of it. Lazaro was loving through my pregnancy but could still be verbally abusive. The put downs were harsh.

When I had Jason, it was a planned cesarean. Lazaro was in the operating room. He held Jason. He was very sweet with him. We were in a family unit in the hospital. Lazaro went into a terrible anxiety attack. I could not sleep or get any rest. He was in terrible shape. The hospital staff finally asked him to leave so I could rest.

There is only 90 miles between Cuba and Miami. It can be a very rough sea. There were so many Cuban refugees leaving Cuba that the US Coast Guard was rescuing Cubans and housing them in Guantanamo. This was years before it was used to house the Taliban after 9-11. Lazaro and many other Cubans were kept at Guantanamo for over a year and a half before being allowed in the US as refugees.

There were quite a few Cubans in Portland since Catholic Charities were involved in helping the Cuban refugees get settled in different states. This was in the 90's and Cuba was having another mass exodus of citizens. From what I learned; Castro was very much a dictator. Cubans were forced to watch his tirades nightly and all apartment complexes had watchers that would make sure families were watching. Castro would have tirades on these nightly shows. By that time Castro owned several homes while most Cubans made $300 a month no matter what they did.

I believe Castro did a great deal for the people when he overthrew the government. Years later, however, he was the government, and he was the one locking dissenters up. He did help a lot of people and did a tremendous amount to stop racism or allow more justice to Cubans. Many more Cubans graduated from college, yet it seemed that education became synonymous to being a communist. Truthfully, since I've never been to Cuba this is all hearsay. I did live with a Cuban and knew several other Cubans, so I heard a lot.

Catholic Charities was one of the nonprofits that found services for Cuban refugees. That is how several refugees found their way to Portland, Oregon. Lazaro stopped drinking when we got together. Of course, in many ways that made things worse. He was terribly depressed after the loss of his mother. I found out I was pregnant about a month after he moved in. He was very sweet and then he would turn, and he had a terrible temper. Early on I was stuck with this guy who couldn't earn a living and was bad tempered. Boy does that sound familiar. Shay ...are you listening up there?

Ian's father did not make much money and spent quite a few years on and off the streets before he was able to really support himself. I started Al-Anon when I took Ian back to Albuquerque after giving birth to him in Phoenix. I broke up with Michael when it became painfully clear he was not capable of being responsible. He was also extremely hurt by the breakup. He said he never wanted children. I took him at his word. Ian did end up having a very good relationship with Michael for several years and I'm extremely grateful for that.

I was attending Al-Anon in Portland. Al-Anon kept me sane living with my mother in Albuquerque. My amazing Al- Anon sponsor used to tell me about my mother, "it's always clothes and food Meg". Marge would say. My sponsor helped me to be restored to sanity about my mother and it helped greatly, before Ian and I moved to Portland. Now once again Al-Anon was really helping me to see how much Lazaro correlated with my father. Lazaro was the first man displaying that forceful abuse and betrayal, which so mirrored the horrors with daddy, unfortunately it would take every man written in this book to really see the entirety of my father and accept that consciously.

In a way Lazaro started me on my path to really understand how severely I had been screwed up by my dad. When Lazaro stopped drinking, he would case the house with a knife and was sure there were people peeking in the windows. In Cuba there was people peeking in the windows and if families were not listening to Castro rant every night on TV, people could and would go to jail. Castro appeared to create a truly captured society, from the little I saw of that. I felt for Lazaro. At least until Jason was born.

Jason's birth was beautiful, and Lazaro adored him. He was younger than I by 12 years and he was so proud to hold Jason and take care of him at the hospital. Until Lazaro had a major anxiety attack and had to leave the hospital because he was keeping me from getting any rest. He had no money. It's painful to recall what bad shape he was in and how incapable he was. He left the hospital with Ian. Ian was eight at the time. Ian was more capable than Lazaro seemed to be. They would come back to the hospital to get money to eat. I knew wonderful capable men, had great friends, several of them in recovery and/or business so why did I choose Lazaro? I could not tell you, but I really felt very much that I was seeing who my father was in this man. I think this was enough.

When we got home and things settled in, Lazaro was very good to Jason and would usually rock him to sleep when he woke up in the middle of the night. He was very patient with him and loved him dearly. Still, it was getting harder to live with Lazaro and he was getting more verbally abusive, it was a very taxing relationship on me. Shortly after we got home from the hospital, he laid hands on me for the first time, and Ian called the police. I do not know if I could have done it myself. It needed to be done. A child services case was started. They were rather helpful. It was still hard between the two of us. It was sad that my eight-year-old son had to be the one that called the police. Shortly after that Lazaro left after a fight we had at a party where he got very aggressive.

He was gone for a while then came back. I figured the only way to get out of the relationship was to take him to Miami. We took a trip to Florida to try to drop Lazaro off there. It didn't work. I wanted to see about other places to live. We flew down to California and stayed at the beach. Lazaro had the habit of pushing men when he felt threatened. Out of the blue he would go up a push someone in a store and apologize at the same time. I became very paranoid of going anywhere with him. When we were at the beach, he did it again, very aggressively.

I got very upset with him and we had a very bad argument in the hotel. We left shortly after and drove east out of California. California was so crowded and expensive that we choose not to be there. We drove through to Florida and stayed at Orlando for a few days. Eventually we went to Tampa and drove over to Miami. We got a place in south beach.

It was the first time I saw Lazaro relax. He was much more comfortable around other Cubans. We stayed at south beach for several days and tried to find a friend of Lazaro's in Hialeah. Lazaro was willing to stay but he had no one to stay with. I was disappointed. I didn't want to live with him anymore. It had been very taxing. I wanted Jason to have a father, but I didn't want to live like this anymore.

Lazaro came home with us and shortly after laid hands on me. That's when I called the police and had him removed. He did come back for a little bit but got abusive again after he thought I was flirting with someone at a party, and I called the police again He never really moved in with us again although he would come by.

That was when I decided to move back to New Mexico. I was able to sell the beautiful old Portland house I bought for a steal, and I moved the boys and I back to New Mexico when Jason was a year, we moved back to Albuquerque. Ian, Jason and I; and our cat Tommy. I stopped dating after I left Lazaro.

We rented a U-Haul and drove down the Oregon coast through California and over to New Mexico. It was a big trip and I'm proud of my boys. There were troupers. It was an amazing trip. We arrived in New Mexico and mama in her bell jar wasn't willing to stop watching TV to meet her grandson.

Mama I love you. Your so much better now. I have spent many years finding out who my father was. Now I get to talk to Daddy often since his death and I love him. The difference between who he is now and who he was then is amazing. Both of my parents have healed so much in heaven.

I bought another house in Albuquerque after we enjoyed an apartment complex and its swimming pools for a summer. I got a job at Intel as a Project Coordinator for the new factory, and we enjoyed our home, and the boys went to school with my sister who was a teacher. Jason enjoyed his brother and cousins. Jason was born in 1999. Jason was cared for at a babysitter's house close to my sister's house, until 9-11 occurred. I got to the babysitter right before the second tower was hit. I remember calling my mother from the sitters. Jason was two. My mother didn't believe that towers were hit. Shortly after that she became a 9-11 buff and studied anything to do with 9-11.

After that the boys stayed with my sister while I worked at Intel. We had a great backyard at our house, and the boys went to the school my sister taught at. Jason and Ian spent a lot of time with their cousins, and I was grateful that they could be there. Maureen had six kids. In truth, they were a very tight unit, and it was hard for my boys to feel like they belonged. Still, they were a part of the family, and it did serve to make them closer to their cousins.

Lazaro showed up at my front door shortly after 9-11. He had gotten a small apartment in downtown Albuquerque. I was surprised as hell that he had gotten himself to Albuquerque. He was always very street savvy. I started taking Jason to visit Lazaro. I was glad he was present for Jason's three-year birthday, and he met my relatives. He was around for a while.

We went to the zoo. It was going to be the first time Jason would stay at Lazaro's house. We had an interesting visit at the zoo. Then something happened that stood my hairs on end. We were in a building in the zoo, looking at an exhibit. I looked over and Lazaro was standing very close to a little girl. I was overcome with a feeling of fear and disgust and danger. It wasn't just that he was standing close, Latin's are used to a much closer distance. It was the feeling of shame and perpetration.

To this day I do not know if it emanated from me or from him. Was it my neurological response to child sexual abuse .

He had this fear of men touching his butt and once threatened a nice chiropractor that would come to the house to treat him. I think it was a 'you spot it you got it' type of thing. I just 'called' that lurking feeling I got from Lazaro at the zoo. Immediately I started walking to my car. Of course, then this really riled Lazaro up and he was getting abusive and scared. He didn't understand. He may not have understood what he was emanating. He was not in a position to hurt the girl.

Still, it belied that deep abuse I knew. I drove Lazaro home. He was flailing his arms in the car and getting heated. I got us out of the car to protect Jason, who was not quite three years old. Lazaro started getting to threaten outside of the car and I called the police. He backed off and left. Later I got a restraining order and Lazaro was so belligerent with the judge that he set a 10-year restraining order.

We set up visitation at a clinic and he would see him every two weeks. It was hard. I knew Lazaro loved him and came to live in Albuquerque to be close to Jason. I still couldn't trust him. I knew Lazaro would never hurt Jason, but I couldn't trust that he wouldn't put him in positions to be hurt. Lazaro was often late, and the visit right before Jason's fourth birthday he was forty minutes late. I think he was busy trying to get presents for Jason. Whatever reason, the time slot was over, we left.

I got a call from the visitation center about a half hour after that. Lazaro came in and got very angry that Jason wasn't there. He then viciously attacked a girl working at the clinic. I imagine she may have mocked him or was sassy. Who knows? Lazaro was taken to jail from there and served a four-year sentence. He was a poor Cuban refugee; he had no lawyer or money. A white man would have been out on bail and paid a lot of money or would have plead down a lower sentence. Jason and I moved to Phoenix before Lazaro was released.

31.

THE ACCIDENT
AND THE RUDE AWAKENING

I met him in Zumba. I love Zumba. It's unusual to see many men in Zumba, especially if they can follow the movements decently. He seemed able to do that. William introduced himself after a few classes we were both in. He was friendly and likable. He was also handsome. I hadn't dated in quite a while, and it was a little thrilling to see him in Zumba. I started looking forward to attending class, in hopes that he would be there. Often, he was. We would talk after class for brief spurts.

After a few weeks of seeing him in class, I invited him to a salsa class taught by a great teacher. He didn't show up for the class but did call to tell me he wouldn't make it. We talked for a while. He told me he was married, not happily so. I was disappointed about his marital status. Our conversations grew more frequent. One day I showed up for Zumba and his wife was there. She was interesting, to say the least. She didn't really follow the norms of a Zumba class and would often turn in an opposite direction from the class. I did see what he said about her seemed to be true. Perhaps even strange. It gave him more ambiance in a way. Here was this interesting guy with a very strange wife. Was he really interested in staying married? He seemed more willing to stray.

It had been six years since we had seen Lazaro. I continued to talk to William in Zumba for several weeks and he showed interest in learning more about salsa. I was involved in a Salsa dance class, and we had a dance party, so I invited him. To my surprise he came. It was a little awkward to begin with, but he was amiable and social and joined in and even danced with a few people and learned more salsa moves. We stayed at the party till a friend of mine suggested we go dancing downtown.

William was game and I decided Jason would stay at my friend's house with her kids so we could go dancing. Outside of the party that night was the first time I had kissed a man since I had been with Lazaro. I felt like I had forgotten how. It was awkward and thrilling at the same time. He followed me to my house, and he met Jason. Jason had never seen me with another man besides his dad when he was a baby. This freaked Jason out. There were all these new sensations moving around and Jason is extremely sensitive to sensations. He has his father's Santeria sense. Lazaro was raised in Santaria and would often sing and chant to the Orishas.

So, we piled in my car to take Jason to my friend's house and go dancing. Jason was in the back; he was all over the place and would not stop talking. He was in fifth grade, and it had been just he and I since Ian moved to Phoenix a few years back. He was very distracting, and he couldn't quite settle with this guy in the front seat. I was also in a very sensitized place with William sitting next to me, I was attracted and distracted with both his presence and Jason's over the top nonstop talking and excitement. We got off the freeway and stopped at a red light on San Mateo. I was going to turn left to get to my friend's house. With all the neurons firing in the car, I remember looking up at the light.

It was red. I thought to myself, this light is too long, it's time to go. I started slowly driving into the lane. William said, 'Babe the light is red!' I was conscious and not. I knew I was in the lane driving on a red light. I had one foot on the gas and one on the brake. Jason was going ballistic; William was freaked out. I was driving so slowly most of the cars stopped for me. It was the weirdest feeling of being conscious and not that I ever had. I could not stop moving forward and I knew it was the wrong thing to do. I could not take my foot off the gas pedal. I was in a trance and semi-conscious.

Suddenly this kid came barreling down the center land. He must have just gotten off the freeway going south, and he was speeding coming towards us. The car was heading straight for Jason. He quickly got a sense of his own mortality as he was transfixed on the headlights coming at him. I can still feel that 'otherworldly' feeling of being tranced out. It was such a familiar feeling to me.

I had never felt it driving a car before and it reminded me of all the women that would talk about having spontaneous regressions while they were driving and how out of touch and how powerless they were over it. I had created an incredibly strong 'Champion' to not be taken hostage by a trance. Now I was driving a car, not of my own volition and could kill all of us in it. At the last moment the kid driving the car heading straight for us recognized that there was an impediment in the road right before him and swerved his car just enough to hit my front door, hard. Jason narrowly missed being the impact point. It shook him up terribly.

We spun at least three times and came to rest at the opposite side of the street. We were all stunned. We got out of the car and stood on the corner. We didn't speak. Some cars stopped to see if people were ok. I walked over to check on the people in the other car. I think I gave them my card. What I remember very clearly was a woman who stopped and venomously accused me of being the scum of the earth. She was vicious and hateful. Then she drove off. The accident was my fault obviously. The kid was speeding. He had no vision of seeing a car in the road when it was clearly not supposed to be there. I learned a lot that night about accident protocol. Later I heard the story of people who die in accidents and them being able to hear people in the cars around accidents. They would hear the people bitching about traffic being backed up or cursing out the people in the accident for delaying their trip. They could also hear the people in the cars that prayed for them and wished them well. This would sometimes be enough to help them along their journey.

After how the woman spewed at me and about me, I realized how crucial our mindset and behavior can be and what this can cause. All can be hurt in an accident. May my first thought be for the safety and wellbeing for ALL people in the accident, not one of trying to castigate the one responsible for the accident. Believe me, currently, the person at fault will definitely feel the pain. Most likely for at least three years of very high insurance and sometimes even harassment from lawyers and pain from their own injuries and awareness of their cause. This is not the time to let your judgement do severe damage to someone who may even perish in the accident.

It seemed to take hours for the accident to be cleared. They took the other car out of the street. Ours was over to the side and not obstructing traffic. We waited for hours for a tow truck to come. We also asked our friends if they could pick us up. They said they would, but signals got mixed and they never showed. It took a few hours for us to finally call a cab and get home. We had gone through something very powerful and sobering together.

 From the time the car stopped I was extremely aware of the state I had been in. I was tranced and knew it. I just experienced that the trance state of mind could and does kill people. I knew that I needed to address this. I had done a tremendous amount of therapy, recovery and healing and I had just put people in a very dangerous and perilous situation.

When we got back to my house, William was still very kind and considerate. Yet I had cooled to him. I thought about his situation, getting in an accident, with his wife uncertain of where he was. His status was ramped up to a person who had a life and responsibility and people who cared for him.

 I did not want the responsibility of having to describe why I was with someone in that situation if he had been seriously hurt. We talked for hours honestly. Whatever might be was over that night in a very sobering manner. He took responsibility for finding excitement outside his marriage and possibly even for addressing why he was staying in a situation that was not giving him what he was looking for.

The Physical Healing Begins

For me the accident awakened an awareness of actions made beyond my volition. This was extremely important to address. There was a body of truth within in me, that I had barely caught a glimpse of. I knew it was time for me to dive into who I was and why I could possibly trance out in the middle of a highly sensational situation and put myself and others in extremely dangerous positions.

I found a therapist that focused on body centered 'Reichian work' is a form of Reichian psychotherapy that involves the physical manifestations of emotions. Whatever was within me was housed in my physicality and I knew I needed to find what and where I had stored these physical manifestations and how the life of these memories or experiences could cause this kind of trance state in a situation like that. I found a therapist that specialized in this work. I actually call it 'tantrum work'.

 I had been exposed to it years before when I moved back to Albuquerque and joined group therapy. This was the same group that I decided I would be my own Champion and, while therapists were very helpful, I would not make them my heroes or a necessity in my life. I did have a session with the therapist and did the 'tantrum' technique.

This consists of lying on a mattress over by a wall. I placed my feet on the wall in front of the mattress, which is padded, and I made the movements of kicking my legs and moving my arms like I was having a tantrum. In a very short time, I could feel a physical sensation of having something in my vagina. I felt young like this happened as a little girl. This was the first time I got physical confirmation of the early rapes. It was an undeniable experience and my whole being could not deny it.

I started working with this gentlemen therapist. I wanted to know the truth that was inside of me. I was more committed to this than I had ever been. I also was physically hurt in the accident and did have some brain damage to my language center. I worked with a couple who did vascular work. It feels like cranial sacral work but it uses the blood system to identify any places of trauma or where the body is holding patterns of pain or numbness or memory.

 Since the blood system is the most vital system in the body, it is a powerful way of identifying any injuries around the vascular system of ways the system is diverting to keep the blood flow safe and uninterrupted. Lastly both Jason and I worked with an amazing child therapist that addressed his ADHD and my head trauma by using what is called a 'Light and Sound machine'.

This consists of goggles with little lights at the corners of the glasses and headphones. The machine can be programmed for any number of therapeutic uses. It was very popular in the 1970's and then fell out of vogue. It was effective for brain 'entrainment' and would literally heal or strengthen any issues or ailments.

We saw this therapist for a good three months or longer. I considered her very effective. I knew the efficacy of the machine when I started seeing this black spot in the technicolor light and music show I would see during the treatments. I asked the therapist what the black spot was. "That is your brain injury, she said, you are literally seeing into your brain with this machine and its settings. That was amazing. I could track the progress of my injury by its size. I don't know what the criticism was of this machine.

 I, however, feel that we may lose a great many powerful therapeutic techniques all in the effort to keep most therapies 'drug' centered. I especially think that this is tragic. Given the fact that I have now lost four beautiful souls to addiction and the idea that pharmaceuticals are not causing one of the greatest pandemics in our history is pure and utter bullshit.

How many are we going to lose to drugs before we address that we have created a nightmare by allowing pharmaceutical companies full reign to destroy lives as well as save them.

I just literally read an article that more people died of overdoses in 2020 than in the last ten years. 93,000 people died of drug overdoses in 2020 and over half a million in the last decade. Fentanyl is killing thousands and is now linked to 3 out of 5 overdoses nationwide.

Meth, cocaine, synthetic opioids, and prescription pharmaceuticals like Percocet are killing people. Drug abuse is a pandemic! Let's stop treating it like a moral or criminal issue and stop locking up people in prisons or giving them drugs that companies are making billions producing.

Just saying! My story isn't unique. I also spend at least three days a week in meetings with recovering addicts that are living good lives and finding incredible love for themselves and others. I have never experienced the pain of addiction as deeply and personally as I have in the last two years. Addiction is an internal dis-ease.

This internal disease needs compassion, understanding, and care. Not another damn drug!!!!! You can't influence a mind under the influence. Many people use because they already feel pain inside. The harm I have seen from the use of drugs, this practice of medicating people that are in deep emotional pain as the main solution, has exploded drug addiction.

We must stop using drugs as the solution to drug addiction. Is it really that hard to see that we have a deep love/hate relationship with our pharmaceutical companies? No wonder we have so many zombie movies. We are manufacturing drugs that create zombies by the millions. STOP. Stop the judgement Reagan and Nixon were wrong. This is NOT a moral issue. Stop locking people away. Drive around your city. Look at what is happening on the streets, the homeless, the degradation. Can we stop throwing people away!!

OK I'm back. Sometimes it just needs to be said. It's heartbreaking. So back to my recovery. The light and sound machine was very helpful.

It did not entirely cure the damage to my language center. My short term/long term memory bridge suffered several bombings from the use of drugs. I literally imagine that some places along that memory bridge are burned out and hanging by a thread.

It used to be so funny when the word fell off the corner of my mind and we would laugh because we couldn't remember what we were saying. It's not so funny anymore. My speech is halting and hesitant at times, I will lose words and appear somewhat compromised. In fact, while teaching I will let people know that they may hear something come out of my mouth that makes no sense and to kindly let me know. I am often the last person to hear my jilting or off topic statement.

The vascular therapy I received from my therapists was incredibly freeing. It is also what led to my experience of remembering my enlightenment at birth as my mother died. The fact is that many things came to light for me at 50 years old. The most brutal parts of my life were revealed then. In the last eleven years I have intimately come to know me, my parents, the generational abuse of satanic rituals and my deeply disturbing pattern of reliving painful childhood traumas. Usually with male partners that were themselves terribly abused and were wounded wounders.

Interesting that the two men I have loved who passed away were both 50. They themselves were reliving excruciating memories but also had the bandwidth and spiritual stamina to see it.

Back to the tantrum therapy. This I committed too. I entered the most painful revealing process in my life. I found the pain I had buried for so long. Especially in my stomach. It felt like Daddy had his thumb on my duodenum. That is the organ that goes from your stomach to your large intestines. That is where felt the most pain in my body. It's like he would hold there, and I couldn't breathe, I couldn't allow the juices that ingested the food to function properly. No wonder I cut off all feeling to my stomach. Also, the stomach area has a huge nerve bundle.

Blocking the bottom of the stomach sends shock waves all the way up the system and is horrifically painful. Now I was getting the physical information from my body that I kept hidden for so long. The pain made it clear how demonic Daddy's actions were. Maybe in a sense I did sleep with the devil. Dearest daddy. It is amazing that this man who truly was sadistic has become a great blessing. It was he who reached out to me long before I was willing to address him with the various mediums that read for me, always seeing the love of my life around the corner.

So, I lay on a mattress and made the motions of a tantrum until I could feel the pain my body knew and often went home feeling so broken that I would cry and pull my covers up. We lived in a marvelous old Victorian home. It had incredible angles and was built by an architect in 1894. This was my respite. I was real, and hurt and vulnerable and betrayed. I came to love me with the deepest love I had. This was still before I learned to raise my emotional state with Divine Openings.

Without this deep trauma work I may not have been able to experience that later joy of emotional frequencies. When I started Divine Openings, I was still just getting over that deep betrayal work. I did not fully know about the ritual abuse until I had been initiated as a Divine Guide. I think that is when I had the fortitude to fully accept the ritual abuse.

My therapist told me all the time.... there's no point for Grace. I didn't do this gracefully. At the time I was working for DoD as an auditor and had some Hella managers. I took one of them to OSHA and through the auditor's union. It may have helped me somewhat, but it didn't change the system. I eventually read a book called Betrayal Bonds written by Patrick Carnes, which I mentioned before.

This really helped me identify all kinds of betrayal. It was an amazingly healing book. See I give you my best stuff. I hope your writing down all of the these very helpful books and techniques. It's taken me over thirty years to amass this info, please take advantage of it.

I did this deep work with my Reichian therapist for over a year. It took me deep, cleansed me, grieved me and left me dripping, vulnerable and renewed. I knew what I lived through in the basement of our rickety Victorian home in Las Vegas, NM. A place rather known by some for the ritual abuse there. I love my therapist for helping me accept me for who I am and the deep sensitivity I experienced and how I gained the great love for this fallible spirit of me.

I wouldn't give you up Meg for all the riches in all the worlds. You are my greatest love. Still, it took me several more years to practice loving myself like I did my children when they were young. I learned later to talk sweetly to myself morning and night, like I would a child. Instead of with a harsh voice of judgment. It took three years of that to truly feel deep love for myself.

Each part of this 'coming to' was necessary for me to become who I am. Even today I am not always a nice person. I love me today and I love you. Love isn't always nice.

My baby Jason. He was his father's son. Jason struggled with sensory integration from early on. Since he was two, we were seeing a therapist for him. He was my beautiful boy, and he had the double whammy of both Irish and Cuban temperament no more need be said.

He was diagnosed later with ADHD. This really was what Jason struggled with. He has learned how to address his limitations and creates amazing situations for himself. Even with the difficulty, Jason had this observational mind that was so clear about what he saw. He is brilliant in so many ways. Jason loves music. While school was hard, music was always his love.

Jason is beautiful, truly. He is super handsome and very aware and sensitive. I realized that Jason was going to learn about life from life. That he has. He decides what he is going to do and goes after it. That wasn't always easy, especially when he was in school. He is a phenomenal musician, and he is also a model. He is very sweet and sensitive. More than that he has a very deep sense of music and of himself. We both lost Ian and it broke our hearts. I know Ian is here for Jason. I know that deeply. Jason has so much to give, and he knows it's going to happen.

33.

MORE ABOUT MAMA

L ater in life, my mother became the 'Grammy' to all our children. Her lovely house that we built on the bluffs of the west mesa in Albuquerque overlooked the whole city. We all pitched in to build the frame and then pitched in to move the posts an inch or two when we discovered that the square footage was off just that much. My parents bought the land in Albuquerque for $3,000, in the early fifties, when there was nothing built there. The lot was right above the Rio Grande River in Albuquerque, and it looked out over the city and mountains that surrounded the city. I was in love with this home. The house was built in my last year of high school, so I lived there some of the time I was in college.

Mama was often reticent to do anything unless it was her idea. When she set her mind to it, she threw wonderful family parties. With my four siblings and fourteen grandchildren among us we had some eventful holidays. Christmas was a mad house. There was not many of these Christmases as we went our separate ways but the ones with all family members present was amazing. Now truth be told, I am a thrower outer, in a family of semi to full blown hoarders. Several of my siblings went all out buying presents as did my mother. My twin had six kids and they often went into debt at Christmas. They had a lot of stuff. There was a time in my early teens when we were tasked with removing hundreds of boxes of my father's books from our basement in Las Vegas, NM. I developed an aversion to 'stuff' that is still strong today.

However, I loved watching everyone open Christmas presents when we were all together. Oh, there was ongoing battles that reached emotional peaks. My twin's family were notoriously late getting to my mother's house. We often waited two to three hours.

This came to a head one Christmas when my younger sister got fed up with waiting and refused to go to Christmas dinner at my twins. It always seemed a little silly to me why a mid-morning time was set for Grammy's house when my twins' family clearly was still engaged in their own Christmas. My brood would always show up an hour later than the time suggested and still wait. This time delay did influence my sisters' relationship. That is another story.

Albuquerque had a tradition of luminarias. These consisted of small brown paper bags filled part way with sand and a small candle. Luminarias were placed around the city, and we often would put luminarias on the outside of our homes. The tradition was that we were lighting the way for Christ at Christmas. I think many thought we were lighting the way for Santa Claus. Either way these simple ornaments are beautiful and would adorn Old Town Albuquerque when they were placed all through the plaza, church, and courtyards.

Our family would eat at a Mexican restaurant on the plaza and watch the candles be lit then walk around the plaza afterwards. I will always love old town plaza ablaze with luminarias surrounding the adobe buildings. To me, New Mexico homes appeared to rise organically out of the earth with their brown and tan adobe walls. New Mexico truly is the land of enchantment and to this day I think it is quaint and unpretentious.

So, next to the wild present openings, and disrespectful lack of attendance at the times given for present openings that were never viable, there was a great love between us.

34.

THE LIFELONG COST
OF BETRAYAL

D istrust! The spiritual principle of trust is extremely violated in rituals and abuse. Unfortunately, there are still aspects lingering from a childhood of ritual abuse, non-existent parenting, and incest in the home. This was such a world view for me for so long, that I did not even know I was struggling with it. I still struggle with this today. Only it is not as generalized.

When I started the self-appraisal process of inventorying my life, I became aware of how negative my thinking was. I truly was not even aware of the pain and stark distrust I had within me because it took the form of everyone outside myself being wrong, and committing wrong, in essence being untrustworthy.

I learned in recovery that I suffered from the disease of 'others'. If everyone else would just get their shit together, I would be fine. I was at the mercy of others' actions, 'they' had the power over me and my life and could really screw it up.

Truthfully, they did. I grew up involuntarily participating in cult rituals. It is one of the more extreme abuses of power. I had no control or power. Or did I? I have come to learn that even then I was filled with a grace that attracted or repelled others.

When I was maybe eight or nine, I was in my father's bookstore, and a little girl came in with her father. The girl kept staring at me. After they left, the girls' father told my father that the little girl had dreamt of me the night before. She saw me as a lion, a lion that had my face. This was much earlier than my imaginative experience of meeting the lion in the meadow. This was the first I heard of a lion. Perhaps it had a bearing on the later experiences I had with my 'lion' higher power. It was another assurance as to who I was, who I have always been. There have been many experiences of others 'seeing' me, this was the first.

This essence of light I emitted was desired and yet there was a deeper desire to capture that light, to 'eat' that essence, to overpower. It seemed so strong a desire to extinguish what I had inside me that it eventually led to the attempted sacrifice in the cult. As if 'they' could take that essence for their own. Or were trying to recapture an innocence and grace that they may never have had.

So again, it seemed only natural that I would distrust everyone and everything. It is a miserable way to live. To feel so isolated within oneself, I am a rock, I am an island.... Lack of power that is our dilemma, driven by a thousand forms of fear, we step on the toes of our fellows...

Corporations were evil and corrupt, politicians were in it for the power and to gain more power and wealth, schools, bosses, banks could not be trusted. I was at war with the world, and the 'world' was killing me. Most of all, I could not trust men, and women were bitches. I was alone. Yet I was still an artist. I hung out with artists and spiritual people.

I was involved with theatre, film, and dance both in and out of college. I have a double minor in theatre and dance. I dated artists, usually poor, often crazed, but some truly talented. I loved dancers, I wanted to be a dancer since I was very young. I admired them. I started dancing in high school. Much later than I wanted to start. My mother dragged us all to my brother's baseball games. She never invested in a talent for the girls. Artists were my brethren; we were of a kind.

In essence I refrained from engaging in the world of business and finance. I struggled with the thought that it was corrupt and power hungry. I stayed in the world of art, of massage and therapeutic touch and spirit. The world was a dangerous place for much of my life, sometimes even in the arts, talk about headstrong egos.

Until I learned, "as you see, so shall it be". I was re-creating the world I believed existed and did exist in my early life. It may have even been deeper than I know. Cults are very skilled at manipulating dissociation, torture and programming their members. It is still hard to remember some of the rituals I was exposed to. Yet I learned to be accountable for my own life. No matter what was instilled in me, it was still my life. I had the greatest influence over it. It took years of journaling every night in early recovery, just doing dumps of the crap in my head onto paper, until I could sleep. Just getting the negativity out.

If it was my life, then I had some ability over my thoughts and feelings. It started with mantras to overpower those negative obsessive thoughts. 'I AM', God remove my fear and direct my thoughts, memorizing poems, 'Ommmm', learning to replace those constantly generated thoughts with focused statements. Eventually it was breath. I could listen more to my breath, and imagine the breath was waves, coming in ....and going out. Imagine a field with a train running through it and dropping the thoughts into an open car. Writing inventories of who I am and what I've done, working the 12 steps, gaining silence!! That was freedom.

With accountability came diminished distrust. I knew I had much more control over how I saw the world. In later self-inventories it became painfully clear that the distrust showed itself in my conversations with service providers.

God help the Verizon rep or the electricity rep, and the cable company...oh vey!! Of course, these were the only people that I was still relying on to 'provide' or 'care' for me in some way.

The customer service reps on the phone bore the brunt of my bad behavior when I identified what need was not being attended to. I sound like such a bitch, and I was. I could get very loud and aggressive. It was hard recognizing that I was still trying to get needs met and using my voice, harshly, when it was not met. Distrust was still there. This took a lot of practice to change, and I still fall back into bitchy to get something I need.

Distrust is still there with men. Will I ever be able to really love and trust a man? I have spent a great deal of my life single, out of relationships. I raised my children and for seventeen years I was celibate. Not that I desired to be. I truly always wanted a partner. A father for my two boys. A man to love and care and provide for us.

Ohhh there it is. I wanted a provider and I still do. I wanted to be taken care of, I wanted my children cared for. I had no model of a man who provided for his family. Not one. All the men I knew abused their families. My father was the model of a disempowering man, more than I could ever know. Yet often he seemed so mellow. Playing beautiful music, with his pipe and his glass of soothing liquid. He was stoned all day.

Daddy repelled people. I learned that from a woman who worked in his bookstore. She said people did not want to come into the store when he was there. I noticed it to. Some people could sense his energy and demeanor, probably more than that, the look on his face, his attitude, and his disdain.

I loved to be in the store. He had several bookstores throughout the years. They never made money. My father was supported by his wealthy family. They would send him money. He would buy books with it or booze. He was not a provider. We lived poor. He was a destroyer.

There are four daughters in my family. Each one of us struggled with men who were unable to provide for their families. My youngest sister rarely dates and has had very few boyfriends. The three of us older daughters either married or had kids with men who never provided. I was a single parent twice over with two men who were incapable of providing for their children financially. This single attribute of the cost of betrayal has been the most destructive. I still struggle with it today. I have never been supported. I have supported men. Never willingly.

This breaks my heart still, today. Therefore, I am willing to write my story. I know the change it has already created in me. I am being healed and open to men who care, love and are capable of being present. Before, I thought, 'I am dating someone who is willing and capable of providing and caring for me.' I'd find that he doesn't have the current capacity to provide or even participate financially at all. Then I'd feel betrayed. It has had a very destructive impact on my life and my children's lives. The ongoing poverty affected so much. Not having a strong 'breadwinner' devastates many households. I became that breadwinner and supported my family.

I was concerned that I wouldn't ever be able to 'see' or 'experience' the characteristics of a man who provides. I do want to experience having the comfort of a provider. I believe women should be cared for. In my family it has been almost unbearable.

My sisters had long term marriages with men who left the family in financial disaster over the inability to support their wives and children. The beauty of even both partners sharing resources, is something I've long dreamed of. Most often the comfortable salary I've had on and off as an Accountant was devastated by relationships. I was left with nothing a few times over.

Meanwhile I am my own provider, I am no longer willing to be the only provider in the relationship. It is hard for me to address this with a partner, hard for me to be honest, hard for me to say something. My sisters stayed decades with men who lived off them. I don't, but I feel I often stay too long or allow them to stay to long.

Have our wonderful men been so damaged? Is this no longer a character trait of men? I hope this is not the case. It has been a lifelong cost of betrayal.

35.

HEALTH, HAPPINESS, AND AU REVOIR

M ama! I've come to love this humble, timid, sweet spirit that is the true essence of my mother. I understand why she choose to live in a bell jar. My mother is brilliant. I loved the inquisitive well-read woman that shared a love of intrigue novels and corporate scandal books. There are wonderful remnants of my mother's life. Her brilliance as head librarian in a small town. Her brilliance as a divorce attorney who also created a template to divide military pensions fairly and quickly, one of her best feats. Just her brilliance.

I was very happy sharing these interests with her. We so enjoyed "The smartest men in the room" or the movie "The Short". My mother was directly responsible for honing my sleuthing skills and my ability to read a contract and my love of reading. She taught me how a book could sweep you away to another life, adventure, reality. How awed I am to have such an incredible journey. To cherish the stories of others, allows me to cherish my own story even more.

My mother's body wore down over a period of years, after an initial diagnosis of emphysema. Her health slowly deteriorated, and she was hospitalized yearly for pneumonia. Her emphysema may have been arrested but it was the initial cause of her weakened immune system. Thank God my mother stopped her pack a day cigarette habit when was diagnosed with emphysema. My mother also had an emergency triple bypass in her late 60's.

She still thrived in her practice of divorce law and enjoyed a salary finally worthy of her. We would tease her about all her money going into southwestern art and necklaces. Which is basically what we inherited.

Later she struggled with diverticulitis, and an infection that wasn't diagnosed in her lower spine till it became cancerous.

She had a series of strokes in the last year and a half of her life. We became sister sleuths. I would listen with curiosity, to her symptoms then at possible ways that she could understand the symbols on the phone when they no longer looked like numbers. I felt that my love of the body and awareness that my mother's body was slowing falling apart helped her experience these painful inconveniences with a little more grace. Our wonderful sentient vehicles also wear down with time. This is a natural state and one we can honor as we find ourselves experiencing our bodies in their various stages of functionality.

I got to be her curious partner and we would try to figure out ways she could decipher what no longer made sense. Like many humans experiencing a failing body, I was very aware that my mothers' body was breaking down. I could not ease the discomfort, but I could be there to listen, suggest, and carry out ways that she could continue filling her thirst for stories long after her brain was unable to make sense of these squiggly things, we call letters. We two made it just a part of life.

She loved her audio books. Which is why I will record this book for audio. For my mama. I love you that much my darling. Such a shiny bright brilliant mind you have and the softest loving heart that I willingly bow down before. I cherished our talks before and now they bring me triple the joy because I see you shine so bright, and you hold those babies in the meadow who came to you needing such love. What an evolution I have witnessed. What grace I received when I reached out to my beloved Thorne. You have brought me so much tenderness and so much love. Te Amo mi amor.

My mothers' body continued to deteriorate. She spent a few months in a nursing home after contracting CDEF when she was in the hospital with diverticulitis. I was running up to Phoenix that summer and looking at houses. My quest entertained her, and my sister and we talked mainly about the house hunt and impending move. She was excited. I moved shortly after her series of strokes. I wasn't there for her day-to-day slowdowns. She had a hip replacement after I moved to Phoenix and never walked much after. She slowly continued to deteriorate.

Lastly was the cancer diagnosis. My wonderful sponsor at the time was a nursing professor and stated that cancer was an opportunistic disease. It finds the weak areas and spreads. Mama's cancer was diagnosed late. By that time in her life, there were so many functions in her body that were limited or just not functioning well. The times I accompanied her to doctors left me with a lasting impression of a medical system incapable of managing elder care. Her primary doctor appeared to be the logical place where all her various issues would be charted, the several specialists she was seeing would be listed, and the various medications would be tracked and checked for any potential issues with counter indications.

Unfortunately, our allopathic medical concepts, which sees that body as several separate functioning parts, simply fails to provide ANY concept of this gracious sum of parts functioning. There is no wholistic view of the body and the result of that is this enormous industry of elder care that is so convoluted and has no one responsible for managing so many specialists. All lose sight that the lack of coordinated care is responsible for a great deal of death. My eighty-year-old mother spent many of her days running around seeing one doctor after another and none of them were reviewing any other doctors' notes. Hospice seemed like the only care at the time that would chart all drugs and all doctors. My mother eventually died of the 'complications of cancer treatment'. That is my diagnosis of what happened. Her body was so worn down from all the ailments, all the different systems wearing out, that the chemo was too much for her. It eventually killed her.

Meanwhile, even before I left for phoenix, me and my siblings were charting and caring for her medications and doing the best we could to make sure she was getting the correct medications. This was getting very difficult as my siblings, especially my sister who lived with mama, was worn out. Such a brilliant and astute psychic she is, yet those skills themselves tend to create vulnerabilities and a sensitivity to the state of others. Caring for someone who is slowly dying in one's household is a tremendous effort. I cared for my father for his last two months. There were times when I was completely overwhelmed.

My younger sister lived with Mama. Her energy was constantly challenged. She was naturally more invested in caring for Mama. My twin also was greatly involved in her care as well. They were the two that still lived in Albuquerque and were the closest to mama. Maureen was also going through a divorce and lost the beautiful adobe house built by her husband that was home to their six kids. My sisters' lives were both filled with grief and pain during my mother's death. This time was so trying for my sisters, yet I want to honor their experiences. Dying brings out our pain and our beliefs.

There is so much more to be said about the loss families suffer, yet I wish to respect deeply my own family and the tremendous loss families experience. Just know you are held, you are cherished, and you are deeply loved.

A few months later, in mid-March, all five kids gathered for a week as Mama lay dying. She was semi-conscious for five days. Unable to speak but certainly aware. The family dynamics were difficult. My youngest sister lived with my mother. Her grief and fatigue were readily apparent as was the difficulty of having all siblings surrounding Mama. The last few years had eroded relations between the siblings caring for Mama. Now we were all here, stimulating this dying woman with our well wishes and permissions to leave the planet. Sometimes I wonder how much family and friends interrupt the journey to the nonphysical. I'll have to ask her.

An old family friend was there. She had been in our lives for over 40 years. I grappled with addressing the overwhelming abuse with mama as she transitioned, until Joann spoke to me and made some comment made by my mother, who told her I was like a harlot as a child. That was that Mama's abandonment was not my cross to bear. She had closed her eyes to the hell we lived, while living her own. She abandoned us. As far as I was concerned, I was the sacrificial lamb that she just gave to her husband wolf. It was time to tell Mama about the incest I experienced in her house.

I sat at my mother's side and likened our experiences of abuse at Daddy's torture. I knew she could hear me. Her body reacted like she didn't want to hear it. I did say to her that her lack of protecting us was her's to carry and not mine to be responsible for anymore. For three days I could see the reactions toward me with her eyes. The anger shone through her eyes, as well as her refusing to look at me and looking away when I was there. On the fourth day she looked at me with pleading, as if she was asking me to forgive her for abandoning us. That night was bittersweet. My two sisters and I took turns holding vigil. The music we listened to was sublime. The most memorable and achingly wrenching song, that will always epitomize Mama and her life, was 'Wild Horses' song by Susan Boyle. It was a poignant night. Maureen took over in the wee hours of the morning. She didn't touch Mama, she just sat with her and let her go, and Mama died that morning.

To the tender state of my beautiful sister, the decision to divvy up the assets in the house right after my mother's death was very taxing. Three of us lived out of state and the cost of coming back was high. So, we placed tags on items and did our best to be fair. Yet my darling sister was barely able to function in the last weeks of mama's life and suddenly having everything up for grabs and being removed left great areas of space in a heart that had lost too much. This is the pain after death. The pain of losing a life and belongings that once brought such comfort.

It was too much, and it took many months of legal bickering to conclude the property part of death. There is still pain that is only slowly healing and I hope with all my heart that there can be a deep healing between the two sisters that were inseparable for many years. The oldest and the youngest. How I wish you could remember how most of your lives your arms were entwined around one another. How sweet is the heart, how easily broken. What vulnerable beings we truly are. Mama I love you so much. To all my siblings, you are and always will be the light of my life. The box car children. Orphans who loved each other.

This wasn't the end. I have come to know Mama in our 'dead talks'. I found such freedom, accountability, forgiveness and such a deep love by speaking to my disembodied, but very much conscious loved ones. Mama is sweet, humble, and willing to own her inability to protect us. She herself talks about living in a jar. She and Daddy are happy and there is a great deal of love between them. I am a witness to the miracle of death and the beauty of forgiveness, and how incredible it is to visit those I love in a space where they are so real, so aware, and so willing to be honest and are not encumbered by the hideousness of self-obsession. They are helping me heal even deeper and I them.

37.

THE FRENETICISM
OF FREQUENCIES

Freneticism: Wildly excited or active; frantic; frenzied. [Middle English 'frenetik', from Greek 'phrenītikos', from 'phrenītis'-brain disease];

Before I speak of self-soothing, I want to address freneticism. What a fantastic word that is!! Anything beginning with an 'F' is a great frequency. Try it. Just make the sound. I finding it satisfying. Besides the satisfaction of making the sound of F, which is certainly a marvelous sound, and a great example of the sensory experience of frequency, freneticism itself is often a by-product of dissociation.

I remembered sitting years earlier and feeling my head spin. My brain felt like I was on the 'spinning cup' ride at a carnival. Do you remember the spinning cups? There are maybe five large cups in a curved surface of the ride. The cups spin as they are also moving over the curved surface. One gets a double whammy of the spinning cup and the curving surface, which adds a dimension of depth.

My brain felt just like I was riding on a spinning cup, moving over an unstable surface of dips and valleys. This is not freneticism. No freneticism is the frequency which is created by the spinning cups. In my recall, my beautiful mind could not reconcile the spinning of my head with the brokenness of my body.

I closed off my ears so I wouldn't hear. Of course, the sensory vibration of the sounds I heard remain. As all frequencies vibrate, it is the nature of frequencies, the sounds vibrated within my being. The words spoken harshly, cunningly, coarsely. Words which stabbed my heart and perpetrated the physical wounding to a much deeper degree. These words were never quite remembered, however never ever forgotten. Recorded in the deeper part of the brain. For certain in the lizard brain. Perhaps in the hippocampus. Which is a marvelous recording device that has twenty minutes of recording space before it overwrites what was just recorded. Brilliant what we have learned in Neuroscience lately.

The more debilitating frequencies come from the tone associated with the words. Tone denotes the frequency of the feeling, emotional state. The feeling state is a stronger frequency, I would say our emotions are the strongest frequencies in our bodies. Tone carries the emotions felt as it flavors the words used. It is the tone which reaches deeply into our viscera and stirs our emotional responses. Humans are capable of a tremendous range of sensations. Orgasms, an experience which can be quite frenetic, is but one of very rich vocabulary of sensations we have within our magical nervous system. Deep abiding pain is another. The slow death of hope resulting in desperation, yet another.

In this instance of the morning after, however, the emotional 'frequency' is overwhelming. Emotions are the nervous systems' language, and its basic function is to relay the stimulating experience. The sensation overwhelms the whole body.

The event then shuts down the child's developing capacity to integrate the overwhelming stimulation and the body chooses its best defense mechanism, fight, flight or freeze. Freeze is the go-to defense of an organism that has no capacity to escape.

The frozen moment(s) then become encapsulated in the amnestic barrier. This then is the experience of dissociation. In animals, prey captured by a predator will fight then freeze. Freezing literally is dissociation. The predatory animal may drop the prey when it stops fighting, the thrill is gone. The prey may also be killed, if so, freezing dissociates the animal so the animal is no longer experiencing all the pain and the death is much less painful.

Back to the swirling cups. This is what my mind experienced the day after incest. The swirling, the dips, the unexplained pain in my body. The swirling brain becomes a focus. Painful body and swirling mind. Those are the 'frequencies and sensations' experienced the day after. The inability to remember is blanketed. Each traumatic event, each dissociation, is like a bubble. Bubbles remain until the overall effect on the child, or the now adult, becomes aware of the bubbles.

In each bubble is the memory of a little girl, or boy, that still possesses the experience, the 'frequency' or 'the taste' of the abuse. The bubbles are the 'weight in the cells' which describes them so eloquently.

I have found myself in many bubbles. Not only bubbles but caves or crevices, hiding places to be safe, to not be found. The various places in my mind and body where the memories were stored. That is how it started. The revisiting of abuse. That is how I grew into the giant that found my children. I became this huge force, strong, brave, brash. Until I was able to interrupt those bubbled dissociations by going directly into the memory of my imprisoned child. I became the rescuer, disrupting the abuse, sometimes blowing away the environment where the abuse was happening. I took the child in my own giant arms, threw my father off me, off my baby, my deepest soul life. Roared at the abuser and carried my bubbled babies away to a place of safety and renewed consciousness.

In the end though, this is an example of the long-term effects of the trauma. 'Freneticism: Wildly excited or active; frantic; frenzied'. A paralyzingly strong frequency, an after effect, a common reaction for many abused children and fearful, traumatized adults. Freneticism. It leaves one with the deeper tendrils of anxiety, it feels like the stings of a jellyfish that smoothly glides over your skin and leaves toxic tentacles penetrating deep into you, embedding the nerve pain deeply into your psyche. The bulbous jellyfish head, held in the amnesic barrier with the memory safely encapsulated; and the hideous pain of the tentacles gliding through sensory scales, stingingly reminding the abused of the hidden, overwhelming, high-strung hell, felt through freneticism.

A constant jolt to the nervous system, a reminder in all is caustic glory, that something, many things, lay hidden in this phenomenal system which keeps functioning. Within in that cold dark night are stinging tentacles which say, I am here, find me, free me. Destroy this self-made prison which stings me in each passing. I cannot breathe without becoming frenetic. I cannot feel unless the sting of the jelly fish throws me into a deep underwater cavern which threatens to bury me and then you will never find me. You will never rescue me. I will remain hidden in the morass of powerlessness and depression, unclaimed even within myself.

Find me so I can breathe. Find me so I can cry. Find me so we can be happy and experience the height of harmonious frequencies. Find me so I can tell you who you really are, what you really experienced. Find me so we can live.

38.

IS IT ME?

I fall in love with men who have been hurt and to date I have not lived with any man that has supported me or my children. It causes great stress in my life. Still think it was early programming, daddy saying no one would love me, and no one would take care of me. Voila, the deepest programming I have. I hear a beautiful young voice saying, 'he said it repeatedly'. These words got into my babies, my sweet little ones inside, again and again.

Ken my therapist told me one of the best ways to get memories was to ask the little ones inside me and promise I will take care of them. If they are afraid of Daddy, promise they won't have to be near him. They love Thorne. I love Thorne. This hurts so badly. I believe in you my darling children, thank you for leaving, for staying awake in the non-physical, for being in your spirit body. I want your help. I am a part of everything. Help me to know what happened.

I ask you, all of you, please I know I am here for you. Tell me the words I cut off. Tell me what has kept me alone all my life, separate, in the deepest place of the not enoughness. That would create a dependency on him, the one who hurt me, hurt you. Tell me where you feel safe, I hear you all love the meadow.

I asked and you came forward. So many girls, the baby, and sweet girls of all ages. Even the older girl that witnessed everything. Watching from the ceiling, safe outside of the body, comfortable in the space of calmness. Staying next to the great being that was always there, always the saving grace. The silent one that offered a place to hide our true spirit and reminded us of what was real. No matter what... our spirit could not be hurt ever.

All the girls, some so curious, all loving me, caring for me, knowing I saved them and brought them here to the meadows. Some of the children are still scared of daddy, and they don't have to be around him. Some of you my babies are so brave, younger, and older. All of them are now here for me. Many willing to tell me what happened. Thank you, my darlings, for coming forward for saying you're sorry for what it has done to my life, our life.

You are willing to tell me what Daddy said. He did say that I wouldn't be loved, no one would take care of me. According to the girls, daddy said that almost every time. The words he said were so mean, the tone was so demeaning, so hateful.

It was meant to hurt and meant to keep me powerless to lord his power over me and make me believe that I was not worth loving and no one would want to take care of me. My babies are looking after me this time, surrounding me, being so earnest. Thorne is there too. He is with us in the meadow. All the girls love him. Even the heavy set, adolescent Thorne who came to the meadow first. The first male to come to the meadow. He is a trusted being here and we love him.

So now I can hear you and I'm so grateful. We do not have to relive this. We can tell what happened and not have to feel all the pain again. I want your beautiful memories. It is still hard for me to remember. It always bothered me, not being able to remember, but wondering what was said, sometimes imagining what was said. I should have known what I imagined was true.

I still don't know all that happened in the ritual, and I want to know and understand. I'm just so grateful my little girls will talk with me, will show me what they experienced and what was said to them.

We can take it as slow as you wish and any of you can let me know what you remember. I want us to be able to see and hear and feel what happened to us and allow ourselves to cry and be angry and still be there for each other. We have been safe for many, many years. All of you are so happy here, so active and beautiful and caring of each other.

All the other children have come here knowing this was a safe place and they will be loved and cared for and will heal from their pain and shame and those awful experiences they had. We created a place of deep love. I brought you here and you have flourished, and you've known the love of many angels and spirits and guides that love to be here with you. You now give me hope, you give me courage to see and hear all the painful experiences we went through, and we do not have to feel the pain. We are free to cry because those things did happen. We are so good and have been for a long time. That is why it is time to share this with others. We do heal and we do cross through the veil of life and death, to walk in both.

We have been cared for. In many ways we have been deeply loved. The men we have known, boyfriends who cared for us and loved us. Perhaps they couldn't financially care for us, but it doesn't mean that we were not loved. We were attracted to men who were not capable of generating wealth. This is who daddy was. He never provided, he really couldn't provide, even though his family were millionaires.

It is more possible today, after realizing how many times it was said to us that we would not be taken care of, and how we often interpreted that as not being provided for, having our basic needs met. I had no concept of being cared for, our parents were too self-obsessed with their addictions to care for us. To be able to cry and really experience the damage done is to heal our lives and to move on to find our own capacities and see men who are willing and capable of providing love, care, and support in all ways. I feel so much cleaner knowing that I am not bound by those painful words anymore and that I have been very effective in my own life and can be with a partner that can support me in all ways.

I love you my babies, my girls that came forward that told me what was said. I heard you all, we don't need to say it out loud, you whispered in my ear. You are all so brave, so sweet. So many of you hid in the caves inside of me. In pockets of pain until you were set free here in the meadow. You are the greatest part of me. I will always keep you safe. You are my babies, my beloved self, my strongest loves. You are why I was willing to stay, so you could be loved and found. You led me out of the darkness and into light. Thank you, my bright, brave beings, I adore you forever.

39.

ON STARRY NIGHTS OF VELVET.

Chimes call the pipers children back. On sunny afternoons, windswept mesas whisper water memories and Chevy's rust by open doorways. Kachinas dance in midnight ceremonies. Mountains hide the wise ones in shadows shade. Houses grow out of the ground and dust turns the sky into bursting sunsets.

New Mexico is the land of enchantment and the land of manana. Its laid back, deep and filled with Native Americans spirit and lore. There are many places where the different tribes believe they came into this earth from sacred mountains. Pueblos surround Albuquerque and add the strength of time and the memories of trails of tears on hundred mile walks their ancestors endured.

When I was young, I would see dust devils in Paradise Hills that look just like spirits playing. There was magic where I raised on top of the mesa. Though many thought that this small town was haunted since it was built on top of an Indian burial ground. I felt a kinship with the land, like I had walked it for years. I believe I had. There were memories of another life in which I walked always. Walked across the mesas of New Mexico down into Arizona and over to Mexico. I carried stories of others and walked alone until I reached another pueblo or village or reservation. I do not think I went much further than Toas pueblo.

Others walked the plains. They were there in ceremonies or festivals when the people celebrated and heard stories from places further away. It was a strong system of messengers. Their territories well established. Their presence would create a gathering to hear stories of others. I was in the southwest traveling on top of the mesas to different villages. Sometimes carrying gifts from other tribes, maybe love letters memorized for potential lovers or mates that often joined and created ties between the people and strengthened the relatives.

I was uncomfortable among women. My home was the open mesas. That was my strength and beauty. I could share the stories, but not my own. My tongue would tie to converse with the opposite sex, but my voice was strong and clear carrying another's message. This life is very real to me. I can easily imagine walking the mesas. I am close to this part of me. Comfortable alone, sometimes tongue tied to speak my own mind. Often eloquent but sometimes the words don't come easily. The life of the high desert was where I found company. The wolfs, coyotes, and rabbits would walk close enough. There was always life out there. I feel this man within me. I used to dream of his wanderings. He is New Mexico in my soul. Endless, eternal. The land of manana. The land of enchantment.

Once I dreamt. I was on my mother's back porch. Which overlooks the lights of Albuquerque? The cityscape spread out in front of me. In my dream it was darker. I went outside and stood on her porch. In the sky there were many funnels. They looked like the nuclear fusion funnels. I could see inside them from the bottom. It reminded me of an early Star Trek show where the transporter would show lights inside them when someone was transporting. Only on these funnels, I was looking up and seeing the bottoms of these funnels with those Star Trek lights swirling around. The funnels were all over the sky. I have not told many people about these funnels. I don't know what they mean just that they filled the night sky, and they were important enough to stay with me for a lifetime.

Our lives are filled with events outside of the norm. To think our divine spirits are just alive for one life is so limiting. We are eternal. In my concept of life, we are eternal. We have many lives and adventures here and elsewhere. This is a big universe and an even bigger galaxy, among other galaxies and we have not even ventured into the non-physical. We are eternal. We are exquisite.

40.

HELLO ARIZONA

In 2011 I attended the NA convention in Tucson Arizona at a beautiful resort. I thoroughly enjoyed it and so did Jason. They had the best swimming pools for kids. It was so good to see friends I had known for twenty years. I went back to Phoenix with some good friends and happened to look at houses for sale and found that Phoenix was in a selling frenzy. The housing market had hit bottom. I was ready to come back! The convention was in May, and I spent one to two weekends a month walking through tons of houses in Chandler and Gilbert. I bid on over twenty houses. They would be off the market almost as soon as they got on. It was crazy hot that summer and I saw some amazing houses and poof, they were gone. The inventory was starting to slide down when I found my house.

It was the only one I felt comfortable in, just not the first time. The first time I looked over the balcony from the second floor and got dizzy. The owner's dog was in the house and barked the whole time. This was at a time when they were offering owners $3K back if they could sell their houses before the house was repo'd. I looked at my house and one other. They were both in Chandler, but my house was much further south than I wanted. The other house was better but when we went back to look at it the owner had taken it off the market. I made an offer, and it was accepted. I successfully transferred to another DCAA office at Boeing. We were auditing a billion-dollar proposal for Apache helicopters.

I packed a U-Haul and drove to Phoenix with Toby, our beloved cat. I had booked a resort to stay until we got in the house. They were so inexpensive in 2011. On the road I got a call that the house appraised for $8K less and was now $150K. Yay! It would take another two weeks to get in. Boo!!

We ended up moving hotels three times. By the time we got in all I had was the seed money for the down payment. The owners had left it a mess and my real estate agent had to talk me down from walking away. I'm so glad I didn't. I loved that house. I lived in that house longer than any other. It had everything I wanted, a huge master bedroom, two other bedrooms, all upstairs. A wonderful pool with a grassy area right next to it in the back yard and a landscaped front yard. All in a lake community. I still love the community.

It took a while for me to make it mine, after a remodel in 2014, it was wonderful. We were able to have the pool redone and black galaxy countertops all through the house. Black was hard to keep clean, but I loved the sparkly specs that glittered. I thoroughly enjoyed that house and I looked for other houses three times before finally selling my house. I never did find a better house. However, covid really made it impossible to stay. My business really took a dive. It was a wise financial decision.

We moved to Chandler when Jason was going into seventh grade, Jason found a group of kids in our neighborhood. It was the first time Jason had boys his age that he could relate to and hang around with. I was so happy that he had this group of friends. They are still good friends today. He could walk to his junior high.

However, the move was daunting, and I had been out of my thyroid medication for almost six months before the move. I was diagnosed with Hashimoto's disease in my late 40's. Finally. The disease is an auto immune disease that attacks the Thyroid. I realized I struggled with this disease for most of my life. I wonder if Endocrine issues, such as Thyroid dysfunction, etc., are affected by early trauma. Treating my thyroid disorder really helped, as did being aware of the functions of the Endocrine systems and doing everything I could to keep this system healthy. I also found out that all my sisters had Hashimoto's. I was the last to receive treatment. So much for sharing! Thanks chicas.

By the time I realized I had been off medication for that long, I was sick. I had no energy; I could barely get through the day. I was dragging at work and would go to meetings and looked so bad I think people thought I was using. I was also very emotional and would sleep a lot. It came to a head at Thanksgiving when Ian cooked thanksgiving dinner and I got upset about something and threw my full plate against the refrigerator. Ian never liked Thanksgiving after that.

I also found an endocrinologist and started back on medication. It literally took another four months to feel better, but I am so glad that I have been stable on medication and found a doctor that gave me the right dosage. During that time of illness, I would drive twenty-five miles to Boeing and consider ways that I would kill myself. After all I've lived through, I think it was truly the thyroid that was affecting me.

What helped the most was being aware of how to stay healthy and active and keep my spirits up. In recovery I learned to do something different. I interpreted that literally, in that I could turn my head and look in another direction and I would see something different. Taking a walk in the middle of the workday, and getting out of my chair, gave me a fresher perspective on the day, and I loved walking in old neighborhoods with Victorian houses. NA taught me that I have a thinking, feeling issue. Only I could change the way I thought or felt about something. I could be the catalyst that would 'change my mind' and doing anything different was a 'pattern interrupt' from my negative thinking. When my thoughts changed, my feelings changed. If I focused on feeling better, it was easier to stay out of negative thinking.

Acting 'as if' was a reality changer. I could just pretend that everything around me was fresh and interesting and overdo it a little. Gush about the trees, make a big deal about all the birds around me, spend three minutes thinking about how amazing the sky was in its most intimate details, the variations of the clouds from fluffy white to dark grey. I'd find one thing that I like or admire about everyone I'd see in a day. Find something to laugh about daily, there is plenty of humor, watch YouTube, read a funny story, look for funny things around you. Giggle as much as possible, create laugh lines instead of frown lines. Whatever will rise your 'feel good' level is worth it. My body buzzes when I feel good. I love feeling good.

I stayed at DCAA, the audit agency for DoD until 2013 and then created my own accounting company. I still do the same thing I did as an auditor, and I quickly was working long term contracts at larger government contractors for several year as well as working with my own clients. I was truly enjoying life especially when I was introduced to Divine Openings in November of 2012. My friend gave me Lola's book and it truly changed my life. I very much enjoyed the incredible awareness I found in Divine Openings (DO), and it not only changed my life, but it also gave me a deep fortitude. Mama died in March of 2012. I was able to walk through that, and the family dynamics that followed by practicing the basics of DO. I lived in the house on the springs happily until August of 2020. It was hard to leave my home, but it helped to have the money to get through the next year.

Jason went on to high school when we lived in the springs. He didn't finish high school. The only thing that kept him there was football. It was getting very difficult for him to keep up his grades and stay in the rigorous practice of football. He decided he wanted to go to the arts school Ian graduated from. It did not work as well for Jason as it did for Ian. Still his love of music was increased at the art school, and he knew that is what he wanted to do.

Ian lived with us on and off and we had great play dates with my grandchildren Sage and Savannah. Being a part of their lives has been a huge blessing for me. Being there for their births and holidays and special occasions was wonderful. Ian was divorced five years into the marriage. His debt was through the roof. It was not easy for him to manage divorce and it was often hard to see the kids. He loves them dearly still. He worked all the time while he was married, and it was very hard on Jess his wife and the kids. Yet his addiction got worse after the divorce. So did his grief about losing his family.

Raising my two boys has been the greatest joy of my life. I am glad we came to Arizona, although not so much in the middle of summer. Recently Jason was here, and he was playing some of his music for a friend of mine. I was amazed at how many songs he has written. He has amassed a massive library of music and I am very hopeful that he will share all of that with the world.

Jason has spent more time in LA and just did a show in Albuquerque yesterday for Juneteenth. His band was received well, and he was happy at the show's reception. This boy that struggled to live in his body as a child, is now so much a man. He is loving, sensitive, temperamental and my only child now. I am very proud of him. He is so much his father's son, but he is very much his mother's child too. I love him with every cell of my body. Jason I could not be prouder of you than I am. I am so grateful that you are my son. You are the best part of my life. We will see Ian again. He is around us all the time. He adores you. You are truly worth adoration. Te amo mi vida! Your cousins will always be your family too.

41.

DIVINE OPENING

I was introduced to Divine Openings in 2012. I had signed up for a spiritual workshop meant to last several months. When they described the 'Spiritual' part of it being the fact that we sold the workshop to others, I knew that was not my idea of spirituality. I have gratefully paid for powerful spiritual books, silent retreats, online courses and would do so again in a heartbeat because it brought me such grace. True ease and grace. I would tell the world of the peace I have gained when I gained peace. I have gained great peace! But I won't sell people a program that considers spirituality selling something devoid of a spiritual practice and the gift of spirit inside.

I visited a friend of mine who had gone through the same program and experienced the same frustration. She then brought out a book. The title of the book was, "Things Are Going Great in My Absence. How to Let Go and Let the Divine Do the Heavy Lifting." Right away I loved the title. I mean how fabulous is that!! She lent me the book and I started reading it. It was a story of enlightenment. Achievable, enlightenment. Lola Jones, author of this book traveled to a three-week silent retreat at a Hindu center in India. She was very focused on her inner journey and stayed in silence. She soon found that her emotions were like title waves, pounding on her until she turned her full focus on them and found that allowing the emotions to be there and be with them brought a profound sense of peace.

It was the story of her emotional journey that struck me the most, and her understanding that to have a spiritual practice, emotions and the acknowledgement of what we feel, is a huge part of the journey. If we bypass the emotions, we are bypassing the most important internal communication system we have. Emotions are for internal use only. I love that statement and I'm still striving for that. I have always been a demonstrative person and I adore being adamant or emphatic and compassionate. No matter what though, the knowledge of the importance of emotions in a spiritual practice was mind blowing and life changing. First, it made them OK. Emotions were not always considered OK in my household. We were a house of secrets and denial. It's pretty hard to be emotionally present when your busy denying what is really going on.

I had been in recovery for twenty-four years when I discovered divine openings. I had amazing experiences in recovery before learning about divine openings. I had practiced other spiritual practices and 'worked the steps of Narcotics Anonymous (NA) many times and walked others through the steps as a sponsor. I loved the 'we' of NA and that we are never alone. I had gained many freedoms inside and outside of myself. Divine Openings changed one major central component of my life that made a huge difference. While reading this amazing book, I woke up one day and I realized that I no longer carried the dread inside that had been a part of me since I could remember. Instead, I felt content.

This was miraculous in at least two ways. Suddenly I felt lighter, lifted, and aware that a constant drain that weighed me down was gone. The second realization was that I had been in dread all my life. It held true that we do have very deep states of being, where the emotion that we carry is much deeper than the emotions we experience based on the daily activity or the cyclical periods of the years. The emotional state was often what we were given by our parents and remains largely unnoticed yet affects us heavily because this is the tuning fork that we use to identify what is happening in our lives and in our worlds. Our perceptions are very much based on our emotional states. They decide whether the world is safe or not. Whether our needs will be met or not. Whether people, places and things will hurt us or enhance us.

I truthfully did not know that my emotional state was dread. It was perfectly sensible given my life. Yet I had no idea I carried such a heavy, dense emotional state around for so long. When it was lifted, I was a different person, and it had a huge effect on me. I was so aware of this transmutation, and I knew Divine Openings played a big part in it. Divine Openings is all about the 'instrument panel'. The analogy is that emotional frequencies can be used like a pilot's instrument panel. One can be aware of what your emotional frequency is, and if it is dense, we can move our frequencies up higher and 'lighten up'. Emotional frequency charts are used in Divine Openings, and by Abraham Hicks and they are very helpful to get a sense of where we are on the 'instrument panel'. The most powerful part of the book was that the energy, or frequency, of the book itself was so high because of Lola's powerful experience.

I truly believe that the book lifted my emotional state because it was written within six months of Lola returning from the Oneness seminar and she was on fire. Reading the book brought fire to a whole lot more people as well.

Lola's language of a cowgirl guru was very simple but also catchy and understandable. She was raised in the south and had a ranch in Texas for many years. You can hear it in the language of the book. It helps. I had such an amazing change in my life reading that book and participating in seminars, then reading her second book which was very inspiring as well. In the summer of 2013, I went to my first five-day silent retreat, which was held at Lola's incredible house. Being in silence that long blew my mind. I also went through my own emotional storm and realized how loud my thoughts were and often how hard they were to quiet them. My body was also very uncomfortable. It was not easy to be that present with myself. Many things came up and my thoughts hadn't been that sensitive in quite a while.

The silent retreat may have not had much talking, but there were a ton of activities. We walked along the beach, took long walks around the mountains near her home, danced a lot, rested a great deal on her wonderful porch. We wrote down questions she would answer, and we would practice laying hands-on people's heads and giving divine openings. Learning how to give a divine opening was also incredible. To allow the energy to flow through us was very powerful. It is a practice of getting out of the way and allowing the divine to come through us. We would practice the Hindu prostrate praying as well. And we chanted. That was very powerful. Lola would give long talks about this way of life and her spiritual experience with diving openings. It was both challenging and enlightening to be inside myself and in silence in my outer world and deal with the thoughts and feelings I was experiencing internally.

We had an initiation ceremony on one of the last days there. I had been journaling to God the whole time and staying silent when I was back at the hotel. I was very excited to go through the initiation ceremony. I decided I would marry all the children at the meadow and my guides, and past lives that were also present in the meadow. The kids at the meadow were very excited about this. I had been involved in the meadow for many years and had taken many of the wounded children that I had rescued inside of me to the meadow at that point. I had also had guides show up and even a few others that came upon us. The children created this beautiful archway with flowers running up and down the arch. We all wanted this to be a marriage of who we were together. How we were one and especially the kids found it very exciting to be married to 'ourselves'.

On the day of the initiation. I was very much in my imagination with my family at the meadow. For me it was truly a marriage of all of us. All these various aspects of myself. The ceremony itself was very beautiful as Lola put it together. I was experiencing so much within me, and it was also very much a marriage with God. It is still one of the most meaningful ceremonies I have done. I still feel married to myself and to God. It was deeply momentous. I made it through the five-day silent retreat, which in reality is really four full days in silence since we talk for the first morning and the last afternoon.

There was something said by Lola in answering one of my written questions. It did not sit well with me or feel true, and it kicked off an intense dialogue within me about whether I was going to listen to others over myself or honor my experience of me and life. It was really a painful query that took a very long walk to address at the end of the day. Lola lived at the edge of the mountains and her backyard looked into these amazing mountains. I walked a mountain trail in the afternoon. By the end of my walk, I decided my experience of myself was the most important one I would have. I wanted to be the largest component of my own experience. Deciding that made the experience of Divine Openings even more powerful because I was there to experience me and find the silence inside that was so powerful.

That first retreat set the stage, but every silent retreat has been very powerful. I have cleared large swaths of my soul to find a peace and acceptance of me. For that I am extremely grateful. By the time I started studying Divine Openings I was ready for the skies to open to me, and they did. I believe I may still have been recuperating from the therapeutic integration I experienced. I was now increasing my vibrancy and embracing an amazing freedom and spiritual awakening. I completely fell in love with God and life was continuing its brilliant remaking of me. My thoughts quieted and my feelings were accepted and embraced. I learned to 'dive in' and accept any feeling state. I was learning to 'deepen the bowl'.

42.

THY WILL BE DONE

I continued to reach for the literature of Divine Openings and find my spirit and energy rising with the material available. I choose to take the course to become a divine openings guide. The course material for the guide program was extensive and it took me probably a year and a half to move through the course. The focus on the material and the sessions with Donna were invaluable. The peace inside me grew and I also pondered elements of life, society, and previous experiences to come to new understandings of who I was. Always my guides evolved around me. I would often 'meet' my guide on a canoe in a river surrounded by trees. I would come to her, and she would hold me, and we would talk softly. I was comforted in the grace of her arms. Life and eternity were golden in her presence.

I attended my second silent retreat to be initiated as a guide at a beautiful retreat that was once home to a holy order. The retreat was 26 acres and we stayed in dorms on the retreat. The returning retreaters would assist with setting up the large rooms and help where needed. I was much calmer then and happy to be attending. There were perhaps four or five attendees being initiated as guides. This meant we could give divine openings by laying our hands on the heads of the attendees and getting out of the way to allow spirit to move through.

The second day we were initiated. Part of the ceremony was an eye-to-eye initiation. It was very intense even though it was short. There was another participant there who had spent much time receiving divine mother hugs from Lola. She went before me in the initiation. The interaction between she and Lola took quite a bit of time and I could feel myself becoming fearful that there would not be enough time. Finally, Lola brought her along with her for my initiation. I felt very sad that I did not have an initiation that was solely mine with Lola. The eye-to-eye initiation was intense, and I felt that I was not given an opportunity to have my unique experience with the initiation. Amid that beauty, I could feel the grief of not being recognized solely as a separate initiate.

This experience, the intensity of it as well as the way it occurred started my journey into both an incredible spiritual experience and eventually learning the truth of my childhood. I felt unsettled somewhat inside. As if there had been a slight at the retreat. Yet I knew it was my response to what was happening within me. Something deeper was stirring than had been sparked by the eye-to-eye initiation. The retreat was in October of 2015. In early May 2016 I was privileged to house sit for a friend's mother right above the ocean in Encinitas, CA. It was beautiful and stunning. I was blessed to be allowed that time at the beach. I also was able to visit my sponsor in Temecula and finish up some step work with her.

While we were going through my 9th step, making amends, I mentioned to her that I had always had this weird ghost dream that I was buried in a coffin. She stopped and looked at me and said that was the first rituals young children go through in satanic cults. My world came crashing down. It was literally like I heard waves in my ears and my head was throbbing and I was dizzy. My sponsor had just confirmed an impossible vision was a reality. I was mortified. We spoke more about the rituals and her experience growing up in a cult until she broke with them as a teenager. I was crumbling. It seemed impossible that it would be true.

The feeling I had in my initiation, of not being important enough to have my own initiation ceremony and how sad I felt afterwards, was a forewarning to this information. I am not sure I would have been opened to receiving the truth about my past if I had not gone through the Divine Openings initiation. While it opened me up and I felt extremely vulnerable, it also prepared me to receive the most devastating information of my life. I was involved in a ritual perpetuated by cultists as a very young child. This was mortifying.

I was buried in a coffin. I remember seeing bones in the coffin. I remember the coffin lid coming down. I felt like I had been shut off from God. I was ostracized. The ritual participants saw me buried and I felt like it meant my life was meaningless. I spent the rest of my time in Encinitas going within. I walked on the beach and went into myself. For years I was brave enough to rescue those broken children within me and bring them to the light. Becoming a brave giant and a champion. Going within and finding the little girl buried in a coffin was horrific. I did what I had done for years. I rescued my children. This time I did it with a sense of a deep grief. I was there with me. The ability for me to be there, be my comforter and my larger self, got me through something I was not sure I could ever look at. I was there for me, my divine guide was with me, and God was with me. This was a testament to the strength I had within and my spiritual fortitude.

Three weeks after I found out about being buried in a coffin, I was sharing at an NA convention. It was on the eleventh step, which states "We sought through prayer and meditation to improve our conscious contact with God, as we understood him, praying only for knowledge of his will and the power to carry that out." I spoke about finding out that I had been buried in a coffin. I could not sleep the night before. I sought out company. This soothed my soul. I was terrified. Yet I told fellow recovering addicts what I knew in the speech. I was raw, scared. My sponsee's helped me get ready in the morning. It took everything I had to share that information at an NA convention.

I broke the binds that held me, and I had to resurface to accept what I had done. This level of honesty held a high price in my life. It brought me back to what was, and it helped me to recognize that healing I had already walked through for 28 years. This ability to literally be there for myself felt so familiar, so soothing. I was able to go into my imagination and see into the coffin and get myself out. The scariest place I had ever been.

I still cannot do closed spaces well. I could not for years before I knew about the ritual abuse. I always wondered why. I was at a party once where they created a tunnel out of boxes as part of a party theme and in the middle of the route I busted through the boxes. I was suffocating. I could not get into closed MRI's. I once spent two hours trying to get into one. I finally had to take a sedative. It was deep inside me the fear of being enclosed. I finally knew why. I was not very committed after I learned the truth of what I lived through. I was grateful that I was alone, and I had time to be with me. I read the ritual abuse handbook. It was scary but I needed to know. The first few times I shared about being involved in satanic rituals I wanted to hide.

I didn't show up for some of my sponsee's commitments. My world was shaken. What was happening inside was such a game changer? I felt irresponsible and I knew deeply that what I was walking through was the biggest awakening in my life. I shared sometimes with people about the ritual abuse. That was never easy, ever. How do you say something like that? I felt raw. I knew though, that everything I had done, All the ways I supported myself, all the recovery I had, all the spiritual practices, took me here. The grace of Divine Openings and 12 Step Recovery is what gave me the ability to survive what I lived through as a child.

43.

RAVING ABOUT THE DIVINE OPENINGS

I want to rave about divine openings and about Lola Jones. I have received so much grace by practicing Divine Openings. I want to rave. It is amazing how Lola has been able to keep this practice so fresh and the material just grows exponentially. It is the opening I have had with Divine Openings that has truly allowed me to journey back into the densest most vulnerable, and painful experiences of my life, and to reframe them to see the incredible love that all people involved in showing me my journey agreed to provide.

I decided I wanted to truly know who I was before I died. I really don't think I had any idea of how much I would find out about my life and the immensity of my spirit. I made that decision when I got clean and started a program of recovery. When I started reading the books I was transformed, so much happened in that first six months.

I read both books; Things are Going Great in My Absence and Watch Where You Point That Thing. I love how Lola writes and the brilliant way she would use art to tune into a divine opening. I attended several phone group sessions and did both online courses for the two books as well. Lola has been genius at continually updating the online portals. In the summer of 2013, I attended my first live 5-day silent retreat. It wasn't easy there was a whole lot of 'stuff' roiling around in my head. After that retreat was when things got sweet in my life.

I had been working as a government auditor and was stationed at a large contractor's facility. It was a twenty-five-minute drive. Just eighteen months before the silent retreat, I had been very sick with a thyroid disorder. I would drive to work and wanted to drive off the road. I had done a great deal of therapy and had great healing regarding the early trauma in my life.

I found myself so tired and having emotional ups and downs. At Thanksgiving my disorder was at its worst, and I got very angry and threw my plate against the refrigerator. My oldest son never forgot that, and it left a bad taste for thanksgiving in his mouth. I was treated for the thyroid condition in January of 2012, and it took several months to get stable. I found Divine Openings in November of 2012 after a friend of mine gave me the book.

After the silent retreat I would drive to work, and I was astounded with life. The clouds were phenomenal. Divine Openings talks a great deal about contrast and the clouds were a perfect example of contrast. The billowy white clouds against the contours of grey captured my attention. I was enraptured.

I practiced raving about what was right instead of ranting about what was wrong. I would wake up and rave about little things in my room. I would describe a picture out loud, and it would create a wonderful ambiance for my day. It allowed me to see the incredible beauty around me. I have previously written about the ceremony at the end of the five-day retreat where I purposely married myself and all my wonderful children that I had rescued. Skinny dipping was the most wonderful time to rave. I loved the nature in my backyard and all the birds around the pool.

Now I was seeing full blown musicals in my head, and they were funny as hell, excuse the pun. I would meet with my beautiful guide in a canoe on a peaceful river. She would hold me and love me and listen. I took it very seriously to "take it to source first." This was different from our recovery practices of going to our sponsors first and it did fundamentally change the way I worked with sponsors.

Although in truth, it was always difficult for me to establish intimacy with sponsors and trust them. My mother locking herself away and being so irritated whenever we tried to get attention from her, very much affected my relationships with sponsors. I was scared. I tended to be attracted to sponsors that were gruff and I was always afraid to approach for fear of judgement or rejection. I had some incredible sponsors, yet it was difficult for me to connect with some of my sponsors. All of them gave me tremendous gifts of learning.

Divine Openings taught me to create a personal God and imbue that higher power with the qualities and principals I wanted in a God. I called this God a 'personal divine representative' (PDR), which is basically, a very personal God.

Often, they were the love, caring, compassion and tenderness I didn't get from my parents. The concept of finding the qualities I needed in my concept of God was tremendously powerful for me and strengthened my relationships with my guides and my higher power immensely.

I now had a very personal God. This healed my heart more than anything. After the first divine opening silent retreat, I signed up to become a Divine Opening Guide. This is a powerful course that Lola offers, and I learned and grew tremendously. It burst open my love pipes. In the summer of 2015, I did my second 5-day silent retreat and was initiated as a Guide. It was very powerful. It also opened the door to the deepest and gravest reality of my life.

I left that wonderful retreat with a powerful opening and a nagging awareness of a deep pain and powerlessness. In May of 2016 I visited my sponsor in California and she confirmed that the ghost memory of being buried in a coffin really did happen to children in satanic rituals. My world collapsed and I spent the next two weeks going within and becoming aware of the deepest wounds in my life.

I truly believe that if I hadn't grown so much in Divine Openings, if my thoughts hadn't quieted to the point that I had such sweet silence and the ability to let thoughts pass on by; and if I hadn't learned to move towards my emotions and practice diving in and allow my emotions to be exactly what they were and accept them and see them dissipate with ease. I do not think I would have been able to handle the information about the satanic rituals I was exposed to. I am extremely grateful for the fortitude I experienced. That year of learning affected my life in many ways, I didn't always show up graciously.

With the help of the book, "Safe Passage to Healing" a recovery book for satanic cult survivors, I learned and accepted what I had lived through. I continued to study online courses in the Divine Openings (DO) website, and I grew greatly. This spiritual practice has been a godsend. In the fall of 2018, I returned for a third 5-day silent retreat, and I totally walked through God recreating my childhood in those four days of silence. It was a tremendous gift from my higher power. My parents were there for me as were many others as we watched my higher power transform so much of my early experiences into amazing new dimensions. The evolution of that five days was beyond words.

When I fell in love with Thorne in 2019, it was a phenomenal experience. I truly had never experienced love like that. The time I was with him was so precious. He surrendered to love and to spirit. We would listen to audio tapes of Lola and watch videos together. Yet Thorne struggled deeply with the effects of years of addiction. He could not be honest. He was terrified.

He went to NA meetings and identified as an addict but could not tell me or anyone that he had nine felonies and was in prison fourteen years. He had this love of life and a mischievous adventurous spirit. No matter what, he loved to be alive. He slowly started nipping at alcohol again and he would get delusional. He relapsed after we had been together nine months and died within five days. I was devastated. Two months after he died, I found an incredible medium and I've been talking to him ever since.

He was there for all the achingly difficult discussions with my deceased father about the cult rituals and the horrific incest. He was always the first to show up at a medium reading and he became like a brother to our medium. He is with me often and always there for me. He found the meadow and eventually saw the children. Thorne has grown immensely in his spiritual journey and was there for Ian when he passed and finally Shay. Having these three men pass within twenty-two months has been achingly traumatic.

Yet they never left me. I have become familiar with the process of moving on to the beyond. So much willingness to continue to go to them and to heal with my dad, which changed my life, had to do with imagining things happening in the virtual first. This is how I learned to manifest in Divine Openings. I had no idea it would eventually help me to listen to the truth my father told of the cult rituals and the incest. I was able to hear him and forgive him. Especially because I learned the truth of what happened to me, my mother and some of what my siblings had gone through. Mainly though, it was me.

Again, it was my long-term practice of divine openings that continuously brought up my spirit and my emotional frequencies enough to walk through what was happening. We talk about the virtual and the beyond is as virtual as one can get. Yes, we will all get there. No matter what your belief is about consciousness and death, or about God or various religions, death is inevitable. So why are so many people so terrified of it and why do we make it such a bad thing. We say, "I'm sorry for your loss" and we are. We do lose those close to us. Yet if this was truly where are spirit dwelled forever, in bodies, or if we just disappear into nothing, then what is consciousness? Divine Openings introduced me to a wonderful God. I believe the beyond is just as wonderful.

I do use a medium to reach my loved ones. Just like I use someone who is good in sales if I need to sell something or a loan company if I need a loan. Why do we not study death and the beyond if we will all experience it in some form or another. I learned to manifest in the virtual, then Thorne taught me that love is what manifests everything in the beyond. I am extremely grateful that I have studied a practice that focuses on using the energetic signatures of emotional frequencies to raise our vibration, for nothing could prepare me as well as emotional frequencies for what was to come when I go to the beyond.

I do not think we cease to exist and, after talking to several loved ones who have passed. I can clearly experience that their personalities are still present. They do evolve. They do grow through their lives here and experience who they were. Yet there is no ego. No more suffering from the dreadful self-deprecation and self-hate. I believe we go home and all the imaginary marvels I have had, I believe they exist there. The meadow I imagined so long ago is there. I am grateful that I have experienced all I have experienced. I fully own who I am, in all parts of my life. I am deeply humbled by those that have taught me about myself. I am beloved. I am loved.

44.

MANIFESTING WITHOUT GRIP

Manifestation is so easy when you do not grip on it. We just finished our Divine Openings Guide Tribe meeting held every other Sunday, and we were talking about manifesting the energy 'field' we are all a part of. Manifesting is so easy. One of our guide tribe members practiced breaking up clouds to hone her manifesting skills. She said it was easy to manifest the clouds breaking apart.

Now perhaps we can drop the story and the grip. Drop the story, feel the feelings. This is the mantra of Divine Openings (DO). Letting go of whatever the story is. Living in the manna, the wind, as the Buddhists call it. That subtle manifestation of energy or force within us. This is the essence of Divine Openings. This is the gift. To let go of the story and experience that presence inside, and all around us. We are a part of the energy field which creates all life, that 'wind', the essence. We feel it when we can go in and experience the flow. It is the central intelligence that guides and governs all of us.

We can feel that gentle energy when we are meditating or listening. We can hear it when we are not busy talking, fantasizing uncomfortable scenarios in our head. I felt it when I was learning

Trager. That wonderful mind/body reeducation technique. Trager practitioners do not assess or diagnose. Instead, they ask questions. How can this be lighter? How can this be freer? Amazingly, the body responds often by lightening up. Easing the tension on whatever part of the body is being held, or restricted. The body allows for flow, more wind, into itself. It is really the mind that does that. The mind lightens up.

What does that have to do with manifestation and letting go of the grip? Everything. We 'manifest' our body being lighter and looser. If we are not aware of the state of being in our bodies, we often tense up or hold tension. Feeling the weight in our joints and just letting our bodies 'give over our weight' is like releasing the grip. We melt, we make it easy to be moved. To feel the full range of motion we have. We experience the freedom of movement, especially if someone else is moving our limbs.

Now how do we manifest without the grip. It is the same process. We recognize how much we are holding onto the idea or thought that we continue to focus on. God is not deaf. God hears you the first time. There is a myriad of ways to 'let go of the grip'. Breathing is one of the best. It allows you to 'change' your mind. Quite literally. I know how juicy it can be to keep repeating the thought over and over or imagining what you want or saying it to yourself again and again. Yet we can allow manifesting to be light as a feather.

We can be playful with our manifestations. We can imagine it already there. The mind does not know the difference between something real in the outside world and something we imagine to be real. It will go out and create it when it is recorded in those wonderful brain cells as real. We just think we must help it along by constantly thinking about it all the time or getting intense with it. If we play with it and imagine it happening and be as light as a whisper, we can have fun with it. Be curious. Be joyful. Be kind. Then it is a request, an experience. We can see it easily in our minds eye, or we can manifest the clouds breaking up. Manifesting is as easy as sending our angels out to do our bidding. Then purposely don't send assassins out to kill them by changing your mind or second guessing or self-doubting. Truly allow the angels to carry your bidding, undisturbed by thought or deed.

45.

REIMAGING WHAT WAS

I continued to practice divine openings. Luckily it was easy to do. The books were easy reading, and the online courses were diverse with pictures, videos, audios, and lots of white space on the page. I would still like to know where she got her pictures. Lola continues to add more content and it is very soothing and sometimes mind blowing.

I attended three or four 5-day silent retreats. My guide certification took place in my second retreat. That was mind blowing. One of the most powerful practices was the tantric breath. I felt this amazing pool of energy below my first chakra. In between my legs. It was like this pool of female energy. The tantric breath practice for partners is profound as well. The woman breathes in through her vagina and out through her heart. The man breathes in through his heart and out through his genitals. It is a circular breath between two participants. I would love to practice tantric sex. I hope to have a partner one day that is willing to try it. Tantric sex is called 'cool' sex as opposed to the 'hot' sex most of us experience. It is much more about exploring each other, breath, and being present.

The most profound experience I had was during my last silent retreat. It was held in the mountains just outside San Diego. The silent retreats are paced very slowly and there is lots of time to rest. Which in itself is rejuvenating. We start out talking for the first morning while introductions are made. After lunch we go into silence. You would be surprised at how much you can do in silence. We do a lot of chanting, dancing, exploring emotions. We walk in silence, hike, swim. During this retreat we went to a nearby lake and swam. Several of us jumped off the platform in the lake and laughed a lot.

Then we played on the playground and swung on the swings. There is so much to explore and share without words. Lola often will talk about her experiences with the silence and with exploring emotions, or meditating, or being with the divine. The food is wonderful. It's not always easy to sit with the silence yet it is always incredible to become intimate with silence. To be that loving of self is a gift beyond belief. I am extremely grateful for this practice and for the people in my guide tribe. Our guide tribe meets every two weeks, and it is amazing support.

I am also grateful that we have freedom to imagine God in many ways and that my journey through recovery in NA includes the acceptance of all concepts of God, even atheism and agnostics are welcome, which is why the third step states, 'We made a decision to turn our will and our lives over to the care of God as we understand him.' I don't see God or heaven in a specific way. I only consider things I have imagined, or are in heaven, that are confirmed by my deceased loved ones as there. I think heaven is magical and as varied as the many beings who reside there. I do not always call it heaven either. Sometimes I call it the other side, or across the veil, the virtual world or the beyond. Heaven may be off putting to others, and I know whatever you call it, it is a place of love for all of us.

This retreat was a journey into reimagining my life which led to a profound awakening. It started in the first silence we did. I was ready for this journey. I, we, were guided by an amazing being. I saw this gentleman; I like to think of him as God. It may have been another very powerful being after all, but for me it seemed like God, and he recreated my life in a huge way.

This radiant being appeared in my vision as soon as I went into meditation. It was as if this was divinely decided. I was not alone on this journey. There were many there including my parents. I had never had my mother present on a journey like this, so it was very precious to me that she was there. Daddy seemed to be very present in this journey. He was committed to changing what we knew as well.

The first place we visited was the basement in the house I was abused in till I was eleven. The basement I knew was dark, dingy, and dismal. I would have dreams sometimes that there were all these people in the basement. I believe now that there were. I think my father was having parties down there sometimes. When we went back there on this trip our guide changed everything. We went down in the basement and with a sweep of his hand all the walls were painted white or light colors.

It no longer felt like a prison of filth I could not get out of. Then we went into this large room where my oh so mature father had scribbled naked images of my mother and Mrs. Gallegos, our very abusive babysitter. Daddy would throw darts at the images on the wall. On the wall to the side of the images, our guide created this beautiful picture of the meadow. My meadow where all the children were so happy. He then made this picture into a portal, an opening to the actual meadow.

We could go through the picture painted on the wall just by touching the picture and we would come out in the meadow in heaven. In one flick of his wrist, he created a portal to the other side and made the basement of nightmares into a live portal. This act brought such a sense of freedom. We were no longer be trapped in this basement in any of our thoughts, memories, or experiences. No matter what had happened there, our guide freed any remaining memories or ghost children still stuck in the basement and gave them a way to freedom by simply touching the wall with the picture.

Remember my parents were reliving this now as a part of this entourage. They were seeing this nightmare turned into freedom. The next thing I remember seeing is the basement filled up with water and we were swimming in the basement breathing like fishes under water. This was so fun; we were able to breath and move freely in the basement and up the stairs into the main house. It was a child's wonderland we were swimming in the whole house. Even the upstairs was like an aquarium and we were playing in it. We had always had fish tanks and loved getting new fish in Santa Fe when we visited the dentist.

Now our whole scary Vegas house was a fish tank with vibrant colors, and we would pass each other in the hallways or in the living room and dining room. It was amazing freedom which we all enjoyed. We were swimming next to each other, my siblings and my young self as children, that had joined us from the meadow on the other side. It was an incredible wonderland. My mother use to read a German fairy tale to us called Undine about a water nymph. Mama thought I was a water nymph. I always associated myself with the picture of the impish girl that would turn into a mermaid. We would see her in this ocean fairy land, similar to the giant house fish tank that God created for us.

Having the house that survived such harm and pain be an ocean wonderland was a mind-blowing experience. Now I see that old Victorian house with no insulation as a water garden complete with the two stories that were always there, only we got a chance to be mermen, women, and children, in our once scary home. The basement was now light and airy and the small rooms where we were captured and tortured were totally white and bright and free. My children no longer were imprisoned, they could get to the meadow now. My parents were not the torturer and the silent one, they were an active part of this journey of recreation.

The next scene was a graveyard. Much of the satanic rituals took place in graveyards, especially when they put children in coffins. Our guide brought us into the graveyard. He then called up whatever spirits that were still in or near the coffins and he apologized for the graveyard being desecrated. He gave the sprits back their dignity and restored the graveyard to beauty.

He turned the graveyard into a garden. By his hand, all the desecrated graves were sealed. It was like some disappeared into this vision of a garden. He made the trees grow and bloom and shelter what had previously been desecrated. We could see the trees come out of the ground around the graves and grow into large trees with many branches and many leaves. The spirits who were still in the graveyard joined us in watching as this place was made whole and beautiful. Moss and grass grew on the ground and the sun was diffuse as the wind lightly created movement in the trees and whistled just enough to create a sense of tranquility and agelessness. It was the first time for Mama to know what had happened in graveyards like this, during the Satanic rituals, and she was present, perhaps shocked but she was there to see it turned into a beautiful garden. After this garden was created, our guide created a little pond, close to what was the graveyard, and more trees were created in the vision throughout the fields that we could see in this place.

As our guide was creating all this beauty, the Satanists appeared. These were the people that I remember burying me in a coffin and attempting to cleave me from my spirit. These masked and robed people were silent witnesses to my shame of not being worth life or spirit. I remember their stares as I was taken away from them after I was released from the coffin. My mind remembered a community that wanted me dead. In the act of burying me they confirmed my worthlessness. I knew how it felt to be ostracized, to be deemed lower than dead. This is the damning that I lived with for my early life.

I can see it in the pictures of me as a girl, miserable, bent over, hiding. I know this memory was the worst and this was purposely done to children to make them believe they were worthless, that they needed the cult. The cult had all the power. Years later when the children were about thirteen or so, the cult would have a ceremony welcoming them into the cult. This was their saving grace they would take on the power of the cult. The power to hurt children, to sacrifice them. To murder others. The cult was powerful in its exalting power over others. Many members of many cults are very powerful, often rich people. They exalt in having power over others. The power of life and death.

Now they were there, where our guide, God just created a heavenly garden and pond. Our group was aware of them. Yet what was obvious was that they were zombies. They were entranced and weakened by the addiction to death. There was so little spirit left. They had been trapped in their own power games. In an instant there was a blast that looked like a nuclear explosion from the hand of God. It went through the throngs of the cultists. It spread out, three feet from the ground and the power moved out in a white/yellow ring and up in a haze of yellow. The cultists awoke from their zombie state. In an instant they were brought back to life, they were free of the bonds that held them in perpetuity. The children blinked their eyes and looked around suddenly freed from the hell they had been breed into. We stood and watched as these people, many possibly long dead but still entranced, woke up and looked around.

This recreation was almost like being born again. It undid so much of the pain I knew in my house and the graveyard. I marveled at the power to change whatever surroundings had held me in bondage, into a lightness and a freedom that extended to my family and fellow travelers in this journey.

I kept stepping back into the vision when I resumed meditations. This was the power of enlightened imagination. It was not I that was responsible for this new awakening. I was just a grateful participant. I have not asked my mother about her experience of this journey. She was kept at such a distance. I am curious as to how she experienced this bold redoing of what was. This ability, the true reincarnation, was of such strength and the experience of turning a nightmare into a wonderland is the greatest manifestation. God did this for us. He recreated a vast impotent and overpowering decrepitude into a vision of heaven. This is what he really gave. Evil is a construct of our own disempowering actions. All exists within the realm of the divine. All can be changed with a sweep of an arm. A nuclear explosion can wake us up. We ourselves are splendor. Even when we are experiencing another cruddy day in paradise.

These few paragraphs were hours of my visions as I meditated in the silent retreat. The recreation of my life happening before my eyes with people I loved. The recreation of my home and the place where the rituals took place forever changed my awareness and reality of that hellish existence. The God of my understanding intervened in a way that was so fresh and full of vitality. There was no more of the dark, small, filthy rooms. Now the house will forever be a portal and an ocean of watery delight, which in truth looked more like a fish tank. What a wonderful choice to turn it into a big fish tank since we children loved our fishes and the big tank that held them. It is a truly endearing vision of delight.

46.

THE COURAGE OF THE DEAD, AND THE LIVING

The now is quite daunting. This exercise of inquiry has repercussions. I am engaged in a conversation with my dead parents and fiancé about what occurred in our childhood. I am hearing, mostly from my father, details about the ritual abuse that is much more extensive than I knew or would have thought.

I asked my father how many rituals I was involved in with the cult. He counted at least five, maybe six. The first one I was a baby, and it was more of a blessing. I was blessed in. Another one before one years old where I wore red. One at two years old. I was held up which was a 'mastery' ceremony. It was giving power to the group.

The one I remember, and what haunted me, was when I was buried. That ceremony was one where I was pronounced dead. The ritual was an enactment of death. I remembered being ostracized by the group by the burial. There were bones in the coffin and when the coffin lid came down, I couldn't get to God. This ritual was 'putting my light to death', putting my light out. It was meant to destroy my light, to cleave me from my beautiful spirit.

My long-term experience of that burial was to cut me off from God. To extinguish that. I was a threat to a lot of what they did in the cult. I am a teacher, and I was very verbal. I was not submissive. Still, this was the most devastating act. The memory of the coffin lid closing me in and seeing the bones when I was put in the coffin was horrid. Now I know the intent of the ritual played a large part in why I would remember being buried. I never remembered any other ceremony.

When I was rejected by the NA Phoenix Area meeting to serve as the regional delegate, I looked behind me at a man who stood against me and glared at me as if he hated me. I didn't know him, however, it stabbed at my heart. It was very painful, and it brought me back to the rejection of being buried and being unwanted and the cult literally doing a ritual to cut me off from the light of spirit.

After I was rejected in the position of RD, I attended a medium session to increase psychic or medium skills. It was given at a spiritual bookstore by a tall Native American man who channeled a spirit, possibly Jesus. He gave us an assignment to meet our guides or something. Immediately I was back in the ritual place with the people of that ritual. Only it was a time of rejoicing.

To really specify what I experienced going back to the ritual grounds and meeting with participants of the ritual who had become free, I need to go back to the last silent retreat I attended in September of 2018. Almost the whole four days of silence was a journey back to my past and a recreation of all that I had experienced. It was phenomenal.

I saw the ritual participants wake up in that divine opening retreat. I was in silence all four days, reimagining some of the most difficult parts of my life including the burial where my soul was meant to be cut off from me. Yet what I experienced was God, there is no other being it could have been; God led a group of us through recreating what had happened at the rituals. God cleansed the burial grounds where the rituals took place, then he created incredible gardens where the cemetery had been. Then, when the cultists appeared in the newly formed gardens; God literally awakened them from their addictive slumber of murdering madness. It looked like a nuclear explosion went to the cultists and through them.

They awakened, as if from a harsh dream, almost a little dazed. They moved about as if freely renewed on this world. This all happened in 2018, long before I was rejected by the addicts in the service body. That service rejection, though, being rejected by a group of people, threw me right back into that deep, deep pain of being ostracized and cast out. I experienced this in March of 2020. It was very painful. It also allowed me to feel the pain of the ritual group burying me as if I had no consequence again. A child, left to fend for myself. Torn from a group of people who appeared to hate me.

It was one of the most painful experiences in NA that I have had. I do dearly love myself and it is for this reason I am so grateful for what happened after. I was recently told that it was spearheaded by one of the women in the meeting. Someone I considered a friend actually. I heard her speak and was surprised that she spoke against me. It was painful.

During that spiritual session at the bookstore, while this gentleman was leading us through a meditation; I was back where God awakened the cultists. If I hadn't had experienced the rejection from this NA service group, I doubt if I would have gone back to that place, where God had released them. As soon as I went back, it was a joyous reunion. Especially with the kids of the cultists, who were awakened with the adults when we reimaged the graveyard with God. I found myself back there with the cultists. Instead of being ostracized, they were running to me. Embracing me. So happy to see me. They knew I was a part of bringing their spirits back to life and they were so happy to see me. The adult cultists were happy too, although I remember the children being the happiest.

The cultists embraced me and loved me in their newly awakened state. It was like a huge party. They were so happy to be awakened. God and the others from my family where there as well. My parents, Thorne, for this happened about six months after he passed. My guides were there too. Then the awakened cultists and many of my family and myself, went to the room where the service group met in my vision.

The NA members were there, and the happy cultists were mingling around them. Now it was the NA members that were waking up, or at least some of them in their spirits, recognized the joy of the gathering and were waking to it. It was amazing to see these two groups of beings who had rejected me become awake with each other and with me. The cultists were the happy ones and some of the NA members that had been particularly harsh were the ones now waking up.

Daddy acknowledges these sessions, which deal with the satanic abuse and even the rejection I felt in that NA area. It is still very difficult, and this process is painful for me. Above all he wants me to know he is hugging me and giving me love. I started to hear a man's voice during this discussion. Of course, Thorne is sitting with me and talking, they know how the group rejection was so despairing. It is not meant to be like this. NA is a place where we listen souls into existence. We welcome people into the room and love them. Yet sometimes those of us with a great amount of clean time find ourselves feeling ostracized by other addicts who have not had the fundamental change of being that can and does happen to those who have long term recovery.

We are not saints; however, we do know and have experienced a great deal over the years we have been clean. I feel that we again have an opportunity to allow newer members the chance to have a spiritual awakening that comes from doing our own inventory and being entirely ready to have God remove our shortcomings as is in our sixth step and then 'humbly asking him to remove our shortcomings in our seventh step. We are giving our 'character defects' over to a god of our understanding. From that we have a spiritual awakening we speak of in our seventh step.

This vital process for me was done several times before I had an incredible experience of literally feeling like my shortcomings were removed and I was propelled into the fourth dimension, as had been said in recovery circles. This is part of the process we experience. So, my deepest, most painful experiences of being ostracized, allows me to see my fallibility as well as the fallibility of others. I may not be comfortable around this service body. That may take me awhile to even want to be back there. I still am serving in this position of Regional Delegate. Helping grow NA around the world.

A larger body decided on my regional position and my service, several areas chose me to serve them, and this overrode the one group who chose against me, and I was elected to this wonderful service position. For that I am grateful even if the journey was hard won. It is my opportunity to forgive and to serve all that supported me and even those that didn't.

47.

SENTIENCE

"They go for the soul. But souls are so resilient. People can do the most horrible things imaginable. But we can overcome just about anything and still be striving for health and wholeness and spirituality."

Safe Passage to Healing: A guide for Survivors of Ritual Abuse.

Senses, sentience, sensory experience, sensory overload, overstimulation, overwhelm, sensations, symbiosis, symbiotic, sensational, extra sensory perception, sensual, kinesthetic…

Sense, Know and Breathe.

What's the definition of sensory?

1: of or relating to sensation or to the senses 'sensory stimulation'. 2: conveying nerve impulses from the sense organs to the nerve centers: afferent sensory neurons.

I am in a lifelong pursuit of sensory knowledge. The reckoning at birth gave me the sense of my greater being. A sensation of that which animates us. The essence living. The rays of life, our lives, the perception of awareness. The sensation of being alive.

This is all we have at birth. A becoming, every draft of air, every touch, and sound, and internal need, is experienced as sensation, developing ~life. Painful, apart, within, joyful, completely of the nervous system. Each stimulus creating nerve and cellular growth. Each experience outside of our skin defines who we are. It maps our bodies internally and externally. Babies left alone, devoid of feeling the touch of humans, or experiencing what animate beings can provide, fail to thrive. Touch is essential to our growth and knowledge of self. Even the touch of toys, baths, the feelings of those around us; love, fear, softness, harsh tone, embraces, kisses help us develop our internal sensory system. This is what animates the being and creates our physical selves. We are mapped by those who are mapping us, who touch us, coo to us, emanate feeling states around us.

There are those graced with being astoundingly present in themselves, well cared for, no doubt of love, or self, or the world. For many of us there is the lack of stimulation or overstimulation. This essence is not a philosophy. It is our selves. We gain our sense of the world from our parents. Their emotional states, not just the day-to-day emotional reactions, are the gifts or curses we immersively inherit.

How could I, the 'born aware' being, who was brought shining into this world, become so overcome by it. My sensation of awareness carried me from birth. My mother, very depleted by our twin births, was not a toucher. Still, she loved us. We were wanted. Yet wanting is not a guarantee of a quality state of being.

My father's grooming was done systematically, consciously, discriminately, and with malice. The lineage of the cult my father was raised in, participated in, is unknown to me. It seems to be one of many in the heartland of America.

I was given a book about cults; it is a cult recovery handbook. My NA sponsor gave me the book when I mentioned I had ghost memories of being buried in a coffin when I was very young. I always dismissed the memories as being too farfetched. My sponsor made them real. She told me that the burials were often the first ritual children are exposed to. My life changed completely that night. I was overwhelmed with what was a reality in my life.

It was also the last time I saw that sponsor. It seemed like that was the culmination of our long-distance relationship. She had brought me to a reality that has only sharpened in contrast and become much more uncomfortably real. The coffin ritual still continues to be the most devastating experience in my life as my knowledge of that ritual becomes clearer.

48.

TALKING TO THE DEAD

It may help to hear what it is like for me to talk to the dead. I have done so for many years. I have been truly blessed to find a phenomenal medium, after Thorne died. She can see, hear, and feel the dead. Which is quite a wonderful set of skills. She has brought heaven to me in that she fully brings in each of my loved ones, in the way they allow themselves to be conveyed.

Thorne is ever the center of attention and the biggest character I have ever known, alive or dead. Always shows up dressed to the nines. Star gives him pleasure by describing his garb fully and he basks in that. He is young in so many ways. He brings me flowers and assures me we will be together again, and we are together every night in the meadow as I sleep. Thorne is with me often. He calls my bed the barge and did so when he was alive. Thorne thrives in his nonphysical environment. He had committed to raise his frequency to match mine, an undertaking if I do say so myself. Thorne does the Michael Jackson shuffle as his parting dance step. It is my earnest hope that I have a wonderful happy life with Thorne, free from addictions and blessed with manifestations to move our souls to further bliss.

My father I see as a combination of his rambling self and Colombo. One of my very favorite detectives. He has told me more of what he likes and doesn't like dead, more than he ever did alive. Both Daddy and Thorne were immersed in their own sense of dread and powerlessness while alive. This is blissfully gone now so I get to see so much more of them. Now when I say see them, I am often referring to Stars wonderful descriptions. My father rides in the back of my car and only likes blues music. I am sure he hangs out at my house too, but Thorne is much more present. My father is still evolving there. We don't stop our evolution even though the physical world makes it easier to move through 'our issues'. Some spirits, like Thorne and my father, are very motivated to evolve.

Mama has a sweetness to her that I never saw here. Such a darling spirit. Still walking through the pain of a life not truly lived. She and my father are now good friends and accept each other and truly love each other. My mother knows she has not moved as quickly through what she has learned, perhaps because she struggles to accept who she was. In all honesty when it comes down to it; we truly are only responsible for one soul, our own.

I have this vision like the psychic reading is happening in a black box theatre, when the 'actors' are enhanced since little else is in the theatre. Most of the time I am just focused on what my loved ones are saying to me or I to them. It is not any different from a phone call or a zoom meeting with the photo off. That communication is just as disembodied as talking to the dead.

However, I have come to believe that the true beauty of heaven is the ability to manifest immediately what you wish to see or be. Thorne spends a lot of his time in the meadow that I told him about. It is a place we both know. The greatest thrill of my life was finding out that what I imagined truly came to be. Even if we can't see it here, doesn't mean that you are not creating it.

So why should I believe a dead man, such as my father. Especially one that had such a negative impact on the lives of his family. Hurt so many people, maybe killed in the practice of satanic ritual. Certainly, ruined my mother's life and contributed to the slow demise of his second wife, while she slowly descended into an alcoholic hell, and came close to resembling my retarded Aunt who lived with cerebral palsy all her life.

Two things I have learned, the point of power is in the present, and we may not be responsible for our victimizations, or our addictions; but we are responsible for our recovery. Many are wounded wounders. While family dynamics and systems may be addressed, at some point only we, ourselves, can care for our own wounds. Then we can truly heal from the inside out. This is a world of well-wishers, and there will be many who help when you reach out.

Only you can know what your own freedom looks like. If we are hurt once or a thousand times, and we tell ourselves the story of our hurt over and over, then we become our own abuser. Our essence is in our feelings, our emotional states. Drop the story, feel the feelings. Find your hurts and soothe them. There is no greater priority. Imagine how you want God to love you, and you will create a relationship with the most loving God there is. My God is funny and irreverent and compassionate to the highest heaven, literally.

This telling isn't about my life being ruined. In fact, just the opposite, despite a vicious upbringing, despite unwittingly participating in death rituals, I created the fascia that molds my life's puzzle pieces together. I became a warrior. Perhaps one that to this day still holds a bit of grief and sadness at seeing my own psyche pulled apart. Courage is the strongest element of the elasticity of the fascia and the basis for a joy to live and hearty laughter. Our joy can only be as deep as our grief.

I hold a sadness for my siblings. Whether conscious of the pain of betrayal they lived, each one holds some of the pain. Some wells are deep, and the cover is guarded. All are brilliant in their own way. Each of the five of us has completed at least a master's level of education. I wish them to know how to hold themselves within their own sensate self and breathe in waves of empathy.

I was privileged to dive fully into my imagination and create myself into the dragon slayer I've become. I still desire to relate and integrate with an intimate partner. I still feel vulnerable in relationships.

Having said that, I also truly feel compassion for the those men I've loved.

Each one struggled with their own demons and taught me to love to the best of my ability. I truly love myself. This fact is what allows me to love others more than any other. My life has been enhanced immeasurably by talking with the dead. I started out by reading books by psychics and found solace in how they helped others move through their grief. I suggest you try a few mediums until you find one that feels right for you. This journey is amazing and the greatest blessing in my life. Make sure you feel 100% supported. If you want other services, you can ask for them.

49.

BIRTH AND REBIRTH

Since Thorne died and daddy was there to get him, my relationship with daddy, across the physical divide, so to speak, has progressively gotten better. I had not cared to speak to my father although I sought out mediums for over 14 years. It's hard for me to call him Daddy. That term did not fit the safety and/or care that a father should provide to his children. However, his being there for Thorne at his passing, and their now very close relationship, gave me strong impetus to forgive him.

I was extremely grateful that Daddy was there at Thrones' passing. It was rather a shock to learn that he had been there, while it seems as though Thorne's own father has yet to greet Thorne. I am not sure if there has been healing between him and his father. To find that my fiancé and my father were as thick as thieves, so aptly put after knowing how they lived their lives, was immeasurably comforting to me.

As a result, I am willing to speak, love, and learn a lot more about David, my father. The man who graciously assisted in my birth. What I remember of him is a continuously broken-down man, who got progressively worse, and in the worst of times, even before I started getting my memory back, he was downright creepy. Yet I was a Daddy's girl.

I felt extremely grateful to experience my own birth. Reframing my birth allowed me to experience a profound change. I realized that the base of our physical existence is a funnel to life. A life which flows like an enormous sunrise. I know that is our enormity as beings. So large and powerful that surely, we can fit only a portion of who we are into these bodies. I was restored to a sanity deeper than I had ever understood. My life was transformed by this experience. I am forever grateful to remember who I am and where we come from and will go back to. I was fundamentally changed. I now know why I was born awake.

50.

HISTORY REPEATS ITSELF

I got a text that said I was what Shay had been looking for, my intelligence, spirituality, creativity. I loved that he was smart and resourceful, but I was concerned that he seemed to work himself into bad moods and exhaust his system. In May he moved out to Phoenix. I seem to be, even still, very susceptible to the vocal tones. Tones convey the emotion underneath the words. That is what I respond to. Not the words themselves.

I do not know why I kept in touch with him. I was in awe of him and his intelligence. He could be very sweet and attentive along with the times he was curt and abrupt. I'm really not sure why I answered his calls. He was close by. This started an hour waiting period in which I was not sure he would even show up. He did, after a time. He showed up with a friend who was more like his bodyguard. It was somewhat entertaining and somewhat irritating. What was it going to take for this guy to show up!!! I watched from the door.

Finally, he was walking to the door. He was scared really. Very concerned about meeting me. I felt like all those calls were him protecting himself, the irritating part was him doing it to test me. I love people being upfront about who they are. He was intimidated. He was also very sweet. He thought I was pretty, which was complementary. I told him about me and what I was interested in. He was very encouraging and talked about his career in the arts. He was very charming, and I thought he was endearing. Why then the curt discourse I had had with him so many times. Here was a man who appeared scared to be hurt again, yet willing to reach out…. sort of.

Still, I loved the night I met him, how curious and attentive he was and how much he liked me. We ended up making love. He was eager. I really liked him. Still worried about his abruptness. He is very auditory. He does not mince words and gets impatient if something is repeated.

He started coming over and spending time. He was very artistic and creative and flamboyant. Of course, temperamental. Then Covid hit in June. Then the company he was working with disbanded the division he was heading, and his income instantly dried up.

I enjoyed his company when he was not too temperamental. He was sexy. Then I met Yumi. I walked up to the car and this little dog was barking like crazy. She was very off putting, and I wanted to get away from the car. She was doing exactly what he wanted her to do. Keep people away. I did not get close to the car that night and really wasn't sure if I should see him again. He did bring her over after that.

She eventually got used to me. The incessant barking is very irritating. She also nips at people. I have since fallen in love with Yumi. She is sweet and playful and totally committed to Shay and feels like she needs to protect him. They have a very symbiotic relationship. She pines for him when he is gone. She really acts more like a protective mother. It is both sweet and sad. This man has been hurt many times in his life. His quota for trust and tolerance is low. In July, he moved in while my house was for sale.

Shay moved in with me in July. He wasn't happy how his 'stuff' had just been thrown together by his roommate and he still hadn't sorted everything out yet. He was angry about how rough that transition had happened. He does have a temper and is quick to blame others.

It reminds me of the Alcoholics Anonymous Big Book passage, page 62, "if the rest of the world would only behave; the outlaw safe cracker who thinks society has wronged him; and the alcoholic who has lost all and is locked up. Whatever our protestations, are not most of us concerned with ourselves, our resentments, or our self-pity?

Shay stayed. His life was a shamble after losing the company division. Covid hit strongly and the country was in serious decline. Suddenly millions of people were unemployed and there was very little activity in the work force. My company was very much hit as was Shay's income. The only action for revenue was the sale of my house. Since this had been in process, I was grateful that I had a buyer.

I had an offer and I accepted. The appraisal came through and knocked the price down. We shared the difference with the buyer. A week before closing, the buyer's sale fell through. It took a month to get through the loan process. We were given a week to leave. I was unwilling to start any packing till the sale closed. I found out that a week is absolutely not enough to move a two-story house I'd lived in for eight years.

I spent at least two days packing. Now this was after getting rid of stuff for at least two months but of course I didn't realize how long it would take to pack. That was tough but I was thorough. It was all the little crevices and the three bedrooms upstairs and two and a half baths. The office upstairs had so much stuff in it and Shay had taken over that room. It was exhausting.

Had I but known how encompassing Shay's health issues were, I would have really considered other alternatives. Shay could not move much. His shoulder had been seriously hurt in a car accident and the bursting of his tumor left his body septic for months prior to surgery. His adrenals shut down when the tumor burst after the car accident, and he was seriously hurt badly.

The next day I drove to the sold house. My wonderful home that I dearly loved and had great times there. All of the skinny dipping at night that Thorne and I enjoyed so immensely. The barbeques and raising Jason there, as well as giving Ian a place to stay when the fraternities became too much, or when he dropped out of college as a junior or got mad at girlfriends or got too caught up in drugs. I moved out to Phoenix to be closer to Ian. He was pretty caught up and doing a little too much imbibing. I was glad I could be there for him and, for the first time in his life, Jason had a little group of friends in the Springs community. It was the first time we were in a neighborhood where there were other black kids, and they had a great gang for a while in junior high. That is still the group of kids he refers to as his childhood friends. I was very grateful that Jason had that.

We were told we had to be out of the house by five. It was a nightmare. We left so much stuff there. My beautiful picture that I had redone twice of the two swans. A whole recycling bin full of books some I loved so dearly. Coats in the hall closet. It was literally delirious. We could not get it out quick enough. Shay stayed to get the last stuff in his car.

I was exhausted and very angry at the agency that pulled giving only the week to move out. I also don't want another man in my life that doesn't pull his weight and support me and love me. There are plenty of good men that are capable of that. It's what I want.

I got a little pissed when he told me he was teaching people how to read the market, the pumps and dumps and to tease arch, how a crypto will be used in a world of decentralized finances to determine its future value.

We moved into this beautiful townhouse in Scottdale. Across the street from my bank, and gym and two other banks I could use. I swim in a HOA pool that's heated and no one else uses. The pool is right next to the golf course with a lake and a lovely walking/bike path. Shay has his own room. I'm in love with him. Not like Thorne. Thorne was so easy to be with 80% of the time. Shay is difficult. So much smarter, snappy, doesn't share. I think he also plays at retribution. He tells me loves me.

Shay is a conundrum and I wish I could say he truly does love me, yet I think he has so much angst about himself, his resentments, angers and fears. He does have a lot of anger. On an emotional frequency scale, he is often low. In the dense range of emotions. He has the capacity to gain altitude but possibly not use the resistance to propel him higher into lightness of being or ambivalence.

51.

IAN'S SLOW DESCENT

I was also walking through some difficulty with my oldest son Ian. His relationship was becoming more and more toxic, and they were drinking and using drugs together. This was coupled with a lack of income that most of America was struggling with. For a few months we had unemployment. It took my son months to get his claim worked out. The stress was getting worse and so was their fighting. They would get drunk, and my son would "black out" and start destroying property. They were living in his girlfriend's mother's house.

He put holes in the walls and my son, and his girlfriend were both arrested for domestic abuse. My son was also arrested for property destruction.

This happened a few times, my son would spend the night in the psyche ward but in the morning, he would be his sane, lucid, highly engaging, and intelligent self. He did not want help, but I could see the escalation and the tension between the two of them. He destroyed property in the house they were living in at least twice, with the outcome previously described. Then one night they had a fight and she left to her fathers. Ian took off after her and hit her car, which was in her father's driveway, into her father's garage door.

He was arrested for this and had to go to court. Her father was very understanding. I think they left town for a short time and then came back and stayed at my house. Michelle took off one night in the middle of the night and Ian was hurt about that. Then they went to a party together and Michelle screwed some girl at the party when Ian was there. He called me and asked me to pick him up from the Circle K that Michelle had dropped him off at.

The cops were at the Circle K when I got there. Ian walked over and got in my car. He was drunk and in a mood. He told me a little of what Michelle had done. He was more freaked out about what was going on with him and Michelle. We got to my house. He disappeared for a minute then he was outside screaming in the front lawn and there were knives on the ground. I got a few of them inside the house. He came in and climbed up on the upstairs balcony and was hanging off the balcony hitting my picture with his bare feet. The picture eventually fell and shattered all over the hallway downstairs. Ian went down and danced around in the glass shards with bare feet cutting his feet and getting blood all over everything.

He was like someone else. Not the effervescent, vibrant man so full of life. He was like a taunting fifteen-year-old. Trying to hurt himself and get attention. He ran outside and was yelling in the back yard. My neighbor showed up with a gun. They had heard him running around out front and making all this noise. Of course, Ian went right into the barrel and was telling him to shoot him.

I was very scared and angry that the well-meaning neighbor had put all of us in danger by bringing a gun to the house. Eventually the cops got there and surrounded the house. They walked to the back yard and Ian jumped over the fence and ran away. I spoke to the police for a while, and they filled out a report and eventually left. I started to clean up the bloody mess. I was very upset at what had happened and started to see all the holes Ian had punched in the walls and on the stairs.

All this while, I was on the phone with Shay. He stayed on with me while Ian was going nuts. It was very scary. I heard someone at the back door. It was a very eventful night. Ian broke the door handle on the patio doors to get in. Now this was getting way out of hand. He was sneaking around the house trying to hide. I was really upset about the holes in the wall and the broken patio doors. My house was under contract to sell, and a great deal of damage was done.

I walked out the front and there were several police officers there. I lied and said Ian was not there, but they were able to find him and stopped him from jumping the fence again. I really did not want him arrested. His state of mind was very scary, but they carted him off anyway. It was for the best. He was cited for doing damage to my house and he ended up in the hospital ward and eventually in the psyche ward. I could not visit him because of covid. I spoke to a counselor, and she wanted me to involuntarily hold him. I knew what it would come to. He would wake up sober in the morning and would be as right as rain. They would not be able to hold him. Sober he was lovely. He was not ever held. I was there to get him out the next day and was very upset about his nightly haunting. He was sorrowful and was also under a restraining order to stay away from Michelle.

After this event I had to find someone to help me repair the holes in the walls. Ian was staying with me and was still very reticent and obtuse. I found a man who helped repair the holes. Ian came in and helped a little. It turned out that this gentleman was from Africa and played rugby for many years. Ian hit it off with him and they talked about rugby and hung out. We did get most of the holes patched. I had inspection in two days. I kept patching the large holes, still very upset that Ian would do that and not really show remorse. I woke up at 5 am to paint the living room walls before inspection. I could see the difference in the patching. I did finish in enough time for inspection. Not much was mentioned about the walls, but the buyer saw the difference. I wish I had known how bad Ian's state was at that time.

Ian eventually went up to Washington and stayed with my brother at the lake house. It was a very healing time for him, and he enjoyed himself thoroughly. He worked hard and was physically active and enjoyed family members that were all working on the lake house with him. He was wonderful while he was there. Full of love and healing.

He came back and moved to Oakland shortly after that. He was much better and stayed on a friend's boat in the marina. Ian fell in love with boating. He was also befriended by the harbor engineer. They became fast friends. Ian loved the community. It was a good change. Then eventually, when he is doing well, his girlfriend comes skipping out to Oakland.

For a while they did well together. They were not using drugs and had the use of a boat and sailed in the bay and spent a great deal of time on Angel Island, camping and hiking etc. It was like a mini honeymoon, and they did very well together. Ian started a company with another fellow cleaning and repairing boats and learned to dive better than he had. He was happy but he needed to make money. Then Ian applied to Amazon and got hired as a manager. Away they went to Fresno. The job was great, and Ian enjoyed it until the intense amount of walking started wearing on his bunion.

Fresno itself was a nothing town and the honeymoon was getting old. I went up to see him in November and we spent a few days in Oakland in a hotel near the harbor. Michelle was obsessively calling. Even then it had gotten bad again, within a few months of being in Fresno and she was obsessive about talking to him. He was really getting over the whole relationship. I could see it was wearing on him. I went back to Fresno with him and there was nothing to do in Fresno. We went out to the restaurant Michelle worked in and had dinner. She was a good waitress. I could see the cracks in the relationship though. My plans for a cranial sacral training fell through when Oregon shut down again and I flew back to Phoenix a week before Thanksgiving. I could see the cracks spreading. Trouble in paradise was brewing again.

52.

SEPTEMBER 24TH

Happy Deathiversary my darling! It was September 24th, the date that Thorne died. Not the date I found out about his death, one week after he died last year. It took that long to find a compassionate woman in the Tucson police records department to let me know that the police had found a body in the Tahoe. Thorne moved on, passed away, or more truly passed over on Monday morning, the 24th of September 2019. Star, our beloved medium, brilliantly brought him through.

Thorne was very excited to be 'on the call' as we say. So happy to communicate with me, his girl, the love of his life, and afterlife. He was dressed in black with gold. Thorne is a snappy dresser and loves to be recognized for it. Star is amazing in her ability to 'see' and 'hear' Thorne. She has been my ears and eyes to experience a man I dearly loved since he departed. They have become good friends, Star and Thorne, and Star loves his BIG character, as well as his commitment to grow spiritually so he can be with me.

He has grown and come to love himself in heaven, and he is still a youthful spirit. His ability to play is what I fell in love with when he was alive. Perhaps I should say incarnate.

Since he has committed to his evolution, he has learned so much about himself. Yet he is still a trickster and still wants to be the center of attention. His eyes have turned golden in his afterlife, at least that's how Star can see him. Beautiful gold eyes that reflect his soul, his beautiful, sweet soul.

Thorne had flowers behind his back and presented them to me. I've had more flowers visiting Thorne dead, than alive. He gave me flowers on our first official date, the first real date we had, on Valentine's Day. I miss you Thorne, yet I know you're looking over my shoulder as I write and watching my face. You love to do that. I know you miss not being able to touch me. Hell, I miss not touching you terribly. I'm still in a body and miss being touched, and held by you every night, feeling the furnace in your belly, with your arms around me.

Thorne said we'll meet tonight in the meadow. Thorne touched my heart today when he confirmed that he is the keeper of the meadow. The children love him. I've known that. I have always been able to see into the meadow, I know that our meadow has become a sanctuary for children. I want it to be known. This is why I imagined the meadow. I needed sanctuary and then I needed a safe place every time I rescued one of my 'inner' children. Thorne was the first boy to come to the sanctuary, long before I knew him. He was in his adolescence and heavy set. I loved him dearly, he was my sweet, heavy set, black child. We were connected even before then.

Thorne wanted to hear a story of his life with me. How I saw him. I told him about the night we danced together. He hadn't ever danced like that with anyone. His eyes sparkled in his face, and he held his chin in a way that looked like he was discovering himself, allowing himself to open his heart and really dance with someone. His eyes were bright, like the young spirit he is, he was so vulnerable. I loved looking at him dance that night. We danced to all kinds of music and his eyes twinkled so bright.

Thorne's love language is acts of service. He would cook for the family when Ian and Jason came over. We had more activities when he was there. He was always at my side. The spiritual practice we had of just having silence with each other was so beautiful. He loved me deeply and still does. I will be with him in the meadow tonight, celebrating his deathiversary. He said that the two dates they celebrate on that side is birth and death. Death is celebrated because we come home.

I told Thorne today about finding his papers about the trial for him stealing Francis's car. He had missed the court date and I saw his summons. I called the courthouse in Holbrook and told them Thorne had died. His summons stated that he was a felon many times over and the tone was so hateful and damning.

I understood why he was so afraid to tell me about his felonies. I found out about them the day we learned of his death. It was the greatest grief I had, that he wasn't able to tell me about them. I was grief stricken that he couldn't be honest. He thought I would leave him. The pending charges for grand theft of the vehicle weighed heavy on his mind. He knew he didn't want to serve any more time. We talked about this on his deathiversary. He decided then to leave, things were colliding. He couldn't work with his felonies and had so few skills. He couldn't ever really adjust to NA, again the shame of the felonies weighed on him. It was tragic, he denied himself the loving community that would have embraced him. He would have known such freedom, he never got honest in NA, in many ways he never got honest with me.

I knew or sensed that he had made his money in drugs, most likely running them, like he did the night he relapsed. The pressure had been building for about a month. Ken, my therapist, was concerned that Thorne was using me and pressured me a lot about Thorne not working. It bothered me too. He had come back from Texas and handed me $500. That is all he had to contribute. He had no car to run drugs in. So, his fears got worse and worse, so fearful I would find out about him. Finding out that he was dead, then also finding that he had spent 14 years in prison on and off, with nine felonies, just was so painful to know that he was unable to face that and get honest.

Thorne was a meth head, he joked about it today. His ex-wife told me how horrible it was to live with that. His addiction was really bad, he suffered from delusions. I experienced the delusions too, they were scary as hell, and whacked. Same type of stories I heard working with the mentally ill on the streets when I was a crisis counselor in early recovery. I'm not sure when Thorne decided he would rather die than go back to prison and possibly loose me. I just know he relapsed the night he got the Tahoe, and my Thorne was gone.

He came home the next day and couldn't speak, and then he took off again. He was there and gone for four days. I packed his bag after listening to him attempt to make a sentence for five hours the day before. He came in more lucid than he had been since Wednesday, when he relapsed. I ranted at him, said I deserved better. We spoke briefly. I told him I loved people, he said he did too. He left when I was in the shower, with the suitcase I packed. He called the next day, Sunday, and said he was trying to get money for me. I found out he died on Monday morning. He smoked himself to death with Methamphetamines.

Heaven has been wonderful for Thorne. Everything except knowing how devastated and hurt I was to lose him. That tore him apart, that he had hurt me. I have no doubt many readers would wonder why I was in love with him and may judge him harshly.

I have learned that we do not know how our spirits can grow. He was an addict, spent many years sick from his addiction, and was addicted to the lifestyle. When he met me, he hadn't used in several months and he fell in love, deeply with such soul beauty.

Daddy was there for Thorne when he died, they have been as thick as thieves ever since. Of all the horrific things Daddy has done, I adore him for finding Thorne, and for being so honest with who Daddy was, and telling me what he did in the medium sessions we've had. He told me so much about the ritual cult ceremonies and the harsh incest and how he truly loves me now. We do not know who we become in our evolution or even what makes us evolve. I know Thorne is with me most of the time and still learning from me.

He came to me a few nights ago. I knew it was him. I could feel the energy. It looked like space was folding in on itself, like a vortex. It was a little scary, yet I was so happy to actually see him.

I know I go to the meadow and am loved there, and we dance. I wish I could remember going and being there and I wish I could make love with Thorne again, he says it too, he misses holding me, brushing my hair. Baby you have become infinitely more than you were, and love saved your sweet soul and your ruptured, brutalized heart. I love you as you are there and were here and yeah you were a big pain in the butt. In death, you have fulfilled my life and given me so much more of myself, as well as bringing my parents into my life and heart again. I am so happy to celebrate your Freedom Day with you.

Thank you for making the meadow a much bigger refuge for children. I am so happy that you are there with them and how they love you and thank you for working with that sweet girl who was killed by her parents and healing her trauma. I am so proud of you, my darling. Thank you for opening the door to eternity. You have given me forever. Happy deathiversary darling, I'll be there soon.

It has been a tremendous blessing and they are helping me write this book. Already I have learned heart wrenching things about my life I didn't know and more things that I just thought happened in my imagination that I now know actually happen in the nonphysical. I wanted to die when I lost Thorne, today is two days before the day he died, one year ago. My life has become so much bigger, and I am ready to go home. It has been made very clear to me that it is not my time. Perhaps when this book is written. Right now, I know there is more to go.

53.

THE GIFT OF THE GUIDES

M y medium, Star, is very sweet. I would not have the chance to speak to anyone without her. She is essential and a Godsend. Today Daddy was there early. I knew he knew I was hurting badly.

I was very upset. Daddy told me today that he was unable to grow or go further until I could. He wants to heal, and he wants to help me heal too. He asked me why. Why am I stuck in these horrible financial binds? I told him that it was him that put us there. He never provided financial support for the family and often he was not even working when he said he was. His family was giving him money, but he was so selfish he would not provide for us.

He confirmed that that was true. He was unfeeling when he was alive. His abuse was so pervasive as a child he shut down and became an abuser. I told him about the poverty we lived through after he left and me standing in line or being kicked out of food stamp lines because I was white. I was embarrassed as hell to get food stamps. We were hurting. It was a hurt I have had for most of my life.

When I became an accountant, I was able to care for my family, my sons. I had a much better relationship with finances, and I still was not dating much in those days, so I was not losing money on intimate relationships. Dear God, this is sickening. Daddy needs to heal this with me, and he knows that. Today was very healing and I have been able to write a great deal about this.

Still, I was in terrible shape before the session. I did a divine opening's meditation. In the meditation I felt the shame of this financial journey, especially in my current relationship. I then saw myself with my wonderful guide. Through the night I had felt like my little girls were there giving me comfort surrounding me on the bed. Thorne was there as well. Usually, Thorne is the first one present in our sessions, he was giving Daddy lots of space to be with me this morning. This was really between me and Daddy.

I saw myself on the boat with my guide in the meditation. I often find her in the boat. It is on a river and there are beautiful trees around the river. It feels so peaceful there and she holds me in the boat. I just want a mother's love. My guide is such a loving mother, so peaceful and gentle. Today while we were on the boat, I saw her holding me as a baby. I realized this shame and perpetration was still held by me as a baby. A very young baby. It was incredible to be next to my beautiful loving guide holding me as a baby.

This was extremely healing. My guide has been there for me for so long. Such an amazing soul. So sweet. While we were in the boat my girls were with us on and off as well sometimes, they would just surround me. This has been an extremely difficult relationship. It is more about me than Mr. X. This is my lifelong pattern. It is a generational pattern. It goes back many generations, and it is stopping with me. I know this means a great deal, yet it has been so difficult for me that I have been overcome lately. To have my guide hold me as a baby as the boat floated down the river was so healing. Then I saw lovely souls coming to the edge of the water and throwing flower petals in the water to greet us and honor us. So many beautiful souls were there for me, for us.

I was telling Star about the boat and my guide, and she asked me if I knew an Angela. Then she said my guides name is Angela. I always called her Mary. Of course, she truly is an angel. Star said she was beautiful. I am a little jealous that Star can see Angela. I never really see her face. Star said Angela has very long blond hair and beautiful green eyes, she is beautiful. She is completely maternal and is often at the meadow with the kids. Thorne has seen her and so has Daddy and Mama. I am so enamored with Angela.

She is the strongest healing force I known for years, especially after I started doing Divine Openings. That is when I really found her love. I had asked Star if we could try to contact some of my guides and I was so happy that she saw Angela. It was such a joyous occasion to finally know who my beloved maternal guide was.

Mama was there today. She too gave Daddy wide berth. This was really between he and I. It was hard to admit the weakness I have with men and money. So humiliating, Daddy started crying hard in the middle of this. Finally, Thorne peeked his head in when I was talking about wanting to die. He peaked around the corner and said, 'no its way harder to learn and deal with things here'. Do not wait to deal with this. I understand but I was so done. I felt so horrid over these issues, and the lack of love and nurturance.

It was meeting my wonderful guides and hearing them be confirmed by people I love, my family, that touched me the most. Angela, who I've always called Mary, being seen by Star was so affirming that my guide is real. Star says she calls me little bear. She thinks bears might be my totem animal. I would be happy with that. I love that Angela calls me little bear. I also meet my funny guide today. His name is Victor. He has flaming red hair. Thorne loves this guy. This is the guide that has put together full-blown productions in my head. Seriously, incredible songs and visions and God! I love his humor. He has gifted me in so many ways in the last nine years and has made my life so much more humorous. I was very grateful to meet him. I love that he and Thorne are thick as thieves. I love that Thorne is humorous and loves to have fun.

I met one more guide today, the serious businessman. His name is Val. Star said he was boring. He was the one that confirmed the publisher would be good. I have a business side and I am very grateful to have such an awesome businessman as a guide. Quid pro quo and all of that. It was truly a magical meeting with everyone there today. Star was also told that I need not worry about money. It will all come together very well and will be there when I need it. I really needed everyone that was there today. I am so much happier knowing my spirit guides and knowing that others can see them. It was an incredible session. I cried over and over, and I think daddy and I have grown in leaps and bounds today.

54.

THE TROUBLE AND PRICELESS BEAUTY OF TRAUMA

Trauma remains until that energetic vortex holding the memory of the trauma, is approached in a compassionate manner that will allow it to be recognized and accepted. For me, this was an internal process. I was the best suited to address the remnants of the trauma held within me and breathe into the 'weight in the cells' that held the memory of abuse. I learned that emotional, sexual and physical assault are handled very similarly in the body.

The body will isolate and compensate for whatever has been hurt. Until the harm has been sufficiently addressed, it will be protected within the system, often holding the 'persona' of the age at which the harm was done. This energetic form then takes the personality of the four, or fourteen, year old that is unable to address or redress the harm. The energy waits until the entity can address the hurt. Sometimes the hurt resides within the body and is never given the opportunity for redress.

The ability to redress held hurts is the ability to journey within our own skin. To experience the pain, we feel inside. Whether that pain is physiological or psychological or even memories or constraints within our fascia. It will wait until we 'go inside' and experience our inner environment. Often, we receive the help of good therapists, whether psychological or physical, their help as guides to our inner universes allows us to continue the journey within.

It starts with a breath. Where does our breathe stop when we breathe in? What stops it? How does it feel if we simply breathe into the resistance? When does the physiological resistance lessen and when does it move into the emotional resilience? How does it feel when physical pain gives way to the emotional vulnerability? How many are willing to take the time to breathe into their own body with awareness. What may start as a meditative or yogic practice can become a deep journey into our inner most selves. The many aspects of the ecosystem of our bodies and minds become ever clearer.

This may be the truest journey we take. Surely it transcends lifetimes. Our traumas may accompany us over many experiences, perhaps even over many lives. It is the truest journey of the heart to find its own beat. To imagine the pumping of the heart within our own chest. To create a rich and deep environment which we may flourish. Truly the longest journey is from our head to our heart.

Many of us cannot experience the inside of our bodies past the initial breath into our lungs. Yet every muscle we have moves blood and breath through our bodies. Every bone moves with breath and the movement of our spinal fluid through our deepest tissue. The entire body is a living, breathing entity.

Yet many of us will only know that entity in relation to 'what hurts' and may never experience that breathe goes beyond our own mechanism to breath, way past what makes us think. It goes into the essence of what is no longer physical. It travels on the wind finding its way to the other side of the earth in a few days' time. We are living beings transporting ourselves into much bigger realities than we imagine, and our hearts beat because of iron molecules within us that were created when galaxies collided so long ago.

Yet we imagine ourselves so small. See ourselves only as worthy as the last task we accomplished or the current currency in our bank accounts. Perhaps worse, we will remember ourselves as the last callous remark made about us by someone who saw so little of who we are. This is the preciousness of becoming our own warriors, our own champions. To know ourselves in the grandest magnificence that we truly are. We are so much greater than we can imagine. We ourselves are tasked to distinguish the exquisite beauty which resides within.

55.

AND THE BEAT GOES ON

S hay moved into my house in July, I failed to have 'the talk'. You know the talk, where you sit down and say, "I need you to contribute to the household and pay half of the bills as long as you live with me." That essential, contract forming, up front and out loud agreement of shared financial burden. I neglected to do that. Me, the accountant, having spent all that time understanding how contracts and finance work, screwed myself by not getting an agreement in writing.

I was starting to see a pattern of irresponsibility and lack of ownership. This did not sit well with the very powerful practice I learned of stating 'I created that'. That statement of taking responsibility of what I create, is not damning or punishing; but very helpful for me to accept my part in things and see that I could create something completely different just as easily.

We were finally in the new townhouse in the center of McCormick ranch. I loved the greenbelt on Hayden Blvd, even though my lover felt it was way too white. Unfortunately, the election of 2020 really did become one of racial divisions and, in my opinion, it was purposely stirred up to the point of a break in by thousands of people on our congress. There was more animosity in the last election than I have ever experienced in America.

I was scheduled for surgery on September 24th, and he had agreed to help me. I would not be able to drive for a few months since it was my right foot. He actually was very sweet during that time period and would wash my hair. He was the most loving during that time.

Shay was very sweet and caring for a few weeks. I did not need to leave the house and I couldn't really walk on my foot for six weeks. I had a knee stroller and crutches and was very self-sufficient. I appreciate him shopping but, since he hadn't paid any bills, I wasn't appreciative of the money he took without asking.

It was in the end of October we revisited the business venture. He said he was scared to approach me. I thought that was odd. I am an accountant and had very good business skills. I found a good partnership agreement, and filed the company with the Arizona Corporation Commission and the IRS for a tax ID. We worked on the partnership agreement. The business was legit.

We went back to create a business account and my bank refused to start a bank account because he had a bad mark on 'Checks' reporting system. We went home and the problems started. I sent him 10K through cash app to start the business at the end of October. I wasn't really concerned about the investment. I felt strong and willing. Within a week though things went downhill.

What I didn't realize was the event, where I thought I was having a heart attack, happened that week in October too. On October 24th I took an all-day workshop on souls' journey. It was a two-day workshop with some great regressions into finding relatives that had passed and finding out what you are working on in this lifetime.

We made love that afternoon after the seminar. It felt like something a lot like cocaine was placed in my body during the love making, I was upset that somehow a substance got in my body, that I definitely did not put there, while I was having sex with him. I started feeling these waves come up my body. I thought I would just ride it out and not really mention it to anyone. I was embarrassed that I was clean so long, but it seemed I had a substance in me, and I was not very happy about how it got it in there.

As I sat there the feelings just kept getting stronger and stronger. It was getting overwhelming, and I got scared. I could feel the waves getting stronger and move up to my chest. I started researching strokes, which I had already had, and heart attacks. Both had the same symptoms that I was feeling. I told my lover to call 911. I felt like I was having a heart attack. He did. The paramedics showed up and took a series of readings. They asked me if I wanted to go to the hospital, I said yes. I was taken by ambulance.

They did a series of more tests when I got there, and a Dr. came up and in a very snide tone told me I tested positive for meth. I just kept saying I was clean for 32 years. I felt humiliated by this doctor. They gave me two shots of Ativan and I was out of it. I spent the night in the hospital and had more tests in the morning and was released.

The most interesting thing was that Thorne visited me the night of the 23rd of October. I woke up and he was literally next to my bed. He was dressed as the grim reaper. Even had grey ringlets, I had never really had a vision of him before that was this real and it scared me. Rightly so, he worked very hard to try to warn me I was in danger. He even had the reaper staff. It's a little funny now, Thorne looking like someone playing the ghost of Christmas past. I love you honey. I know that took an intense amount of effort to make yourself seen like that.

You saved my life Thorne. I may never have heeded the warning. I do feel Shay was dangerous in a very flippant way. He is so mad that I see him the way I do. He is my amalgamation of the horrors of Daddy and his obstinate reluctance to take care of himself.

I went to the bay area right before thanksgiving to spend time with Ian. I visited Thornes family with Ian in Fresno. God Ian was so cool. We sat with Thorne's sisters' daughter; his niece who was a few years older than Thorne. She told me about Thorne witnessing his aunt kill someone when he was two. This is when it's hard to think of Ian being gone. God it was hard on him, his life, his struggling to make it every day, the partying. That is so true of every one of the beloved men I lost.

Thanksgiving was hellish. Shay was obtuse and punitive all day. Talking about his dead relatives and how he hated Thanksgiving. I cooked several dishes and made a nice meal. He was out most of the day and morose. We made love, then he screamed at me when I was scared to tell him I wanted to eat dinner. I did not want to be there with him after Thanksgiving.

I redid the souls gift training, and it was amazing. I met the elder spirits in a meditation and felt right at home. Saw Grammy and Buppa, my maternal grandparents. My boys came for Christmas. They both ran to Shay when they saw him. They wanted and expected him to be a part of the festivities. He acknowledged them for a minute and went right into his room. Ian said he ruined Christmas for him because he would not participate.

Why did he hide himself away? He could have come out. Instead, he played his music loud, obnoxiously, like he was trying to be seen without being seen. The boys hated it and started to hate him. It really turned them off. Still, we had a great Christmas dinner and had fun playing games afterwards.

I told my lover I would pay January expenses. I had complained so much about it. I drove a check over to the rental office. And gave the landlord my 30-day notice. This lover was truly my petty tyrant. The one that showed me the most who daddy was, his controlling, his yelling and how mean he was.

How unsettled and unkempt he was too. How he was killing himself, with self-loathing. I really wanted a man that would come through for me, truly deeply. This was so wrong. I still think that was his intention, to create an empire for both of us.

I see the worst of daddy in him, the manipulations, the blame, the filth, the drugs, the lies, the criminality. I wanted us to be above board, create amazing art, books, movies, music. He never really showed up for me. Ever. Great lover, still yearn for him, but he doesn't know how to make love or give love. This was a terribly sad part of our relationship.

I was unhappy in this relationship, and it never got better. I really liked who my partner was and then he just went downhill. I knew I could not trust him. It hurt him and me. I know I was seeing my father in all his powerful control and manipulation, and I was willing to see it. I was still unhappy.

I knew this was not what I wanted, but I hoped for a better solution. Still, I had tools, tremendous tools. I never stopped using them. I was different. I was not a victim. I was not unable to see what was happening or how lonely I was. I still participated in recovery. Did those things that made me happy. Still wanted to share them with a man who would not come out of his room. I walked, swam, biked, wrote, worked out. Saw friends, went to meetings. Committed to my spiritual growth. I was the best of me even in my unhappiness.

I had the medium sessions and way more time was spent talking about my current relationship than I wanted to be. I have this opportunity to talk to my dead parents, and I did. I had gut level discussions with the man who almost killed me, my father, in my medium sessions every two weeks. I listened to his honesty. I heard what he said to me about who he was and what he did. He was honest. In the middle of a difficult relationship, I was talking to my father, and he was honest about being a rapist and a pedophile and mean and controlling.

This juxtaposition was not at all lost on me. I needed this honesty. I needed to hear my father own what he had done, how he had hurt so many. This was real, this was painful, and this was true. He was telling me who he was in all his ugly glory. I was seeing it acted out sometimes by a partner who could not get honest. Did not tell me how bad his drug use had gotten. Meanwhile, my father is giving me details of what he did. He heard me when I told him how devastating his actions were in my life. Daddy cried. Often. He cried about what I told him. I flat out talked about what he had done, and he admitted it. He grew as I grew, and I was willing to know. No matter how horrid, I want to know. It gives me strength.

I thank my partner for showing me just how bad it was early on. I'm grateful that Daddy was gut level honest. I had opportunities to give my parents back their irresponsible actions and not continue to carry it for them. I would not hold their shame any longer. I have enough to hold off some of those deeply set in character defects that I practiced for many years. Losing my temper, bitching out service providers, being stronger or meaner than needed. A deep insecurity that still rears its ugly head even though I feel so clean inside. So cared for, by me and by others. I know without a shadow of a doubt that I truly am committed to me.

I deeply love me. Guess what! We are responsible for only one person on this planet...ourselves. When we die the first thing we do is work on self-love. I heard this from Daddy, Mama, Thorne, Ian. They all had to start with themselves. They all saw their life review. Yes, it is true, we go through that. They saw who they were. Daddy accepted his life right away, Mama struggled with how she did not protect us for a while. Thorne's review was tough to. He was an addict and a drug runner for years and did prison time for it. Perhaps that is why he shows up for me and shows me so much love. Ian was shocked to find out how deeply loved he was and how he deeply loved. He still did not give himself much self-love till after he died. Then with Ian flair, he would come barging into the scene announcing himself and say, I'm working on loving myself mama. I just did not know how many people loved me. I love him totally.

56.

WHOSO SHALL RECEIVE ONE SUCH LITTLE CHILD

"And whoso shall receive one such little child in my name receiveth me, and whosoever shall receive me, receiveth not me, but him that sent me. Truly I tell you...unless you change and become like little children you will never enter the kingdom of heaven."

Christmas past two days ago and Star, our beloved medium, was on the zoom meeting bright and chipper. Thorne was very excited to come through. As usual he was eagerly waiting to be with us, and he often overwhelmed Star. "I keep telling him to back up a little, otherwise I get headaches his presence is so strong. He was so excited to share his news.

Thorne had been very present with me and the family on Christmas day. He said he stayed very close to me. He loved how light and pleasant the day was. In truth, Ian, Michelle, Jason, and I spent lots of time watching Peaky Blunders and hanging out in the living room. We also took a long walk with Ian's and Michele's two dogs and Yumi, Shay's dog, came too. For an old dame of 11 years, she was a trooper and kept up with the younger dogs.

The 'adult' kids made a wonderful Christmas dinner after we enjoyed the pool, even if I was the only one brave enough to have a swim. I rested while they prepared a meal together. We played the 'ungame' and had much discussion about just how it was to be played. It is a game of cards with a series of questions revealing information about ourselves or others. I thoroughly enjoyed the game as did Thorne from his unseen position next to us.

Then Thorne spoke of the big Christmas tree in the medium reading. He was extremely excited to tell us this story. Star was having a difficult time placing the Christmas tree that Thorne spoke of. At first, she thought he had seen it in a town center. Then Star had an 'ah ha' moment and breathed a sigh. Thorne was talking about the Christmas tree in the meadow in heaven.

Thorne never remembered a wonderful Christmas in his life on Earth. Either he was too high to enjoy it or Christmas's as a child were stressful. The household was large, and money was scarce, and he never remembered an enjoyable Christmas. He was so eager and happy to tell us the story of Christmas that he experienced in heaven. Star laughs at Thorne's outfits. He always shows up dressed in a wild outfit with a derby hat to match. Today he was all in purple. Thorne just laughs about it; he is so happy. He proceeds to tell us about Christmas in Heaven.

"The Christmas tree was huge. You could barely see the top of the tree. The kids were so excited. I've never experienced Christmas like this. Here Christmas is love. The tree was in the middle of the meadow. It had so many colors on it. All the kids contributed to the tree with their imaginations. There were spirit presents for all the kids, like teddy bears, and toys. We all held hands and circled this huge Christmas tree. There were so many kids. Kids that had been hurt in life. These were the kids that came to the meadow. That sought out the meadow. There are so many kids there now they fill several meadows.

Star was amazed that she could see the kids. Kids of all races and nationalities. Usually, she can only see spirits but this time she saw the kids. So many different children, so many colors. It was like the children were teaching us how to come together. These children, who had been hurt, and many that were killed, were here together so happy to be loved and embraced and with each other. They were singing and dancing around the Christmas tree and Thorne was the biggest kid of all.

He was wearing such a colorful outfit. The kids adored him. He was the loving ringleader and the most excited kid there. He has brought so many kids to the meadow.

This beautiful place was the haven I created for my own internal children. This was where I would bring my children when I rescued them from the abuse. Over and over, I brought my little girls here. All ages until the incest stopped at eleven. It was not just my rescued girls; it was myself in previous lives and other kids that found their way to the meadow early on. In the beginning there was the lion that would run the long field close to the meadow and the Doe that would talk so lovingly. We could fall into her eyes and be loved. Then came the big birds. We would fly on their backs and scream into the wind and feel the soft air on our faces. I loved flying on the birds.

The children came slowly over time. There were also spirit beings and guides that were so loving and caring. We would sit in a circle and be content with each other and see each other heal as each one came to life. Thorne first came to the meadow as a heavy boy between 10 and 12 years old. He was the first boy to come, but not the last. Years later Thorne, my love, heard the story of the meadow.

I first told Thorne about the incest the night he came back from Texas. He surprised me and did not tell me he was coming in until I was at the NA convention. He got upset that I was not home. I was already at the convention. I stayed to hear the speaker, a little miffed that he had not considered my time. Thorne strolled in the house after I got home, he had been drinking. He was being belligerent. We had a little fight and then I got very serious, and I told him about the incest I had experienced as a child. Thorne was so incredibly compassionate and loving. It was then that I feel deeply in love with him. Our relationship was cemented that night.

I told Thorne about my meadow one night as we lay in bed. He was so accepting of this other world and how I had rescued so much of myself. I told him all about the community that had been built. The kids that were there and those there to give us comfort, our guides and loving animal spirits. Thorne had such a natural affinity for the divine. We spent many hours listening to tapes of Divine Openings. Thorne brought home the little book on "the Dance of Anger" a small pamphlet that introduced us to nonviolent communications.

A few weeks after Thorne died, I attended a grief recovery camp by Payson. I could feel Thorne there so clearly. He loved the mountains. The grief camp was powerful. It was originally started for kids and then the adults created their own camp. It helped me a lot. I wasn't the only one that had lost a loved one to an OD. There were also suicides and accidents and many people were grieving several losses. It was the first time I felt Thorne so clearly. I knew he was with me. Still, I was very bereft over his death less than a month before.

Life resumed after Thornes's death slowly and then I was referred to Star in December. Since then, Thorne and Star, the medium that is so talented, have become like siblings. They love each other and Thorne, as well as my parents, have become an intimate, loving part of my life.

We now have a standing reading every two weeks. I have seen Thorne and my parents grow in leaps and bounds. My own life is much fuller with them in it, and I am healing in very deep ways. We have covered some very difficult ground. All of us committing to heal from our abuse. Daddy and I committing to address the satanic ritual abuse we both experienced. Me by his hand and his by his parents and generations before that.

I was so happy to hear Thorne talk about the meadow when I started working with Star regularly. I could not believe it was real. Here was Thorne at the meadow. The place I had imagined since I was twelve. It was real. It seemed like everything fall into place. The most important was finding out that Daddy was there to meet Thorne when he died. That meant more to me than anything else.

Back to the meadow. Since we have been meeting regularly, Daddy has been so forthcoming about the ritual abuse I was exposed to. He made a commitment that he would also heal himself. Thorne made a strong commitment to healing himself and addressing the addiction that eventually killed him. He never felt like he was able to 'get' recovery when he was alive. He felt so 'less than' and struggled with being honest in meetings. He wanted it so bad. He found others after he died in the spirit world that helped addicts and eventually, he was meeting other addicts that died of overdoses and helping people transition and then found he really wanted to be there for the kids that were abused and often died from the abuse. He was very happy to work with kids and care for them as they found their way to the meadow. It was helpful for him to love the kids that need such care and nurse them back to thriving.

'Christmas in the Kingdom of Heaven'

So here is Thorne. Happily celebrating Christmas around the hugest Christmas tree in heaven. Surrounded by kids he loves and being the biggest kid ever. The kids were jumping and crawling all over the tree as were the animals. There was tremendous joy and the meadows all around held kids. He was so excited to tell us about the heaven Christmas and his joy of being there. The meadow now is one of many meadows filled with children and Thorne has healed so much of his wounds in the caring for children.

My parents participated in the Christmas activities. As Thorne was telling us about the beautiful Christmas tree, my father cried, deeply sobbing for the joy and healing of the children. My grandchildren were there among the children celebrating since those of us in physical form are also there with our loved ones in heaven. Even as we are still alive on earth. We are there every night and in our thoughts.

My granddaughter Savannah and grandson Sage were there for the Christmas celebrations. Savannah is often in the meadow and is a tomboy that reminds my parents very much of me. Hearing about my grandchildren is very endearing to me since I haven't seen them since March. My daughter in law is currently estranged from my son and his heart has been broken since he has not seen his children, as has mine. To hear of Savannah and Sage and know they were there for the festivities melted my heart.

My parents were there at the Christmas celebration. For them it was a sacred event. They watched the children and were in awe of the love and tenderness of so many wounded children. Therefore, why my father cried. My mother has come out of her shell. For the first time since I have visited heaven through our medium Star, my mother has been clearly present of her own volition. Before in each visit she was hesitant to come forward. She was so bereft at her inability to protect her children in her life that she could barely be seen.

Today she was present. She was also present at the Christmas celebration. Savannah helps my mother to come out of her shell. Mama gently put a coat on Savanah during the celebrations. The greatest healing today was with my mother. Her coming forward without hesitation and speaking out about the greatest pain being a mother's pain for not defending her children from the abuse they suffered. She was clearly shining today. "I'm not hiding behind a book anymore Meg!!" She is so lovely and sweet and her being clearly present was so incredible. My mother is healing in large waves and the children have helped immensely.

Star had a realization. It's as if each one of us needs to accept the children within us to really learn to love children. My mother has been healing with her parents. She never learned to be a child and was not afforded the opportunity. In another foray into the virtual world, I was greeted by my mother's parents. They too have become so light, and my mother's family is healing back generations. To see my mother so alive and loving was the biggest gift to me. Her healing is a tremendous event.

Today was an incredible blessing for the children who have found a deep love in heaven and a place of safety and happiness. The Christmas celebration described by Thorne, and my parents are a breakthrough for many. Thorne told me again and again that it was I who created the meadow that now heals the deepest of wounds for children and restores their spirits to rejoicing.

Thorne himself is in bliss. His frequency so light and fluffy and full of love. My beloved passed away last September. He committed to grow and learn to love himself deeply. This was something he was never able to do here. He was shown the rooms of recovery and found himself lacking. Since his death he has committed to healing his spirit and doing everything he could to become a being of love. This he has done magnificently.

Lastly Star and I recognize that the committed connection between the living and the dead is a very powerful healing tool. We have all grown tremendously. Heaven for me now is a place of wonder and awe. Also, a place of deep healing and growth. I have seen my fiancé and my parents, and even those children wounded within me, heal deeply and come into a very intense love. This parley between the veil has healed me greatly and brought a profound love for my parents into my life. The deep wounds I chose to heal in this life have now created a space for our darling children to live and heal freely and deeply.

We all come as children, and own ourselves as our most intimate children, and are loved to the highest degree by divinely exalted beloved beings. I go through my life knowing that we have healed many and the divide between the living and the dead is simply a thin veil which is traversed often and heals even the deepest wounds.

Merry Christmas my babies and my beloved family. The deepest love for all who abide on all sides of beinghood. May we all bring our hearts to freedom.

57.

IAN IS GONE

L eft foot, right foot, breath. Ian is gone. Left foot, right foot, breath. This is what my sponsor taught me. On February 22nd I was on my way to my bank after seeing two pending expenses hit my account that I knew I did not incur. I got a call from Ian's girlfriend, Michele. She was crying. I told her I was on my way to the bank. She asked me to call her when I got home. While I was in the bank, I got a call from Mike, Ian's dad. He asked me to call him when I got home. I knew something terrible had happened. Ian was dead.

Mike told me when I got home. He said it was really fucked up. I agreed. I got off the phone and wailed. I knew it when I was driving home. I called my boyfriend and told him. It was one of the last calls I had with him for a while. Ian's death will forever be tied with the difficulty I had with my boyfriend and the uncertainty that he would ever financially make it right between us.

This is a story about Ian. How I lost the person most dear to me, my oldest son. The man I loved completely. We used to say to each other in Spanish, "Tu eres mi vida", You are my life. This was true. I love Ian dearly. I always had his back. I would do anything for him. I have done much for him. I financed his marriage to the tune of $11,000. He was a mama's boy. I adored him. I lost him. I still can't believe he is gone.

He wasn't supposed to be a part of the book this way. He was supposed to be the hero.

He was amazing. Truly. This man, my Ian, loved thoroughly. In truth, he did. He also partied like crazy. Scarily so! That is why I moved to Phoenix. I could feel that Ian was really getting in over his head. He was living at a fraternity in 2011, when Jason, his brother, and I moved out here. It was a fraternity off campus since ASU does not have on campus fraternities. This fraternity had taken over the whole apartment complex. At least it seemed that way to me. He was living there, although I think he just crashed at whoever's apartment he was partying in at the time. I posted bail for him a few times after getting kicked out of a bar or getting in a fight.

He did get through his junior year at ASU, but the tuition was becoming overwhelming. This kid was in debt from the time he started college. ASU requires freshmen to live on campus. Ian switched dorms and ASU charged for some damage to the dorm. I still do not know how much damage there really was. However, those charges gained interest, then interest on interest and snowballed to a crazy amount.

Unfortunately, that rule of living in the dorm's freshman year created a debt he was never able to pay. If there is one issue, I would like to address for our higher education process, is that we are creating slaves out of our college students. The costs to attend universities has so skyrocketed and states have very little monies to assist with our institutions anymore. The debt Ian incurred, with associated fees running up to unbelievable costs, was the start of a debt that just snowballed for the rest of his living days. His debt and the burden it caused was the hill he could never get over.

Now he is with his beloved Grammy and his grandfather and Thorne. They are the three musketeers and the trilogy. They love each other dearly and are inseparable. This helped Ian so much. He is extremely happy in the subtle region. So, loved. He did not realize how loved he was until his 'going away' party. Then he heard the stories and saw how many people loved him. I love him tremendously and I know how he has helped us from the other side. All of them have helped us so much. Still a rugby player too.

Still, I had to take care of the family. I had to let everyone know. First, I had to get Jason. He was most important. I cried and screamed and woke up from my daze. When Ian was under four years old, I had an incredible psychic. She saw that Ian could choose to die at 29. All year, the thought would come up that I could lose Ian. Especially when he started drinking more and his relationship became so painful. I could see the sadness in his eyes. Especially when he stopped seeing his kids from his drug use and how he hurt others with his actions. Especially Jess, he did some really messed up things, Spiking drinks with acid, destroying property, difficulties with sales. The knowledge was just there for me. When he died it didn't lessen the grief to know beforehand. I did everything I could to be there for him.

I knew I had to get Jason from his friend's house before I told him about Ian. I drove thirty miles to pick him up. I was about two thirds of the way there and I felt like I was going to faint. I couldn't concentrate. I was on the freeway, and I thought I was going to pass out. I called my friend Billy and he kept telling me to breath. That was the only thing that got me to Jason. I had him drive us home. He kept asking me if something was wrong. I could not tell him until we got to my house.

When we got home, and I told Jason he just broke down. He loved Ian so much. We both did. This was the day he died. It was so incredibly hard. That was the worst day of our lives. Then all my siblings kept calling and in two days they were here. So much happened in so little time. Jason has always relied on his brother so much. I thought he was going to fall apart. There was so much outpouring. Ian died four days before his birthday and my phone blew up. I was completely overwhelmed. There were so many people who truly loved Ian. My phone didn't stop ringing. We organized a memorial five days later on his thirtieth birthday at Encanto park. So many of his friends came, his rugby brothers, his fraternity brothers, his high-end custom clothing clients. He was so incredibly loved.

His cousin Devin created an incredible website for him, and we put the high-end clothes he still had up on the website. Devin also managed the zoom meeting for the party. There were people who called in and watched from all over. We will release the zoom soon. Devin was amazing and so was his wife, Naomi. All of the family was here for him. If only he knew how precious he was.

Jason and I were honored to spread Ian's ashes in the San Francisco Bay, and we also hiked up Angel Island to spread the ashes. Dave his boating brother was so awesome to offer us this trip. It was beautiful and so sad. We talked a lot about Ian, and we knew he was here with us. He was heartbroken with Ian dead. I can't wait to see you again son. I know you are here a lot, and you talk to your aunt a lot. I miss you.

58.

WHOA TO THE SURVIVORS OF DEATH

Ian died almost seventeen months after Thorne, my love. In less than a year and a half my lover and my son both died. The two men I loved the most besides Jason. Thorne was not in my life all that long. I met him online a few months before we met, then in person the day before Valentine's Day. Valentine's day was our first official date. He was strong in my life since that day, still is. We spoke every day since then even if one of us was out of town. Recently I had a gentleman tell me that you must be with someone for several years before you love them. That is not my experience.

I saw the despondency in Thorne right away. I loved him soon after. I was totally committed to him when I told him a little about my life and he responded with a compassion that I had never experienced before. That was his spiritual principle, compassion. I still love him deeply. In many ways he was a disturbed man. Not even addiction could dull his strong personality and gusto for life.

Yet he knew fear, his addiction landed him in prison for several years and he 'caught' at least nine felonies. I love the way addicts say that 'caught' like they were catching a cold. Well, this war on drugs quickly became a war on race and he was no exception. Not that he was not involved in the drug trade. He was.

He was deeply ashamed of his felonies and with good cause. Nowhere do we see more judgement than the prison system. The war on drugs allowed people of color to be locked up in record numbers. Why do I write this? It is true. Obama did an interview in prison and the cameras caught a scene in the prison yard and 95% of the inmates were black. There is injustice that is almost unspeakable. Thorne did not speak of his. He never told me he was a felon. It was a huge disgrace to him. I have no doubt the shame he experienced created the fear of being honest.

He told me he stopped doing drugs before I met him. It wasn't until after his death that I met his ex-wife. She was instrumental in helping me get Thorne cremated and the car back. She also told me how very sick he was in his addiction. She lived with him through the worst parts of it. At times he was so loaded he seemed retarded. She talked about people staring at him and how she felt sorry for him. She also lived through his delusions and him losing cars drug running or the cars being impounded.

I knew a different person but one who was still hiding his addiction and his deep fear of losing me if he told me the truth about his felonies. Yes, this will always be my biggest heartbreak because I belong to a society of recovering addicts that welcome addicts in. His felonies would have been par for the course. Hopefully his honesty could have cemented him into the society that above all, helps addicts stay clean and helps them learn to live a life of recovery using spiritual principles.

It still breaks my heart that he did not experience the love we had for him. He felt the fear of judgement and the lack of confidence that we would love him. Many are the ones I have seen awaken in the rooms of NA and find themselves as they find their voice and shout the truth about their lives until they see, there is nothing they did that we wouldn't accept. We listen a soul into existence in the rooms of recovery. Nothing broke my heart more than knowing he missed that love.

He has it now. There is no escaping a soul's journey. Not even in death. He knows a loving society in heaven, he is doing the 'work' of coming to know himself. He made a commitment in heaven to evolve, to grow through the addiction he struggled with on earth. He now knows a lucidity that he never had here. More so, he is so fully himself, with his golden eyes and a strong spirit that overwhelms our medium. He is still such a large being, yet so happy. There is tremendous happiness there.

My son is experiencing that too. A love much greater that the horrid self-obsession so commonly felt here. He was tremendously judged, and his honesty could be used as a whipping board.

Where he is now there is so much profound acceptance, such a larger capacity to see the elements of our lives and growing points. I believe that if there is a hell, it is the one we encase ourselves in by the judgement of self and others. There is no such thing in heaven. Please know when I call this 'place' heaven, I mean it in the Greek terminology. Heaven means harmony. I truly believe we go back to our natural state of harmony.

That which we are, and that which we will always be. Judgement is an unnatural state. Not found in nature. A view of 'other' as better or lesser than self. Judgment has allowed for the most egregious acts performed on others on this planet. Judgment killed Thorne. Almost as much as his fear of more judgment. Only Thorne put a meth pipe to his lips, for the worst judgment is our self-judgment.

From my beloved Thorne, and my grieving of his loss of the life he could have known here in recovery, to my beloved Ian. My first born, truly the greatest of my creations, or a creation that I participated in deeply. Ian, we must be a family of great characters. Ian was head and shoulders above others since birth. Quite literally as I have stated elsewhere.

His character and spirit shown through in his mannerisms and facial expressions. He was happy to be here. I have been blessed with beings that just were so happy to be alive. For all the inner pain both Thorne and Ian kept to themselves, they delighted on being present here.

Ian was an Irish twin with his cousin Eileen, born six months before him. When I moved back to my mother's house with Ian in tow at two months old, my twin and her family were also living in the household for a few months. The two babies were fast friends and quite attached. These two bonded my sisters and I and my mother. While the house was too well lived in, there was great joy with the babies abiding with us. A few months later my twin and her husband bought an acre of land and settled into a trailer, which was a very common occurrence in Corrales, New Mexico. The family spent the next ten years slowly building a magnificent adobe home and playing outside in the fenced in yard around the trailer.

Ian continued to be beloved to me always. We moved to Portland when he was two. We stayed there and bought an old Portland style home, which we lived in until Ian was nine. His brother Jason was born when he was eight. This was all Ian's doing of course. He begged for a brother for years and was a little upset that he came so late and was so little, he wanted a playmate, and it took a while. Ian adored Jason always. They were deeply devoted to each other, although Ian still was sad, -he couldn't have him earlier in childhood.

Ian's character shown through in his performing arts elementary school that he loved, and even in his difficulty learning English in first grade. We eventually moved him to a better teacher. He was well loved and had lots of friends. It is difficult for me not to write Ian's life story truly. When he was nine, we loaded up a U-Haul and drove down the coast back to New Mexico. It was an amazing journey down highway 101 along the coast of Oregon and California with these young boys and we enjoyed it.

Maureen, my twin, was truly their second mother and took care of them while I was working. We moved then so I could start my master's program in Accountancy at the university. Ian was extremely well loved, and he eventually lived with his father in his seventh grade for a year and attended another arts school. His father was living with a girlfriend and a school year with her boyfriend's son was more than she could stomach of a school aged child. Ian was invited to live with my brother in Seattle. He was there for a year and a half. These two living experiences with the two men that were his paternal role models had a very profound effect on Ian in many ways.

Both men are extremely brilliant, rather stern in their parenting style and somewhat judgmental with Ian. Ian eventually spent more years with his biological father and built a stronger relationship with him and he always considered my brother a father as well. They both loved him deeply and still do. Still, I am not sure Ian experienced the acceptance he wanted from a father. He always seemed to judge parts of himself harshly and eventually he created a part of himself that was harshly judging of who he was and whether he was capable of being loved.

For a person of Ian's character, his brilliance, his ease with people, especially men, this was a very sad and disturbing development in his character. He could make friends immediately and I never knew someone so comfortable with sales or meeting and making friends so easily. He was immensely loving and loved by many people. Ian was always into music. His first instrument was an upright Bass. I was so enthralled with this decision. What an elegant instrument for him to choose in sixth grade. He was getting stoned in sixth grade too and got into partying young. This eventually became a much greater part of his life.

We were able to get Ian into college as an independent student since he had lived with friends in high school and supported himself. This was a huge advantage for me as a parent and Ian until he moved dorm rooms in his freshman year and created a debt with the college that never went away. Ian was basically in debt since his freshman year. I say this loudly and clearly because we in this wonderful country of the United States have created slave laborers of our children and often their parents in many ways. One of them is this debt system used for higher education.

We have indebted our whole society with student loans. Many of those are privatized. In fact, the women appointed to run the education department under the Trump administration was from a family that owned many of those private institutions that kept our society deeply in debt with college loans. It is one of the biggest punitive aspects of our 'free' society. In New Mexico we would joke that if you went to community college, you could get a job as a guard in the prison. If you didn't go to college, you would probably end up guarded, in the prison. Must debt and imprisonment truly be our biggest expenditures in this country?

Ian eventually majored in fraternity and his partying took on a more destructive tone. He still found a huge camaraderie with his frat brothers, but the drinking and drugs had a strong impact on his life. He loved partying and loved hanging out and having friends.

By his junior year he amassed more debt than he could pay to the school and dropped out before the end of that year. He was studying business and went on to sell books all summer which turned into a sales career in custom men's clothing that he loved dearly. Two things Ian loved, custom clothes and the camaraderie of other men.

Meanwhile at 22 Ian had his first son, Sage. This is what led him to this custom clothing career after selling books all over the country, with a sister affiliate to the clothing company. If Ian had some debt when starting college, it escalated greatly with his young family.

59.

BUYERS AND
LOVERS BEWARE

I an's death is a tragedy. As far as I know he has no living will, and I am default next of kin. The outpouring from his friends was fantastic and we had an incredible ceremony for him. Since he died almost a month ago, I have been inundated with reaching out and/or responding to his friends and my friends and everyone who has given condolences etc. I am grieving. I am scared and I am still dealing with the wreckage of my last relationship. This above all leaves me feeling weak, scared, sad, unsure and shaken. As for Ian and his marvelous clothes, my nephew created an amazing website, I put the clothes on an online clothing store, PoshMark.

My father created a victim. I am no longer a victim. I am so much more. A powerful, compassionate, articulate, amazing, beautiful woman. I have rescued myself repeatedly. Yet in the realm of love, of intimate partnership, I know I place myself in a position to be hurt.

There are times when children become vehicles used to dump resentment about the absent parent. In this case the gross amount of abuse and neglect ended him and a sibling in foster homes since they were being starved, literally. There is an inherent sadness about abused and/or neglected children. We either live with that sea of sadness within our chest and bellies, or we find a way to soothe ourselves and open to the divine world. A world that folds its arms around us, until we can feel even the air around us softly nurturing us, like a very soft blanket of light and gentle air.

For each wound inflicted on our wounded hearts, there must be a time within our own bodies that we sit and allow acknowledgment of the trauma that it is there, within us, a part of us. When the sentience, encapsulating the unbearable pain, and keeping the wound safe, feels itself within a now mature being offering shelter, then the painful feelings are acknowledged and accepted.

The consciousness that kept those painful feelings safe for so long allows itself to let go and releases the pain into the greater stream of life that resides in our deepest, truest, ethereal body. We are made whole.

Yet this process is a committed process of going within. A part of realizing that we can create, or recreate, our reality. It is a strong, and often lifelong effort of integrity. An act of being whole, undiminished. We engage on the journey consciously and recommit several times along the way to empowerment. My darling lover was, and is still, a victim. He feels his pain deeply and is often reminded of what he has endured, especially on holidays, when he lost those in his life that loved him.

Death, to so many of us, is a stagnant state of mourning, to be done on those special days when our pain can overwhelm us and incite feelings of rage, pity, or pain. It gives leave to place our rage and pain on others in our environment that have little knowledge of the carefully wrapped and placed parcels of pain. How easy it is for those victimized to then lash out at others from a sense of "you should have known better" or "don't you know what happened to me", "who died", "how I should mourn them mercilessly and harm you for your ignorance of my pain?"

Basta, enough! None of us get out alive. If we continue to grow pain and resentment within ourselves because our loved ones have died, then we will never know peace. I write this now, not even a month has passed since my son died. I am in mourning truly. My sleep is disturbed, my emotions turbulent. I cannot respond to all with compassion or even with enough bandwidth to process. I am alone even when many are reaching out. I go within, to write this, to examine my life and loves, and then I will talk to those that have passed.

I'll talk to the dead. This is what I have learned to do. I do so with gratitude for speaking to the dead, the unbodied, the ethereal, the unencumbered. This has greatly enhanced my life deeply, lovingly, and soothingly. We die, but we never cease to exist. I miss the sound of my son's voice on the phone. Miss hearing his "I love you", feeling his love and his hugs.

I will not see Ian rise above the painful effects of alcohol in his system, when the drug used for release becomes an even greater jailer and the painfully horrid feelings are enhanced like twenty-foot waves, crashing into a chest already sunken with the angst of his worst ideas of himself. He died this way, hampered by the drink of amnesia, in the deepest torment in the world. The pain of self-hatred. He betrayed the one consciousness he came here to truly embrace, himself.

He is free. Truly free and happy. He is near me now. He sees how we have gone out of our way to honor him. To take care of his wonderful suits, and care for his brother that he loved beyond everyone. Even though Jason drove him crazy. Ian is good. I feel his fantastic trickster character.

He was there at his memorial running around hugging everyone. So happy to be loved. He readily admits that all he was attempting to do was get attention from his girlfriend. Yet his method was overkill. A permanent solution to a temporary problem. He stepped out of this life, this frame, this reality. In many ways he betrayed me the most, he took from me his love. Yet if I do not see how his incredible spirit surrounds me, if I stay in a self-centered misery, allowing his act to control me and my emotional well-being for the rest of my life, then I miss the whole wonderful point of his truly fabulous life.

Then I too place myself in misery over a choice another person made of his own free will. This is not a cross to bear but a joy to remember. He was a joy. A bright amazing beacon and he is having all sorts of fun. Son, I will not pull down the curtain of your final parting to wear it as a mourning dress for the rest of a self-obsessed life. My pain being the most important thing for others to hold for me. How I am offended, how I am mistreated. No, my beloved you enhanced me every day of your incredibly impactful short life.

Ah yes, now we are back to my lover. The holder of the many dead souls that blessed his life. He regards each one with the misery of their deaths, choosing to hold them in pain, when their spirits now climb to the highest heights and breathe in the nectar of the heavens. Let go! For God's sake, let the dead breathe in their lightness. They have lost their awful sense of self-obsession.

Do not make them carry yours. It is enough of a burden, and joy, for them to see themselves in the life they just stepped out of. It can be a harsh reality to see who we were in our lifetimes. Let them only carry what they were responsible for, while we here may chance upon the miracle to feel ourselves as light and strong as a feather. What a joy to be made of these miracles.

60.

I LIVED ON AFTER MY SON'S DEATH

I lived. Even after my son's death. He died just shy of eight weeks ago. It is my relationship with Narcotics Anonymous that has kept me alive in many ways. NA meetings provide a place of intimacy and reality. I have lived this path for thirty-three years. Hearing people I know and don't know share from their hearts keeps me connected. Going to meetings and talking about living day in and day out after my son's death keeps me alive. Feeds me and gives me strength to keep walking through this life.

I still struggle with even talking. My mind is slightly off. There is a fatigue in between my synapsis. The hesitancy in my speech which is directly tied to my grief, my slow start in conversation or the fog that fills my mind. The cover of clouds that perhaps is a sign of love from the collaborative brain, the right brain that is the communal brain. The part that is tied to all that is, the greatness of our spirits. In many ways I am living in that brain. I remind myself of the wonderful book, "My stroke of Insight" by Brain Scientist Jill Bolte Taylor. She describes her massive left hemisphere stroke and talks about how she has an enlightened experience, and she is thrown into this ecstasy of 'all that is'. She lost all normal functioning, and it took her eight years to recover fully. Today she has a Ted Talk on her stroke of insight and its phenomenal.

My brain fog just makes it hard to communicate. I hear my cadence and it is staccato. There is a fatigue of transmission into the linear brain. Almost a giving up. How do I talk about this? How do I talk at all? How do I get past this verbal hesitancy in my brain? I write. It comes from a more collaborative space between the brain hemispheres. I do not experience the staccato voice trying to find words to express the everyday discord. I am tired. I am out of sorts. In truth I have been torn asunder. Even though I can continue in my daily life, I can even feel a wide variety of emotions and engage in activities. There is a knowing of my cells being ripped apart.

I believe when we love someone, and we separate, there is a division of a whole we created with another. When Thorne died, there was this shock and cleaving. Then there were the activities associated. I had no privilege in his life as his girlfriend, no rights. His wife, who he considered his ex-wife, as did she; she came to my rescue. Since there was one signature missing on one page in the divorce, they were never officially divorced.

She came forth for me and signed over to me this ability to get the car we had bought in his name and his belongings. Finally, we were able to get him out of the morgue and cremated and spread his ashes on the mountain top then bring him home. It was exhausting yet there was also this strength of spirit that drove me. I would not let a man I loved not be cared for. We had known and loved each other less than a year. He was the man I loved. He is still with me today. Not in physical form yet so close to me always. He has become an amazing being so full of light. His death was shocking, tragic, his overdose exploded his heart and opened mine further.

My son's death was a tearing. A shredding of a bond since his birth. He was present within each of my cells for twenty-nine years. He was my first born. He had a huge character from birth on. Even in the womb. After three days of induced labor, an ultrasound was done. I saw this huge head trying to fit into a much tinier canal. I thought 'oh no that is never going to happen'. Thank God for modern medicine. I really cannot remember if Mama was in the delivery room. I also cannot remember seeing her after his birth. I stayed in the hospital for four days while they tried to get my viscera back in working order.

Well Mama says she was there with me in the delivery room, and she did bond with Ian. I do not remember seeing her afterwards. I was not very cognizant of much, except my boy. He was hard to ignore. The other babies would mew, Ian would wail I could hear him from down the hall. The nurses would bundle him up and put him in the swing. He always loved to swing.

When we got home from our hospital stay, it was harder to get around. I was still hurting from the cesarean, and it was still hard to nurse. I remember the week after having Ian was my three-year clean anniversary. I called my neighbor crying because I was on pain killers, and I didn't want to feel high when I was clean. David came over and helped me out. He was an amazing guy. He used to do security for one of the enlightened guru's perhaps Maharaja. He had great stories about that. He got clean like the rest of us. I was so scared to take Ian to a meeting, but I really needed support. I took him to a woman's meeting and got so much love and support. Still, it was very difficult to go through the process of getting out the door and I felt so vulnerable as a new mother.

Two months later I was moving back to New Mexico, back to the idea that I could get support from my family. It wasn't as easy as it seemed. I believed I had helped moving. A friend of mine drove with us. It was a big move to make with such a small baby. God, I loved him, and I wanted him to be surrounded by family.

Maureen and her family moved out a few months later and bought property in Corrales, a village right outside of Albuquerque. They bought an acre of land and lived in a small trailer for ten years while they built a custom adobe house that would hold a family with six kids. I could not believe how they have lived in that trailer for so long. They did make use of the land around them and built a great porch around the trailer and a fenced in yard where the kids could play. They moved into their beautiful two-story adobe home right before

Rebecca was born. It was an incredible home and surrounded a grassy area that could have served as a soccer field.

My younger sister also lived in my mother's house and she and Ian bonded greatly while we were there. It was difficult to get assistance with Ian if I tried to work. Neither Mama or my sister was all that willing but they very much-loved Ian. When I first moved in, I wanted to have Ian baptized. I was upset that my mother wasn't very interested in this. I was attending a small church that had an early morning meditation ceremony. There were not many of us, but it was a lovely ceremony that also included a time of lighting candles and focusing on what we wanted to create in our lives. I just wanted Ian to be welcomed into this life by some type of baptism.

My mother was concerned about having a luncheon with her friends. I was quite upset that this took precedence over Ian's baptism, and it hurt greatly. I did realize later that my mother really fretted over friends. While she had had compatriots through work and some friends, she never really socialized much. This group of friends that were fellow lawyers were very important to her. I eventually forgave her lack of interest in her grandsons' baptism, and we did have a small ceremony at the unity church for him. I was very aware of wanting Ian to be welcomed into the world and how important that was for me to make sure he was welcomed.

We stayed at my mother's house for two years. I did dinner theatre and worked for the daughter of my old boss. We made do. It was not easy to live at my mothers and we seemed to cramp their style although they really did love Ian. I wanted more support for my recovery, parenting and a career. I decided to move to Portland Oregon. Ian had bonded with his cousins by then. Recently Maureen told me that Ian was very worried when I was packing the car that I would leave him. He was very scared. When I had it all packed, including the window that broke accidently from trying to close the door, I grabbed Ian and put him in the car. My sister said he was so relieved and happy to be with me. I would never leave Ian behind. He was my beloved boy. I don't know if he sensed some tension, but he was very happy to be going with me.

61.

THE PAIN OF LIFE, LOVE, AND DEATH

I spoke to Daddy this weekend about the betrayal bond I experienced with my last boyfriend. He agreed that the way Shay behaved, with his snarky remarks and yelling and the pain of losing family members years before which ruined holidays, was very similar to how Daddy would show up when he was alive. Daddy was always morose during the holidays.

The pain and fear that resides within those people we love keeps them sick and stuck. Shay withheld information about the money I invested and would not communicate with me about the status of the investments. This lack of communication appeared to be very much a 'power over' maneuver that kept me stuck in needing to know what was going on with what I invested, and the fear that I would lose so much money.

Shay was Daddy. He showed me clearly what I experienced with Daddy. The deep pain and horrible verbal abuse that kept me so sick and desperate. It was very painful and at the same time I knew that Shay was reflecting the unkindness and hurtful behavior that I experienced with Daddy. He was the perfect petty tyrant and mirrored the horrible manipulative behaviors Daddy had.

As a child I could not handle the abuse and the memories hid in the amnesic fluids so lovingly caring for those memories we store until we, ourselves can know them. Each relationship I engaged in gave me more awareness of who my father was. Each of them depicted emotions and behaviors of my father and every one of them restored my memory of who he was.

Shay was the last. I knew it into my bones that his behavior reflected the worst parts of my relationship with Daddy. I saw Shay fall apart while I was with him. Physically he was degenerating and emotionally he was all over the map. It was very sad. There was this very sweet and kind man in him, yet so much of the time he would hide in his filthy room. He was using. There was no way he was not, he isolated himself so much and he was hurting. It was like I was seeing my father wither away again as he did at his death when I took care of Daddy.

I know Shay invested for me, but I really do not know how to access the investment since he accidently burned the passcode when he was using. I went into this partnership because I believed he could make money and he did grow my investment. Like millions of other investors that lost passcodes, I may never see the investment.

I became very sad about the end of this relationship and all that had transpired within it. The monies I lost to the landlord when we moved because there was so much damage to the room and bathroom Shay used. That was just added to the bills he never contributed too. It is interesting to me that the strongest betrayal bond would fall into the financial arena. There was always this distrust about his behavior and snarky comments and meanness. Money was always a big issue in my family.

I felt the hurt and pain I had in this relationship. I told him I didn't want to hurt anymore; this was all too much. I didn't need this constant dangling of the carrot, whether it was the investment monies, or reimbursement of bills that never happened, or withholding of love and kindness. I felt the sadness of living in relationships where needs and desires would never be met. I knew this was very conscious.

Daddy confirmed it. In the medium reading last Sunday. I told him everything I experienced with Shay and asked him if this mirrored what he did to me and our family. He said 'Shay was me. I was Shay' I withheld from you and our family. I never gave money although I got money from my family. Our family was poor. I withheld my love. I tortured all of you, especially your mother. I gaslighted and turned people against each other. I manipulated. I constantly played power games with almost everyone. I hurt many children. I hurt many women and men. I wanted to get back at my family that had destroyed me. I felt the most comfortable when I was manipulating others and making them uncomfortable.

The shame is that both men, my father and Shay, have golden hearts. They are the sweetest beings and sensitive beyond measure. Shay was so scared to meet me, what an ordeal that was. Yet he was so endearing. He was that man often in our relationship. He could be very sweet. He was also brilliant. Yet he was killing himself, just like my father.

When we spoke about Daddy being just like Shay. There was this recognition of how the most sensitive men become jaded and then want power and control. The early abuse just rips out the manhood in men. That was a very strong theme in our last medium reading. The trilogy of my father, son, and fiancé (otherwise jokingly known as the Holy Ghost) all experienced that loss of their manhood from the abuse and withholding of love.

This is what I am left with. An incredible empathy for my brothers. For the men I have known in my life. For all the horrible abuse I suffered from their hands, or even Ian's drowning in debt and self-doubt, I feel an incredible love for them. All of the men that have suffered at the hands of people that should have loved them. The pain is deep and devastating. I want to walk away with an open heart and a compassion for the lives they have had.

These men I have the pleasure to engage with on the other side. They have taught me how vulnerable they were. How hard it was to be human, how difficult it was to live with the betrayals they suffered. In one way or another, they became hardened or learned to get their needs met dishonestly. Thorne fell in love with me and had never experienced that before. He had always used women who cared for him.

 In some way or another all of them, these men I cared for, emanated an energy of taking from others, almost in a way like they deserved to take since much had been taken from them. Yet now my trilogy is experiencing building self-love and growing their spirits this way. So is Shay, who finally told me he had accidently burned the passcode to the bitcoin a week before he died. They are all learning from lives of deep pain, which eventually led to addiction to end suffering. I write for those who suffer. There is gold in our hearts, yet we perpetuate pain, in ourselves and others.

I do not hate them. I do not want the same betrayals. I am finally awake and truly compassionate. I do not know what that means in terms of future relationships. I do not want to repeat the past and I love that I feel compassion for the men in my life. We shall see. I just know they too deserve peace inside and a deep sense of love starting with loving themselves. I am so grateful for who I am and for them as well.

THE DEAD TALKS, & ENLIGHTENED IMAGINATION | 271

62.

PETTY TYRANTS
IN AUTHORITY

Next on the list, was the continuous struggle with authority. This affected me in two ways; one was the timidity in approaching authority figures, especially women. I know this is a byproduct of a mother who was checked out all the time. I found it extremely hard to approach female bosses. The busier they were, the harder it was to approach. I would literally stop myself, or struggle to get up the courage to ask a question. Often this was met with irritation from my mother and women bosses.

There appeared very little opening to approach, even if to get clarity on a task or ask what else may be needed. I worked with many women who seemed to be too busy to be bothered. What a double-edged sword. If a female boss or supervisor is too busy to give directions to underlings that are there to serve her, then she does a great disservice to herself and her staff, especially if she responds with irritation when she is disturbed.

I know this was my thing. My mother would simply not pay attention to us. Within me I created a dynamic of wanting attention while at the same time being somewhat terrified of disturbing my mother. I found similes of my mother in many workplaces.   I am sure my sheer anxiety of approaching a female boss sometimes was enough to irritate them. Unfortunately, I also think women have had so little opportunity to perform in positions of management that we often do not have managerial skills developed to be good bosses or leaders.

The betrayals that go on in the workplace with women towards other women is sad. Often time's, female bosses will 'eat their young' and get rid of any woman who appears to be a threat. I worked with a government supervisor who prided herself on how many people had quit that worked under her. What a waste of resources and good talent.

I was the first woman who was moved off her team. I accomplished that by going to the regional manager and finally asking him how many more people he was willing to lose before addressing the situation. He was enraged that he had to act. It took a great deal of courage to go up the chain and it wasn't the last time I did that. Unfortunately, it is not always addressed appropriately. I learned a great deal about workplace abuse of power in the very good book "Betrayal Bonds". This book made it very clear that many work environments are more willing to lose employees than address abusive situations, especially in management or with star performers.

I have also had my share of male 'ragers' in the workplace. I once worked for an amazing massage therapist. He was a gifted masseuse with an incredible aptitude for healing. Yet he had a horrid temper. Every morning we would have a call to discuss tasks. The tasks were overwhelming. Invariably there would come to a point in the conversation where he would ask about a task, and I wouldn't respond fast enough or couldn't find the outcome and he would become enraged. I developed a tremendous anxiety working with him. This was coupled with a female masseuse who was very manipulative. I ran the front desk and helped in the massage school. At one point she stole something from the front desk and blamed me. I believe I quit over that.

The point of these examples is that I placed myself in positions to be hurt. I attracted abusers because that is what I knew, the enraged father and the vacant, busy, irritated mother. I found them again and again in the authority figures I met.

This was a very unpleasant norm and continued to feed into my anxiety. It happened before getting into recovery and afterwards. However, in recovery I learned to stand up for myself even if the outcome was not good.

I eventually left my position in DoD's audit agency to create my own cost accounting firm. I had a wonderful sponsor, an accountant, who said; "I'd rather be a big fish in a small pond, than a small fish in a big pond." I loved this woman!! I loved being on my own. I also was hired as a contractor for a large government contractor almost immediately at a much better pay rate which supplemented my business greatly for several years.

Working as a contractor gave me a great sense of independence. I learned in my spiritual practice that we could be entrepreneurs, with our own companies, or intrapreneurs and work within a company, yet we can instill in ourselves a sense of independence. I decided I would rather make less money and have greater independence than be tied to larger company and be dependent. Dependence on malevolent people created a great deal of my overabundance of fear and insecurity in the first place. Above all it is very important for me to take ownership of my life. I am responsible for finding solutions today and find better situations that are more sustaining and healthier to my being.

The attraction to people who mirror the characteristics I grew up with is a big cost of early betrayal. The only good counter action is to be completely responsible for myself and immerse myself in dynamics and environments where I am fed. I worked with wonderful men in several positions.

My favorite was the boss I worked with in a tourist shop in Old Town Albuquerque. I adored him and he loved my quirky character. We sold moccasins in our shop. We would get tourists in daily that would ask, "Are these moccasins made in Japan?" I would respond, "No ma'am, there are no Indians in Japan". Mr. Brown would smile, laugh, and shake his head, enjoying every minute of it. I went on to find many wonderful male supervisors in my career that were respectful, considerate, and attentive. I am extremely grateful for those male role models that molded my career and were loving, caring individuals. These men helped me heal and I am very grateful.

64.

LOVE YOU IAN, AND WELCOME HOME

Hi mom! Ian was here bright, brilliant, and a trickster extraordinaire! Star was already trying to back him up. He was coming in so strong her head was ringing. I was so happy to hear him and how present he was. I was also having an anxiety attack because I could not get my zoom to work, and I could not find my glasses anywhere.

Ian was gleeful. I moved your glasses mama. He was so damn proud of himself. Breathe Meg! Star kept telling me, I cannot get a reading on you. I was still in the middle of trying to fix the Wi-Fi and I still could barely see a damn thing. Ian may have been proud of himself, but I could have smacked his nonexistent head. Finally, I gave up on recording our medium session and found a somewhat usable pair of glasses.

Ian was ecstatic. Star described him to me. He came through in shorts and he had a ball. That, my dear Star, is a rugby ball. I knew immediately. Ian Loved Rugby. He continued to play when he could despite a broken back, broken teeth, head injuries he sustained while playing...he loved that sport. So, when Star said he showed up with a ball I had no doubt.

I just wanted to tell you how happy I am Mama. I am doing my work too. God I was happy to hear him so jubilant. Ian talked to his aunt regularly as well as me. Did you hear me tell you how much I love you, Ian? Yes, mama all day long. I am very happy to hear you are doing your work baby. I can feel the excitement that my son gave off.

He truly was happy. His joy drove me and eased a little of my sight frustration simply because I know how much of a joker he is and how much fun he is having moving things around. Ian, my son; Thorne, my fiancé; and Daddy...always to remain Daddy, are fast friends. Two weeks after Ian died, I could feel Ian and Thorne having a blast. They were moving many of my pictures and laughing their virtual heads off. I felt them with me all day. They were enjoying themselves immensely. They rode with me to my NA meeting and to the taco restaurant and were having the time of their lives.

Usually, Daddy is right there with Ian and Thorne. Since Daddy was there to 'get' Thorne when he died, they have been inseparable. That simple act of being there for the man I loved helped me to forgive my 'Satanist' father for the sick and overpowering things he did to me and my siblings. I have been having a very frank dialogue since a month after Thorne passed in late September of 2019. Daddy and Mama both showed up early in our bimonthly medium readings.

Mama and Daddy also said that they wanted us to 'give them back' what we were still holding onto from our experience of growing up in a highly dysfunctional household. I was just so blown away to be 'seeing' my parents again, or rather, hearing them again. I am still working on imagining how my dead loved ones look. Star is fantastic at describing how they look and what they say or do. I always feel like I am right there with them.

That first meeting with them was so incredible. Both Mama and Daddy praised me for giving back their 'stuff'. The issues they had that we children tended to take on, as if we had caused their problems.

Often, especially with Daddy, he would attempt to make us children responsible for how he victimized us when he was alive.

Now here he was, joking with my mother, who rarely allowed the five of us children access to her. Now she was jovial and engaging. Both Mama and Daddy had a message for my siblings, give us our 'stuff' back. They were especially concerned about two of my siblings. They felt as if my siblings were still very much struggling from taking on our parents' crap. I agreed this was true.

I was truly amazed to experience my parents so free, happy, and lighthearted with each other. Mama was a sweetheart. I never experienced her in that way before. After that initial meeting that was so refreshing to me, Mama retreated back into somewhat of a shell. She showed up hesitantly and struggled with the fact that she did not protect us from Daddy. It took her quite a bit of time to move through this.

She still would come through, hovering in the background, ashamed of her lack of ability to take care of her children. I am pleased to say she has moved through that and is coming forward much easier now. I am awed to find that my mother is a very sweet being. I fell in love with her softness, this was a big change for me since for years I was convinced that my mother 'gave' me to my father to keep herself from being harmed. I think there is some truth to that.

By last Valentines, my mother was very present. She melts my heart now. I am eternally grateful to know her. Since Ian died Mama has been super strong. She adored Ian. He taught her how to love. I so desperately wanted Ian to have a family around him. It was humbling to move back to my mothers, in my thirties, after being on my own. I didn't always feel supported. However, Ian, this boy who had so much character, was deeply loved by his grandmother and aunt.

It wasn't until he died that I realized my choice to go back to my mother's house and humble myself to provide a family for my baby was a very wise thing to do. When Ian died, just two and a half months ago, all my siblings were here in less than forty-eight hours, as were most of his cousins. It was amazing how much Ian was loved. He truly had no idea. The space he was in at his death was so narrowly focused, he was blown away at how deeply he was loved. It wasn't just my family, but his father's family and the friends he had amassed over many years.

Five days after Ian took his life, we had an amazing party for him in the park. The stories they told were so touching. My sister, the sensitive psychic that she is, could see Ian running around everywhere. He was 'virtually' hugging everybody. It wasn't until that party that Ian realized how deeply loved he was. He also saw how much love he had given to people.

In our reading last Sunday, Ian reaffirmed what he experienced. "Mama I was so loved, so many people really loved me. I just did not realize it and I couldn't love myself. Now I am working on loving myself Mama, I'm doing the work here. I'm so happy". Of course my mother was ecstatic to have Ian with her. She just turned up beaming. He had such a party to greet him. According to Ian, and my sister, his aunt, my mother is 'his' Grammy. He will share her, but she is his special Grammy. He has no idea what he did for her by joining her on the other side. She is so fully present for him. I still cry knowing how much love we truly have, and we often do not see it till we get to the other side. If only we could see it here.

So, Ian 'partied' with people who loved him dearly. At one point at the park party, a goose was honking up a storm. We could barely hear the amazing things his friends were saying. Later, in the medium reading we had the next day, with my whole family; I asked Ian if he had been in the goose that was honking. He affirmed it was him, being so obnoxious that at one point I told "Ian" the goose, to have more respect for all the people who showed up for him so we could hear what they had to say. His party was marvelous. I know my son 'left' that day realizing more of who he was than he had ever known.

I love him deeply, truly, madly. Mad that he could not see how amazing he was. Mad that we don't see ourselves from the inside out, sometimes until it's too late. Ian knows his work is to love himself now as much as he loved others. Ian developed a deep part of himself that rejected who he was. Often this 'self' came out and caused great damage to him and to the houses he was living in. He had been escalating in his drinking and the toxic relationship he was in contributed to some very extreme behavior.

Ian was hurting himself and I saw the pain and the feeling of being trapped got deeper and deeper. He knew that what he was doing was hurting him and he really tried to get out of the relationship. We talked about it for several hours two days before he died. The day he died, he and his girlfriend drank most of the day. In some ways Ian gave up. He stated later that he was emotionally hurting so bad that he didn't even know what he was doing. He locked himself in the other bedroom and put a leash around his neck and fell onto his knees.

"Mama I didn't mean to do that. I just woke up on the other side. I didn't realize what I had done." Now I know that it is easy for the loved ones of people who die to get stuck in 'how' a person dies. It is rather macabre. In fact, it is the number one thing people wanted to know. "How did he die" they ask. Not who was your son. How did he live his life? What did he love the most? Ian said he wanted us to remember how he lived, and how he loved. He really didn't want us to focus on how he died. I appreciate that son.

All too often people will first think of how their loved ones die and go no further than that. They traumatize themselves by the image of the death. That is not the most important part of your loved one's life. I loved how deeply Ian lived, even when he partied, not that I condone that way of life. I do know that the way he was separating himself from self-love was very toxic. Now he sees that the most important effort is to see how marvelous we are and allow ourselves to accept who we are.

Ian felt like he could never be enough of a man. He carried debt since his freshmen year in college and that escalated when he had his son at twenty-two and his daughter eighteen months later, and the debt grew just that much more.

He felt as if he was failing, and that critical self-doubt would be drowned out by drinking; but the liquid drug does not hide the gnawing doubt of "who we are" well enough to make it go away. It wasn't until his party that he realized what he missed about himself most of all.

He was a talented, sensitive, incredibly loving man. He lost sight of that and internally spiraled down as the drugs were sought more and more and did more damage. Now he sees how amazing he is and that this vision of himself was what he could have lived with. Now he is doing the work to love the amazing being he is. Ian you are truly loved and very much worth loving. Now stop moving my damn glasses!!

Ian is joining 'us' after an intense amount of 'work' was done between my father and I. For seventeen months my father and I walked through the pain of his abuse and his perpetration. Daddy suffered horrible abuse at the hands of both parents.

When Daddy died, he went through his 'review'…I know right!! I guess it is real. That was somewhat of a shocker to me too. Anyway, from what Daddy says, he saw all the horrible, terrible ways he abused people, in the Satanic cult during ceremonies and at home with his own children.

My world came crashing down when I really acknowledged the ritual abuse. That was just five years ago. It's amazing that this journey has become one of deep love and forgiveness and self-acceptance.

Now almost seventeen months later, I have spent so much time in these sessions with Daddy truly learning to accept what my life has been. This has not been easy, sometimes I have felt like I have had the painful relationships spurred on from birth with my father repeatedly. In truth I have. This has been the hardest part of my journey. Until I realized that this has really been a journey of discovery. With each awareness of how I experienced the partners I had, and how they mirrored a part of who my father was, the more I was able to see that these men brought to a greater awareness of just what I had experienced so I could truly know what my young life was like.

Knowing gave me the power to love and rescue myself. It wasn't about being a victim anymore, it was about how I recreated my life to find my own self love and my own power. Recovery made this possible, that amazing practice of 'working the twelve steps' and finding out who and how we are, remade me into a woman who could commit to bimonthly medium sessions to meet her father and come to find a deep love, forgiveness, compassion, and awareness of how this adds to me.

I am a Champion. I have made myself into one inside; every time I breathed in and found another part of me that was broken early on and sit with her until she is a part of me. Slowly with patience, I came to love all parts of me. Many of them have joined with the greater stream flowing within my spirit but the journey of finding each part, held in the statis until they trusted me, that is unforgettable. That is self-love, the greatest act of love.

Now Ian is truly receiving the love that was there for him all along and that he showed others how to experience, like my mother. He is really experiencing himself and happily loving who he is. This takes time, especially on the other side. They lack the ability to create environments around us that show us who we are and how we have created our world based on our earliest world views.

From what they say on the other side, it is harder to come to know oneself and accept who we are. Believe it or not, it is easier to create these scenarios here that teach us so much about ourselves. If we choose to listen. We always have the choice to not get the point we are trying to evolve too. I honor Thorne and Ian's choice to learn there, in heaven, so to speak. Even if it is harder. The one thing I know is that we lose that horrible sense of self-centeredness, or better put would be to say we lose our self-obsession.

Now I learn so much from those three men who love me most. They are around me a great deal of the time. I can hear them, just sometimes I only have to believe that they are really here. When I ask for confirmation in the medium reading, I always get it. I am getting more used to hearing and even seeing them. Imagination is the most gracious gift from a loving God, and I am graciously becoming more and more willing to accept it.

In the last month I was joking with these three wise men and I said, hmmm there is the father, the son, and the holy ghost, referring to my beloved fiancé. They cracked up. They loved the analogy, and that was exactly what that was, not a spoof on any religion. So, they have taken to calling themselves 'the trilogy'. Yes, we are quite disingenuous so please forgive any religious discretions, they are not intentional. We do love the trilogy terminology and they are having so much fun with it. Who says we must lose our humor in heaven?? Ian never met his grandfather before his birth. Now they are fast friends. I am truly blessed to have such deep love from them, even if I would still like to experience the deep love of an earth man before I join them.

Thorne gave us an amazing 'lesson' on manifesting in heaven. Says he, 'Here we do not manifest by 'thinking' something into being, it is all done by feeling it. We find the emotional frequency to manifest what we want." I was floored. The practice of Divine Openings, which is centered around 'Drop the story, feel the feelings' was exactly what he was talking about. I couldn't believe it. For over eight years I have practiced Diving Openings and part of that is being aware of the emotional frequencies. To hear that this is how things are manifested on the other side, which I will interchange the wording with 'heaven' was mind blowing.

I asked Thorne for an example of something he manifested there. He told me he manifested bringing me to him by feeling my frequency of love. He taps into that, and I am there with him. The first thing that I need to acknowledge is that he is bringing my spirit to him. This brings up the idea that we may experience 'heaven' a lot more than we think. I believe this is true. I believe I easily travel back and forth. When I feel the energy of love for someone who has passed, I can imagine them here with me or me there with them. I do that with my spirit guides. I imagine I am in a boat with my spirit guide, Mary (also known as Angela). Now I believe that it isn't just my imagination, I am there with her. I love to feel her love for me, and I often go to her to be held and talk about my life.

I feel comforted and guided by her. I have other guides too that have given me great gifts. One guide would put-on full-blown concerts in my head and was funny as hell (ok that was intended, cuz he is). When I started divine openings, my imagination went wild. It has settled down some, but it doesn't mean I have lost the guidance of my guides. I do believe I travel to them. I created the meadow for those parts of me that were very horribly abused when I was a child. I became my inner children's Champion and brought them into the meadow. I discovered the meadow at twelve and I still love to frequent with my wonderful family there. My life has truly been about me easily moving in and out of heaven. I just experienced it like a journey of the imagination.

Thorne told me he found the meadow easily. For a while it would just be him there. Sometimes he would call me to him there and we would dance and spend time together. As Thorne became more self-loving, he found the part of himself that was still a child within him. As he loved and accepted that child more, he began seeing all the children that were in the meadow. Since I brought my children to the meadow after I imagined it into being for myself, it has become known as a place where children can come to heal and be loved. Many children who are killed or harmed by others come to the meadow and find love. Thorne now is a huge part of the meadow. He loves the children there unconditionally, even his own internal children that were harmed. They adore him. It is part of his calling.

At Christmas he was so excited because they all created a Christmas tree together and my parents were there, and Thorne was amazed at the Christmas tree and the love surrounding everyone. Now my Ian, my beloved son is finding his love and has blossomed so quickly, I believe this is our home and we are living a dream now. Yet this is a dream that can be shared and can lead to experience a deep love. We can experience our emotional frequencies here, just as well as there, if we choose to focus on that. Now I know that that is what we take with us from here. I know the more I develop the frequency of love the easier it is for me to find it there.

I'm practicing making my 'love' frequency stronger, so it is easier for my beloved, ethereal bodied dear ones to experience it. I have been practicing strengthening the love I feel for the Trinity. This has been very powerful since Thorne spoke of how they manifested in heaven two weeks ago. Thorne was phenomenal in sharing about the frequency of love. I feel it grow within me each time I practice loving. This, I believe, is the highest calling. It keeps expanding and grows exponentially. We can do this here just as well as there. We are gifted.

I'm so glad you are happy my sweet, sweet son. I love you, Ian. Welcome Home. I will always miss your voice, your hugs, your smile. I am so grateful that you are happy my darling. I will see you soon.

65.

TANTRIC BREATH-FEELING THE POWER WITHIN

B reathe. Breathe in. Breathe all the way down to below the tip of your sacrum. Remember the pool of energy, the sea of energy that resides below your torso. Feel it fill you. Feel the amazing strength you pull from it. Feel that divine feminine energy that fills this pool. The essence of tantra.

Remember what you learned in the silent retreat. The beauty of that retreat with all women. The encounter of the tantric breath cycle. The breath shared between lovers, partners. Remember the enormous energy source you felt using the tantric breath meditation. When you discovered the pool of feminine energy below your sacral bone at the end of your spine. The bowl that feeds your divine bowl. The entrance through the vagina, the sea within the womb. The magnetic energy of the divine feminine that draws men to us. Allowing you to retain your beautiful, sweet, feminine energy. To be the sea, to move the energy through the womb inside.

Breath in the depth of that magnetic force. Breath it up and into the first chakra. The grounding chakra deeply connected to that ocean of source beneath the sexual center. Draw it in and feel the deep grounding of the first chakra.

See the red color of the chakra being drawn up in you into the power center, into the breadth of the grounding chakra. Red like our blood on the outside. The strength of red, a power color, a grounding color, strong. This chakra, or energy center is the one that connects you to the earth, to nature, the beloved trees. Trees that show us how to experience our roots deep within the ground. Feel the veins flowing energy, that mimic the roots of trees, flow freely from you into the ground. Stretch deeper into the ground and feel yourself balanced by these lovely energetic veins that feed the earth and give it strength. This large sensate sphere we walk upon.

Now feel the energy move up to the second chakra. The relationship chakra. The source of our love, trust and betrayal. This chakra is orange like a rising or setting sun. Imagine a huge sun in front of you, slowly rising above the ground. Shimmering in the fog and haze of sunrise. Watch as this huge orange sun rises from a small oval into a shimmering sun which takes up the whole horizon. This is the power of our relationship center. Imagine from this center, the huge shimmering sun; the roots shoot out, shimmering lines of power that balance us. The roots or energy wires tie us to our relationships, past, current and future. We send them out in front of us and all around us. This is our first contact with others. These can guide our relationships. We can feel the essence of others with these shimmering lines of energy. They move energy to and from us just like electricity moves on wires.

If we have been harmed in our past these roots may be damaged. We may seek out those like the ones that harmed us in an earnest effort to heal these energetic centers. To experience exquisite grace. We can revise our vision of what we want, to bring us vibrance and brilliance. We clear the lines as we clear this relationship center. Breathe, forgive, breathe, cry, breathe, embrace, breathe, allow, breathe and fill the lines with compassion for all pain, for all yearning of the search for love. We are the ones to cleanse our own breath, our own energetic feelers. We learn to direct our energetic lines toward the one which can match our compassion and our wisdom and our desires. This energy center is of utmost importance. Send out your intentions, let them flow and balance you. First feel the essence of you, your signature, and find essences that may match them. Find the song that compliments yours.

We again breathe in and above the relationship chakra we move to our will chakra. The energy center at our solar plexus. Fitting that this center is yellow, mirroring the solar nexus of our being. This is where our body hold itself upright. Where the connective tissue covering the heart, lungs, and the ribs open and close with the breath of divinity. In this space, the ligaments connecting to the tissue covering our heart and lungs and the ligaments balancing our pelvis connect at the thoracic spinal column. This is where our wonderful tensegrity, inherent in our breath, keeps us upright. This allows us to walk on two legs and breath in the universe. The yellow center of our will. Our will that follows how 'thy will' be done. This is our center of power where we can breathe into our strength, our essence, our eternal sunshine. This governs and protects our internal organs.

We can shine our sun out as the representation of our beinghood, or we can hunch over, attempting to protect ourselves from fear or abuse we internalized a long time ago. There are no external enemies now. Just those wounded wounders we can call to us as we walk the road to our gain back our own power. The petty tyrants who may harm us now are reminders of where our wounds lie. It is now for us to heal ourselves. To hold our strength and our hurts and wrap our humongous selves around both. Only we ourselves can rebirth our beinghood into a greater depth that the pain allowed us to reach with extreme grace. This we do from the sun within us at our will center. Thy will be done.

Now the heart. The center chakra. The middle chakra, the fourth chakra. The most supreme, the communicator between the sky and earth. The governing chakra since it holds the truest essence, love. This is the source that allows our humanness to talk to the divine. All chakras above our heart are directly connected to the divine. The heart is the interpreter, the guide, the center of our nervous system, the place where we live, breathe, pump the liquid in our system through the ventricles of life. This is truly our essence. Our hearts, strong, sensitive, intuitive, empathetic, the source of life. The color for the heart chakra is green. The green of renewal, of rebirth, of grass, and leaves and meadows. Eternal, exquisite, wise beyond all measure. This is where we can communicate from, where we can breathe into and out of. This can be our largest, grandest beam of energy. We can flow freely from an open heart or shut ourselves down so that only our ongoing pain can reach our heart. Our capacity diminished.

This is the path of tantric breath. We can flow our energy to our partner and to the world. We as the feminine, breath in from the bottom of our sacrum. We experience the breath move over our spine and into the ground chakra where our ocean of magnetism resides below. We mingle that breath with the waves of our magnetic ocean and breathe it through the ground chakra experiencing how we are balanced on this earth, how our tendrils stretch deep into the ground like the trees. We bring the freshness of the earth with our breath into the second chakra. We travel through our relationship chakra, experiencing the essence of our partnerships, our beloveds that fill this center of orange shimmering.

We bring our grounding energy and the balancing flow of the sum of our relationships as we balance the relationship chakra that allows us to sense and caress 'the other'. We move up into our sun, our will chakra, still the same breath that has come up through the earth and brings the balance of our communions. Now we deeply feel our essence in our will chakra. The extraordinary beings that we are, we feel the power of us, the vibration of our own cells. We feel our uniqueness, our enormity. We are the sun, we are ourselves and carry the essence of the other, we are the ground we walk on.

We bring this to our hearts. All of that, every star we have seen, every body of water we have touched, every sense of self that empowers us. This we breathe up into our hearts. Now, as the divine female, we breathe out from our hearts into the heart of our partner. The divine male. The magnificent attractor. The powerful, protective, enveloping man.

He breathes in from the heart, feels the beauty, the magnificence of himself and his woman and he move his breath down. Down into his will center, where he feels his power and essence, down deeper into his second chakra, his relationship chakra. He entwines the breath into his depth and goes deeper into the ground, into the deepest part of the earth. He embodies the strength of trees and of mountains. His legs energetically filled below him, into the vibrant earth. He lives in vibrancy of belonging. At the end of his breath, he breaths out through his shaft, his sexual organ bringing full circle his energy into his partner. He fills her magnetic womb with his self, his power and she in turn, brings it up and back into his heart with her full earthly spirit as she breaths him in through her vagina and out through her heart.

On it goes, the tantric breath of partnership. Strengthening each one of them, making them more whole and more themselves. Sharing intimacy and autonomy. The tantric breath makes them as one yet also truly each are of themselves. The spiritual beings experiencing the physical union deeply, penetratingly, through orgasmic breath.

Now here I am in my full glory at sixty. A vibrant woman. Truly upheld in my own grace as I have found myself wrapped deeply in the conscious tendrils that continued to entwine me after my glorious birth. In all that, I have found myself in the beauty of living in a deep spiritual bond with a loving God. A practice enhanced by thirty years of looking within and finding the grace, peace, deep love, and compassion for self and others. Started by that ever-living event of meeting my vast soul, as the sunshine of my own spirit filled the cavern of my mothers' womb. I no longer need to believe in the lie. I am beloved. The betrayal cannot break who I am. I never was destroyed. I am love. I am loved.

66.

EASTER AFTER IAN'S DEATH

Today is Easter. For me Easter is an eternally sunny day. Today is no exception. Easter truly is a day of renewal to me. I couldn't sleep well last night. My grief for Ian was deep yesterday and last night. I watched Euphoria. An interesting well-done show on high school teenagers. The lead played by Zendaya is a beautiful young addict. Every type of addiction is depicted on this show. I'm watching it after Ian's death, which was influenced by drinking and a toxic relationship.

He ended the deep emotional pain he was in by hanging himself. What he wanted was his girlfriend's attention. He chose a permanent solution to a temporary problem and 'he woke up on the other side'. I grieve what he didn't get to do, like bond with his kids again, get hired for an awesome sales position at Amazon which he appeared so close to getting. Perhaps finally break free from the ties that bound him.

Those were the things I wanted to see him experience. All the life he had in him, all the vibrancy, all the pain he kept hidden inside. I wanted to watch him walk through those difficult areas, the ones that moving them can bring true fortitude and wisdom. My grief comes and goes in many ways. Most often when I'm alone. I have learned to love myself deeply. My company is a gift to myself.

My twin was a second mother to my boys and when I told her of Ian's death, she walked out of her physical therapy and keened while I was on the phone. It was heartfelt, wild, and magical and we were both so distraught to lose this amazing man. The man who taught my mother how to love, who would walk into a room and be friends with everyone in fifteen minutes. No presents can be greater than his presence.

As an adult I was blessed with the experience of the 'renewal' of Easter. I love the idea that we rise again. It is not only a rebirth of 'Jesus'; but to me it is a time to begin anew. A renewal of our spirits, a time to imagine the beauty that we experience in life. To allow others their slights and indiscretions. It may be done from a distance. To hold onto the wrong's others have committed is like renting a room in our heads for someone else's stuff. Is it mine to keep a track of the wrongs done to me by others?

This is Easter. I want renewal. I want my beautiful white lilies that remind me so much of Easter. I want to renew myself. I am starting a new career, based on the wisdom I have gained on this road of life that has at times been painful and reflects the joys of discovery over and over again as well as the healing of betrayals done very early in my life. Just as I created a Champion self that rescued those parts of me deeply hurt; I am also responsible for my actions, reactions, and inactions. I can take this lesson of financial loss and build them into gains through my own contributions.

Not only does renewal reflect my gifts of the honesty about my life but also my ability to reframe things. To see that my goal is to indemnify myself without losing my compassion or fluidity. I've gained the wisdom and the blessings of letting go and forgiveness of betrayals and not carry the need to know why I was betrayed.

I cannot know what is in other humans' thoughts or justifications, but I can rely on those incredible strengths within me to know that I am the largest component in my life. So much pain is caused from wounded wounders. Justifying the need to hold others accountable for the pain they carry. Only when we truly own our emotional reactions, and our responses to any situation, do we gain the grace of autonomy and true renewal.

I love to have company of others, crave to be held and nurtured. Reaching out is not a consideration when I'm in the grip, it isn't that I don't want to be loved. My internal process is active, grief is a deep dive into an area that used to hold so much pain. Now it holds space, awareness of the pain that was, and a flexibility which allows for life to pass in and out of my emotional reality.

It is love that gives us the greatest capacity to fortify ourselves and love our own foibles. It truly is our ability to bounce back and find balance that gives us the stamina to create great spirits and to continue to enjoy our lives.

I can be set free, just as the pastel colors of Easter brought me much renewal, I am recreating my life to give renewal to many others. We all can learn to rise from the metaphorical blasphemies that shape our lives and sharpen our souls and still feel compassion for others. It is the petty tyrants who teach us the most. They can bring us the greatest strengths. I speak to my dead father, a Satanist that committed the biggest atrocities. A man doomed before he even began. He chooses to reach out to me, to tell me his story, and my early story, and we are healing together, so the deep despair and craving for power, resulting in extreme abuse, need not be perpetrated further.

Yes, I am healing in the deepest parts of me. May I attract the bravest, most compassionate and aware partner to live my life with. It is still up to me to look for these attributes and find a partner that also seeks the ongoing renewal that I experience. Even in my deepest grief there are reasons for joy. I grieve at the loss of a profound bond with an amazing soul. That bond was not lost when he passed, I simply have only time before I am with him in a slightly different reality.

This I choose to believe. We all move out of this existence eventually. I feel grateful for how I have grown. How I can see such a beautiful world in the depths of pain. I embrace the joy, the pain, the fear, the sunset, the trees, the people I love and who loved me. Most of all I embrace who I have become. This is the greatest source of renewal. Happy Easter.

67.

BLESSED BE THY WOMB

Hail Mother of God.

Mother. Deep mother. Deepest of the divine energies that flow through creation. Hail mother. What betrayal have we wrought. How have we lost our way, lost our site, lost the trail to the most precious place of source. We lost our way. We lost the connection to source that flowed freely and brought us new life. Such a strength we had. Such a depth was in our wombs. This space for the sacred child that comes to us slowly in its growth. A growth that ends in the cavern opening to allow in the divine energy, big as the clouds. The Sacred source comes through and enters this little body. We are the bowl that holds the divine waters, which surrounds our babies. The beloved beings we chose to carry. Sacred is the womb.

Blessed are those bonded with their loves. Those that have kept their intimacy and birthed in true bliss. They keep the source and know the beauty of deeply woven souls intertwined with love and family. For many, we lost the source, our source, within a dance of betrayal. The pain of relationships, that lack of love men and women perpetuate on each other. The fear, the overpowering, the removal of the one thing that we desire more than anything, love. From the tightness of the womb, the blessed womb, that bears our most sacred selves, we cut off our connection to the divine and we bear our children in resentment.

These beloved babies, our boys, our girls. We bare them with no remembrance of what love is.

Only the feeling of rejection do we give to the most precious, most beloved beings. Sent straight from source. Knocking on the door of this earth, entering in a blaze of glorious light that we can no longer see from our own hurt, our own screaming needs. Our own hatred of our partners. The fathers and mothers who only remember the pain from their beloved. We bequeath our children with our deepest depression, the deepest loss of love, the deepest desire to hurt them for the fault of their mothers and fathers. We hurt them for the fault of our mothers and fathers.

We abandon our babies. We raise them in intolerance of their sweetest selves. How they look like the one that hurt us. How their mannerisms reflect the one that did not love us enough. How it reflects the softness we rejected and reject in them. Who are they to suckle at our breast? Even at times mothers desperate to love their young, replace their loving with resentment of the fathers. We abandon, we betray, we hurt, we reject. Our babies grow up to lose their own children to their deepest need to punish their parents lack of love.

In my meditation. I had a vision. It started with the argument with my beloved. Within me I heard his voice, his deep voice. The voice that carried the bass of men's voices. I felt it in the deepest part of my womb. Already I was hurt by the lack of nurturance, embraces, and protection I desired. This sound of the deep vibrant tones of his voice filled the space around my womb. This bowl of divine waters. The waters connecting to the deep, long cornucopia which wound its way back to the oldest part of our source.

I felt the sound of the bass male voice surrounding this bowl within me; deeply, sweetly. Filling the crevices around this sacred womb. Until the womb became a large bowl, surrounded by this deep male sound. The sound became substance. A sustaining, purposeful substance, meant to protect the womb, meant to hold it sweetly. Rocking the bowl with a gentle embrace. So powerful, so protective, so divine. This intention of the male, malleable, the deepest fluidic, strong support for the divine mother.

Dark, soft, safe, powerful beyond the boundaries of beinghood. This was the father, the safety, strength, and the most righteous belonging. Creation held, converging within itself.

This male energy, so thick and safe and nurturing then broke apart and scattered, like birds crying their own pain to the winds. The scattering of the protector filled the skies and this being, now of multitudes, cried out his pain of not knowing a mother's love. Not being surrounded by the thick protective blanket of 'father' as they themselves falter. Cast aside to forever be wandering in state of need to find their own divinity. Yearning, moaning for the deepest love of life. The conscious love of mother. A mother still enraptured within source itself.

So sorrowful was the sound. Lost are they without the deepest sense of the mother during birth, that mothers are birthing miracles of manna. Life itself. Love eternal. This is the cry of our men, our boys. Kept from the depth of a mother's love, raised with a mother's resentment.

Often accompanied by a hurt father shouting his deep need to be recognized, loved, mothered. We have lost the deepest bond, the purest creation. Our mothers betrayed and battered. Our fathers raised in pain and harshness. All crying out to find again that vibrant vessel nestled in the protective deep hum of man.

Then in my vision, I saw man and woman embracing. Winding around each other in the deepest desire for each other. In the center of the woman was the flame encased in the womb. A deep eternal flame within us, within each womb, each woman. The male energy is surrounding us and protecting the eternal flame. So strong, so whole, as if encased in the thickest of steel, molding itself around the womb so committed to life and to protecting the love and the depth of our largest selves in the tiniest of molecules. Holding each other safe, surrounding the delicate beauty of the twinkle of divinity.

Together we are a deeper, much deeper source of quantum energies combined. I cried seeing this unity that I have been so bereft of in my partnerships. So often caught up with my own soul's cry for belonging and a love entwined and independent. We breathe into our own bodies and breathe life into each other. I could feel the tears of the experience of men abandoned and women crying for protection, for the depth of their own love and the love of a partner so often incapable of being present.

This vision was alive with the duality, the pain, and the allowing of intimacy. A depth of connection. A renewal within our cells, within our wombs, and in our hearts. The tenderness of sharing life so deeply and opening with the most ancient love of the mother, to the divinity of our children. Holding them as the most precious beings they are.

We are lost when we lose the divine mother. That nurturance which feeds our deepest being. No more betrayal, no more resentment or rejection. Full openness and the powerful love of the mother raining down. Experiencing herself opening fully to her divine child, loving them each day they are formed. Full protection and embracing of the father, to the depth of his deepest self. We are and need to be embraced for our most divine selves.

68.

A PERFECT STORM

My boyfriend fit quite nicely in my self-made role. In truth, I still don't know if he is a stand-up guy, with his beautiful light golden bronze skin, his sweet lips and eyes so easily squinted in quirky wonder or warmth. He has a beautiful mind and lives a life of music and business with a temper quick to anger then cool, and a soft, vulnerable heart seemingly willing to love yet terrified to do so, so afraid of being hurt. I feel deeply for him. I want our dream of the arts, the music, the profit. My distrust and fears were palpable these days and for good reasons.

He was an addict. A using addict. One who finally admitted how much he used when we were together, after we were together. How bad he screwed up his mind. How what I saw of his tweaking was real. How reaffirming it was to hear because I knew. The behavior and temper tantrums. The filth he lived in. How irresponsible he was for his actions. How it was everyone else fault. How he would not come out of his room.

It was a heartbreaking shame. What was heartbreaking were the dreams that were shattered; of artistry, creating music, film, productions, investments, shared profit, and equally paying expenses. That was the greatest betrayal, what we could have had. That is what I mourn. He was so sweet, brilliant, creative. Yet he created a hell with me. He slid downhill so quickly, so horribly. He portrayed my father brilliantly. At the end, my father agreed, he was exactly like my boyfriend.

Still, my boyfriend recognized the depth and dimensionality of who I am, the artist, dancer, accountant. Lover. Sees me as worthy of praise, respect, and love. Also, the deeper script of what I was told so many years ago, in the dark basement, in a small dark room, on a small skank bed, savaged by a man, who was truly a savage.

I have become my own warrior, a champion. It is for me to listen to my own rantings of 'being disparaged' and remember the lies that depleted and truly disparaged me, no longer need to be spoken. They are not real. Only a figment, a recording replayed at the hint of judgment. The record is broken, only in deep sensitivity might it be considered again. I am gifted to find my own peace and know the voice of my dead father no longer speaks with an evil tongue intent on destroying the light in me, which is incapable of destruction.

Now here I am in my full glory at sixty. A vibrant woman. Truly upheld in my own grace as I have found myself wrapped deeply in the conscious tendrils that continued to entwine me after my glorious birth. In all that, I have found myself in the beauty of living in a deep spiritual bond with a loving God. A practice enhanced by over thirty years of looking within and finding the grace, peace, deep love, and compassion for self and others. Started by that ever-living event of meeting my vast soul, as the sunshine of my own spirit filled the cavern of my mothers' womb. I no longer need to believe in the lie. I am beloved. The betrayal cannot break who I am. I never was destroyed. I am love. I am loved.

69.

OH HELL NO!!!

Oh Hell NO!!!! Enough. Enough of covid. Enough of my business failing. Enough of my customers barely hanging on. Enough. Most of all .... enough of the relationships that are nothing better than repetitive reminders that I grew up with a Satanist. Enough of living through this repeatedly. I got it.

The worst though was the relationships I have had with harsh, sick, and incompetent men. At least my oldest sons' father did support my son and had a good and loving relationship with him before he died. Even that, the death of my son, shouldn't have happened. That is another painful example of the legacy of abuse. In his case it was the alcohol and drugs that ended his life in a suicide. Painful, harsh reality of what my family has lived through.

So enough! I say Hell No. So... see me now. It's time to take back my courage, my strength, my anger and my valor. Enough of this. Enough of living it over and over like a nightmare. See me.... stage right. I enter in the best outfit a woman can buy. Black leather cat suit clinging to my body. I may be sixty, but I make this look good. My long blond hair flowing down my back. Come on get with it my beautiful sisters, let's take back our power. Then the boots! Stiletto high heels, black, covering past my knees, a black mask around my sparkling green eyes.

I walk slowly toward center stage, one foot in front of the other and get to you, all of you who have lived similar lifestyles. Who have struggled to make ends meet or lost relationships, marriages, and jobs. Those that have been ridiculed or berated by bosses or lovers for who think you are so much less than they or use that as an excuse to do you harm. To scapegoat you for what you didn't do when they never bothered to see what you did do. Never see your worth. Never recognize your value.

Hell no to the lovers that take advantage of us! To the children who don't recognize what we have done to raise them or love them into the exquisite beings they are! To the bosses that cannot see what you provide to the organization or, worse yet, set you up to fail to make themselves look indispensable! To the organizations that failed to pay out unemployment to millions and millions of people this year and the forgivable loans that failed to provide what they said they would.

We have lived through hell for the last year and a half and its time it stopped. Now stand up my sisters and yell it.... Hell NO. Enough is enough. No more. We will not be ignored or threatened or ridiculed or humiliated or scared or taken advantage of. Enough of the hell. Get on your cat suits and join me. It's our turn to take our power back to let them know we have substance, we have intelligence, we have heart, and we have power.

That is the truth. We have power. We can show it with our skintight black leather outfits and boots, and masks. Walk together with me. This has been a long time coming. Get up and scream. Let yourself be heard. We are substantial. You may rip us off, but we will come back stronger. You may leave us with nothing, and we will be fortified. You may rake us over the coals in meetings or humiliate us while other teammates feel embarrassed for us but that only serves to make you small, not powerful. We will not be undone. We will not fold. We will not cower. We will hold our heads high and cry. We will leave those horrible situations that drain our value, and we will be strong. We will walk together. We will raise our voices. We will find strength to take back what you have taken from us.

Walk my friends, show us your beauty. Bring out everything you have within you. Own your magnificence, for you are magnificent. See yourself this way. No matter what color, or what shape or size or age or education. You are marvelous. See the stunning woman you are. I urge you, be the badass woman that you are inside. Then see the beauty of your sisters. Greet their amazingness. Feel their power and know you share it. Congratulate yourselves on how you have come to love who you are, accepted every ounce of you. Loved every part of you that feels small and victimized, scared and terribly sad. Cover those parts of you with your love and kisses. Shine the light on the most vulnerable parts inside of you and embrace them completely, own every part of you.

Now walk with me. Let those boots click on the stage or the sidewalk. Swing those hips with us in your skintight suits. Let those hips represent the strength of steel you have inside. A steel reflective of the loving beauty and brilliance within you. Yes, my sisters walk with me proud and bold and deserving, exquisite. We rock.

70.

YESTERDAY I GRIEVED

Yesterday I grieved. All day. I could not stop crying. The catalyst was my boyfriend. How he left me in the dark. I consider this hideously untransparent and controlling. I have never seen any money's he has invested for me and the amount I invested was 17k in a high growth time for Bitcoin. Right before he died, he admitted he accidently burned up the passcode when he was using.

He agreed to pay for the rent starting in October. Then he asked if he could have till the end of the month. Then it was the end of November. He never paid a penny. Then his behavior got worse.

I paid all the bills the whole time I was with Shay. Not only that but his room was in such bad condition, I lost everything I deposited. All $3,100. This guy really took me for a spin. I think he does want to be a good guy. I'm just tired of what I lived with and how much I have lost financially.

This was a huge lesson because he mirrored my father almost exactly with the horrible verbal abuse. The addiction. The lack of love or affection. The filth and disregard for me and for himself. He showed me how hellish it was to live with and be abused by my father. I dissociated so much with my dad. Shay made it extremely, vividly real, what I had lived with. What I was living with now. For that I am grateful.

71.

I AM POWERLESS AND SEEK A RETURN TO SANITY

This 'thing' about my life, or what drains my lifeforce, and has kept me weak and hurting for, well for my whole life. Are relationships. Intimate relationships. I keep finding my father and the pain he caused me over and over. The men are all different, yet I encounter the deep pain I experienced with him repeatedly.

I need a God, an infinite loving and caring God, to do this with me. To restore me to sanity. It's time to work the steps on this very old and very discouraging problem.

Step #1, Narcotics Anonymous,

"We admitted we were powerless over our addiction, and our lives have become unmanageable."

I admit I am powerless over my addiction to relationships that cause me pain and financial unmanageability. However, it's not the only unmanageable part of my life. Before we get too deep into unmanageability let's look at how we define 'addiction'.

Drugs are but a symptom of our disease. Relationships can be as damaging as a drug. Sometimes even more damaging. Addiction is a progressive disease. Often ending in jails, institutions, and death.

Often an addict may not even identify that the craving is so strong. They just act on the craving and have an unsatiable need to use the drug(s) again. The mental obsession is just as powerful as the physical craving. All addicts can think about is getting and using and finding ways and means to use more. The obsession to use clouds all other thoughts. The spiritual self-centeredness is self-evident, there is no room for thought of others, of family, friends, husbands, wives, or children. The addict's thoughts are on themselves and the need to get drugs at any costs. The loss of life suffered by many addicts is a tragedy on a grand scale, as well as the activities they engage in to get and use more drugs. This can and does end in the loss of life for others or at least the loss of property.

It is common to hear an addict state, I am an addict, and my problem is me! This is true. The disease of addiction is a much deeper disease based in our thinking and feeling and how we interpret our will and our lives. Addiction is a form of insanity. An addict often acts out of 'self will run riot'. We consider that threefold disease of obsession, compulsion, and self-centeredness because this is where we are often quite sick.

We often cannot recognize the deeper malady of addiction until the recovering addict stops using all mind- and mood-altering substances. It is then that the deeper disease of thoughts and feelings become incredibly painful. Obsession is like listening to a record repeatedly. It is the thought that won't go away. The discomforting thought that is heard in our heads again and again. It could be from a conversation held with someone, or what we should have said, what they did say or do, or what we repeated in our brain repeatedly that we didn't say.

The compulsion is the second element of addiction. Getting clean is like letting loose emotions. It is a perpetual roller coaster of feelings. We are up, we are down. We are angry then horny as all get out. We act on all the other addictions, sex, food, Netflix, reading, exercise, dating, fishing, work. It is not about what we act out on, it is the way we approach it. Are we obsessive and compulsive? Do we do something for our own gain? Do we do it to excess. Are we overwhelmed and overstimulated? Are we driven? Are we motivated by fear? Are we consumed by what still drives us inside?

Or are we calm! Can we quiet our minds? Can we feel our feelings? Allow them to be a part of us and not hide from them until they become our monsters. Do we recognize their value? Can we quiet ourselves long enough to embrace what we are feeling? This is our internal communication system, our one true knowledge. This is where we find who we truly are. Can we be with ourselves inside?

Recovery is not done on the outside for others. It is the greatest training in the world. It is how you become your truest self. What you get is much deeper, much more than you would ever think. You get back yourself. The ability to know who you are inside. This is not an outside job. Nobody can do it for you. The most precious gift is a quiet mind. The most incredible sensation is the ability to experience any emotion. Honor it. Feel it. Emotions will move on their own once we allow them to be a part of us. First, we must be able to actually open up to what we feel inside.

The ability to actual feel, to breathe in and feel our breath go all the way to our toes is precious. We can begin to recognize what emotions we are feeling within our bodies and find a way to allow them to be there. We stop trying to hide from what we truly are inside. The ability to follow our breaths to an active emotion, one that is alive within you now, is exquisite awareness. To literally sit next to this feeling and gain the ability to be there and allow the emotion to live, instead of cutting it off and hiding from it, which makes it blossom even more simply because we do not have the courage to accept it.

This is true awareness of self. Some emotions are harder than others. Anger by its nature, jumps ahead of us to protect us. Often the effect is the opposite since anger is seen as a shameful act. Anger does not have the softest voice, nor does it act with compassion for all. Yet anger keeps us alive. It brings our power back. It is a true gift, however one that is very hard to control. It can be very useful, or it can be used to fuel us on to adventures better left alone.

All emotions are the essence of us. They are the truest communication system we have within us. They will lead us to our truest being and allow us to feel a freedom to our very depth. When we have gone within and sat next to the deepest grief and allowed it to live, then we find freedom. Freedom is not the absence of feelings it is the allowance of what we feel and the acceptance of it being a part of us. Even deeper, it is the love for us, and our feelings give us the greatest awareness of self.

We experience the fullness of our being, the ability to be alive. It does not guarantee that we will not hurt. Instead, we feel the hurt and find our vulnerability. Find the soft underbelly of who we are, the sweetness, the child, the innocence, the softest voice never heard.

We listen a soul into existence. We become the depth of who we really are. Flawed, beautiful, ingenious, emotive, peaceful, free, beloved, tender, pained, real, and truly alive.

So then how am I addicted to painful relationships? What a painful question. How is it that after so many years clean and in recovery that I can admit to this very painful addiction. More than that...what do I get by admitting it and what do I get by looking repeatedly for a resolution to the pain.

Addiction is the thoughts, feelings, and self-centered pattern of trying to resolve an issue. We may try over and over, but a problem is never resolved from the same mind that created the problem. I wanted love. I wanted to have a father that protected me and kept me safe and truly loved me. It is essential to recognize the patterns I perpetuated by choosing men with similar qualities.

Admitting I was powerless helps me realize I am no longer powerless. I can make other choices and do make other choices. Most of all I can accept who I was, and who they were, and experience compassion for all of us. I can and do love and forgive. I can care for myself and know the deep worth I have and let the need for 'love' go. I am loved. I no longer need to seek it elsewhere.

72.

FAMILY HEALING WITH LOVE FROM THE BEYOND

We gathered. My family. All my siblings on this side. My parents and grandparents and departed friends and loved ones in the beyond. We gathered to heal the wounds carried by my siblings. The wound my mother experienced at the birth of her twins. Her death and the pain in her physical body, as well as her heart. I experienced her death with her. She experienced coming back into her body. Recently I experienced the wounds in her lungs as the last organs to open.

Yet she was weak for a long time after our birth. When my sister was born twenty-two months after we twins, she was diagnosed with a life-threatening lung disease. A doctor advised my parents to keep her in a room with a breathing machine. Mama was told that Sheila may not live to her first birthday. Sheila was isolated and alone. A baby needing attention, love, touch, affection. Yet she was ignored, struggling for the breath. A spirit not quite in the body she was born in. So alone. Crying out with a voice she would struggle to find long into adulthood. A deep wound of abandonment screaming into the ethers. Sheila lived. Grieved to the point of deep sadness that she was never given the life affirming love that may have brought her into a little being of light.

She has wept the tears of unbelonging for an eternity. Even her skin aching for the touch she never knew was viscerally missing. She just knew a deep gnawing pain of a scream that was never quite finished. She felt the curse of my mothers' previous death as an absence of care. Knowing the resulting sting of grief, the potential of losing a baby, as the baby herself and the soft touch not felt. The lack of embrace, or of loving eyes looking into hers. The comfort of the boundary of her body around her, defining her experience in a sentient, breathing, harmonic, cellular form. For this she grieved until even her betrayed spirit rejected the body she was meant to have. Dearest Sheila carried the pain of the effect of our mother's death into a life graced far beyond the time frame of living given at her birth.

My younger siblings also experienced the lack of a vibrant mother's body, not to the extent of Sheila in her early illness, but in other ways her weakness and struggles became their weaknesses. Their bodies too feeling the lack of something unknown, the lack of vibrancy that took lifetimes to uncover. They too had their weaknesses, some in the lungs, some in the stomach, some in the lack of love that was a thematic stream running through our generation. Five children were born to a woman who almost died in childbirth. How do we not heal our mothers? How did we lose those wonderful practices other cultures have to heal the mother, so she may be a mother? To the mothers we have lost, and the fathers that were grieved or clueless of how to nurture the woman who has given birth back to health, I honor you and cry for you. Tender be the breath that breaths back life into our mothers. Lightly be the touch of the father, the giver, the protector. May he learn to carry his family with joy.

It was we five siblings and a spouse that gathered to acknowledge the wounds of a death at birth. To hold our mother in the beyond in love, and in a space that acknowledged what she experienced. Also, to pay tribute to the body that birthed, and the needs of the other bodies birthed. We gathered to honor and acknowledged what weakened a family. To heal wounds already gone from our loved ones who still wished to heal, and love those that may have been harmed, from the physical wounds perpetrated by the act of birth.

We started with a short meditation, then into the stories of my mother's death at our birth and the deeper story of the great awareness of life, spirit, brilliance that blessed my mother's womb and created a bond of a baby to its ancient spirit. My siblings heard the story for the first time of my mother's death and my introduction to my blazing soul. After the story, there was reverence from the beyond.

In the beyond, many relatives gathered there and felt the depth of grace. Then my fathers' parents requested permission to be a part of the healing. Never had they come into our midst when we visited our loved ones. Daddy's parents also carried the weight of the satanic rituals. That we had now healed so much, that a third generation back was coming forward to heal, which was phenomenal.

This request carried the lightening of the weight of harshness of generations before us. They brought with them the healing they wished to experience too. Our maternal grandparents came to the circle too. They that had blessed us in our growing up years with celebrations and stories. There were others close to our parents in the circle, aunts, and dear friends. The circle kept expanding in the beyond.

We then did a healing meditation to address the lungs, the grief, the stomach, and the resulting anxiety, now seen so clearly in our bloodline. After we opened to the lightness of healing, my parents shared their love. My mother, in her sublime spirit body, wore white to commemorate this healing. This beautiful being so entranced with pain in her life here, has blossomed into the most loving mother. So sweet is her essence. She now cradles the babies that come to heaven early. She is their loving mother here. She holds them and loves them. How gracious is the blessing of the kindness of God? To grant this mother the honor to love the babies beyond. May my siblings truly grow to see her grace, her abundant love now. May they see her beauty now. What lies beyond is the greatest of gifts of the divine.

Our medium described the love and healing felt from our family on the other side. Lots of love and lightness, a lot of bliss and gratitude. A ton of feeling gratitude for bringing the siblings together. There is so much love. They in the beyond are standing in nature with lots of flowers and water. There is a bright, bright light behind them, very bright like the sun. Star feels very calm within this light. Some of our family is kneeling. My father has his hands on Mama's shoulder. Lovingly touching her and saying how wonderful it is to have the family together again. Our parents have healed so deeply. Mama wants all her children to know how much she loves them and admires them.

It is a family reunion. Daddy is so loving and peaceful. He says our family is together like a family reunion. They continue to expand through our healing. Mama says that she and I have been talking a lot recently. She is thanking me for our conversations. I do not consciously remember conversations with my family on the other side. Thorne was very honored to be included in this family healing. He says that my family is the only one he really knew. Ian is awestruck and he wants everyone to know that he sees all of us. He is so happy right now and at peace. They are saying that the healing is what matters now. Moving higher, understanding and awareness. Daddy said it's taken some beautiful work to be where he is now. He has done a great deal to heal his soul. I thank my mother for taking care of my son Ian. Thorne says being with family is a very sacred moment. There is a lot of reverence. They are in the light.

We invited my sisters and brother to share their experiences. I was feeling a slight tension in my stomach. We then focused on all our children and surrounded them with love and healing. Star was feeling some resistance and my sister Sheila was feeling a lot of heaviness and pain in her stomach. We focused on her, and Star suggested deep breathes and letting the pain go. She was feeling so much sadness and fear it was intense. We gave her permission to feel the pain. Sheila said she felt so strong that she did not want to be on the planet. She has felt that her whole life and she does not know why she stayed on the planet. She feels a push/pull thing with Mama.

She asks mama, "why did you want me to stay if you did not want me." Mama is feeling Sheila's pain and saying it was not about wanting you. It was about Mama not coping well. She is trying to get into Sheila's energy but there is resistance.

"I feel myself in that room, feeling so alone, always so alone. I trust spirit, I trust God. I don't trust people." We ask if we can come into the room. I saw Sheila in the room, and her spirit that was free form. "I thought you hated me." Sheila said to me, I answered "I saw the spirit in your room, and it scared me".

"I was jealous of you because mama went away. Can we jump on the bed with you?" I love you, I wanted you to come out of the room and the spirit to be in your body. I had a vision of all the siblings jumping on the bed. Mama said, "Let my children be children." Sheila says that when mama says that she felt like she wasn't one of her children. Mama knows the pain she caused Sheila and knows she caused it. She takes ownership of Sheila being hurt. "We are closer than you know, you just don't get it yet." Like the two of them are more connected than they know. There is a push/pull energy. There is a part of Mama and Sheila that is very similar. Mama has felt her pain. "You are my daughter but there is more than that." Mama is holding Sheila's hands and is very close to Sheila. "I just want to be with my child"; Mama said to Sheila, "You were one of my greatest teachers." They sit in silence.

Mama says she has loved Sheila for eternity. Sheila is feeling a soothing in her stomach, like mama was trying to soothe her. She hears mama saying, "I'm sorry I couldn't do it then." Sheila's pain was so awful, always feeling pain and hunger always. Sheila needs touch to remember who she is here; she needs to map herself to the world. We want her to feel our hands on her so she can feel she is a part of the world. Soothing her, feeling our hands on her back and on her hair. She moved a lot of energy.

The session is ending. This was the intent of the session. For our family to heal with each other. Our family on the other side was thanking us and letting us know they love us very much. We are all healing and expanding. We thank our grandparents for coming into the session as well. There is a great deal of love shared and pain. It was amazing to have all the siblings on and for them to be present. The sensory world is so much stronger in the beyond. They feel clearly and there was tremendous healing. This was an amazing session of love and forgiveness.

73.

PEACE BE WITH YOU AND ALSO YOU

This was the first medium reading since our family healing two weeks ago. My mother was the first to be heard. The rest of my beloved family was there as well. Mama was a changed being. She was so light, so free. She was happy. I had conversations with some of my siblings and they were in various stages of learning and peace with the gathering. Now I was hearing and feeling the grace that my mother was feeling. I had never seen her so light or lighthearted. If this was the main effect of the family gathering, then it was completely worth it. To see my mother so lighthearted and free. She was so happy that her children were growing and accepting.

To the dust kicked up with my siblings, my mother stated that it took a mess to address a mess. Now it was addressed. The dust will settle. More will be seen. To see my mother so light and happy was the very best gift of the gathering. This had been for her. To heal her pain, to bring her babies to her. To acknowledge that drudging she lived through. Now she is a changed spirit. So light. She was again wearing her white dress. In this occasion it was so fitting. My mother had come into her own. She came forward in love for my sister so deeply hurt. She was there to comfort her. To acknowledge the eternal relationship, they had. To tell her she was one of her most powerful teachers. My mother had loved her children. Acknowledged their pain and their beauty. She shone. She allows the dust to settle and acknowledges it. We have changed those in heaven in our seeking solace. It is not only us that grow. Our awareness enhances theirs. As we evolve, they to evolve.

Ian came to me and said he loved me. He and mama then held hands. My son. My beautiful boy. I acknowledged the burden of debt they both carried. Not only from the lack of abundance they both experienced, but also from the separation of their children. A separation from their own inability to be present. Both dealing with their pain in their own ways yet mirroring each other. Ian the soul that carried such great love within him, and mama who now shines with a freedom from bondage. Yes, this coming together of my family was such an incredible gift.

My siblings have yet to see how they have changed the lives of those beyond the physical. My eyes are open. We all continue to evolve. Each of us grows, whether manifest in form or not. We continue to higher consciousness and freedom. Mama, I love you so. My life is now made so whole and the effort was worth seeing the light in your spirit that I now know. If these stories go nowhere, they have made you into a light being of tremendous love. This may be the biggest gift I give to the world. To see my mother light, and loving, and accepting of herself and seeing herself as a loving mother. Peace be with you my amazing mama. You are blessed and with each awareness you grow grander in your consciousness.

Daddy was not quite present with us. He was now with his parents. As had happened in our conversations. He now had the opportunity to heal with his parents. They were with him. This is so powerful. This family that knew such pain. A pain carried through generations, multiplied by ritual abuses. Now they are here. Seeking solace. Willing to heal with their son. This man that lived through hell, carried it within him. Now there is release.

A sweetness that comes with relief of burdens, no longer being carried by the one that bore the pain. It is now his turn to release his pain and his parents' opportunities to acknowledge their parts. How they contributed. Just as my father did for me. How we are moving through generations of harshness and seeing the consciousness of our beings. It is the truly honored that can accept and acknowledge the part they played. This is not an easy burden.

It has always been hard for me to acknowledge my jealousy and fear of my sick sister, even though I was so young. I placed my mother's hiding on my little sisters' shoulders. So angry that this woman who was barely capable of providing was now even less available.

How dare this spirit, my sister, come into our lives and drain one so drained already. She took the little bit of love my mother was capable of and demanded so much more. I was angry at her spirit. Yet it was not my story. This was a story of my mother and my sister. I just carried my resentment of mama's capacity being further depleted. My sister remembers me beating her. I do not know how often that happened. My memory carries only three episodes, yet of those I felt the fear.

The first was when Sheila was in the bathtub and was given a new toy. I was two. She was born twenty-two months after us, so she may have been six or eight months old. Old enough to have a toy. I think I took it away. In our family healing, Sheila said she thought I hated her. I most likely did at times. She was not responsible for my mother's frailty and eventual withdrawal, yet I blamed the circumstance of my sister's birth, for my mother receding even further from us.

The second time I remember I was strongly affected by my little sister was when Daddy brought her into the room where he incested me. I was so angry that she would be witness to my shame. More than that, the worst of the effect, was that I would have to stay present in my body. I was well versed of leaving my body during the rapes. Now he brought my sister in. She was now in my care. It was on me to be present, to make sure she lived. That she survived his horrid indulgences. I hated her after that. Both for seeing my humiliation and for the necessity to care for her life. She took the brunt of my rage at him.

That he would wake me up by bringing this confused and broken girl into a situation of sadism. I believe I did hate her after that. She was so young, so hurt already, yet so innocent. So easily did she carry pain. So well did her mind remember the lack and the hurts. Her memory so geared to the wrongs she had suffered, at my hands and others. I was mean, rageful. I was also aware of the nightly horrors. I do not remember him bringing her again, perhaps it was my rage that kept him from harming her. At least in front of me. Perhaps I saved her life. I knew the burden of being responsible for her life from the minute he brought her into that room of sadistic torture.

The last time was when my mother was in the mental hospital. I took over the family newspaper business and my siblings were paper girls and boys. Sheila slept in. I went home and pounded on her back till she got up and did her paper route. I was abusive. I was also angry that Sheila was there. She came home to be with us from a foster home my father had put her in.

Not an official one but one where again she was seen as a burden. She wanted to be one of us. I was angry that another child was home to be fed. Sheila spent years as the lost child, whether she was with us or away. She was given away. This I feel deep sadness for her, even when I myself wished her to be cared for elsewhere. So, Sheila knew rejection again and again. I was responsible for rejecting her as well. She was truly the lost child. I am so sorry for your pain Sheila.

Now my mother was happy and light and free. She had loved her children. She was there for her daughter. Willing to love her and be with her. Perhaps it was too late. Yet this loved crossed the boundary of death, and my mother experienced her own love. Just as one day I dearly hope my sister can experience her own forgiveness of mama.

We can hold onto our pain for a very long time. Being wronged is a seed that germinates in our hearts and head and the stories we tell for long after the wrong is done, keeps us caught up in it. Drop the story.

Have courage. Experience the emotional knot that holds the unallowed emotions. Sit next to them. Bring your consciousness to light. Acknowledge the burden held as an emotion and allow it to be there. Then it will unwind on its own. This painful knot will undue itself as you look on and breath and welcome it to your consciousness.

My father was with his parents. This was a miracle. That my grandparents came forward was a testament to how much my father grew. How he took responsibility for himself and his injustices. His sadism. Now my grandparents can heal and are healing. We are changing the past we are creating a new future. They can now look clearly at what they created, and obviously have since they asked to join us in our circle of awareness.

My family in the beyond were adamant that what happened wasn't healing. Healing means that something was broken. My mother stated nothing was broken, there is nothing to heal. We are allowing. We are acknowledging what was. We are aware of who we are, what we are holding onto. We allow ourselves to feel the tightly knit bundles we accumulate within us and bring our consciousness into our selves. We sit next to the weighted cells and breathe, allowing the knots to be present. We do not need to know why, only that they are there, and we allow them to be there. This is another way to come to. We can experience our awakening, our dawning. Even way back to our grandparents awakening. The healing seems to go from the present back to the past. It affects our bloodline. Cleansing it, freeing it from its pain and neglect.

I asked my father about my aunt. Aunt Julie. My retarded aunt with cerebral palsy. He said she has earned her wings. My beautiful aunt, who could not eat with her mouth shut. Who raised dogs and found herself in a situation where the bank was attempting to take her home away from her, a home that was left to her and her mother from her grandfather. When my grandmother had the stroke, my grandfather became executor of the estate and shortly afterwards died of a heart attack. Banks may not be the best executors.

Aunt Julie is exalted. She exists on a very high dimension. This did not surprise me. I think perhaps she choose to be here to temper this family of Satanists. What a choice she made. To live her life like she did, with so much limitation. This is perhaps the biggest grace. Julie is our most exalted being. What an incredible reminder. For all those that we may turn from as they live with their visible defects; we may know that they are the exalted ones. They are the ones that are the most benevolent, the wisest, the most aware. Thank you for your blessings, Aunt Julie. Peace is with you.

We are greater than we know. Our effect here and there can change worlds. There is much that we do and much we know that changes galaxies. We are not small. We are grand. We are magnificent. Carnate or incarnate, we are incomprehensibly genuine suns equal to milky ways. We come into being and rise to an infinite beinghood. How deeply we can traverse to find we always were love. We will be forever.

74.

SHAY IS DEAD

Shay is dead. He died on my porch. I found him there at 7 am yesterday, Sunday July 11th. He was standing up and bending over. Like he was throwing up. I shook him. He was in such a weird position. His hand was purple. I moved his head. I went back inside. I was pretty sure he was dead. I went out again and moved the patio furniture out of the way.

Then I moved him to the floor, it wasn't easy. Then I called 911. They send the fire department and an ambulance and told me to perform CPR. I did. He was still warm. His eyes were closed. His face was very red and purple. The first CPR there was an exhale. Then his chest felt full. I kept performing CPR till the police and EMT's came in the door. Then they made me leave him.

He came over on Saturday. I saw him standing outside in front of my apartment building. He was dressed in black. He looked better. The last time I saw him a week and a half ago he was so skinny, his demeanor was negative, and he was in bad shape. This time he looked more vibrant. I met him in the ice cream shop. He smiled and got up and hugged me.

I was a little leery but happy that he was smiling, and he kissed my face. We talked a little bit then went upstairs. He was friendly to the fellow working the ice cream counter. His countenance was much better. We came up to the apartment. He hugged me and kissed my face a few more times and he said he was sorry at least twice. He was doing something to pay me back.

He told me about all the doctors he had seen. His heart doctor had hospitalized him. He had texted me saying he was in the hospital and then I didn't hear from him for a few days. I called several hospitals and none of them had him listed.

He also saw his endocrinologist and a foot doctor. The foot doctor said his feet were all bone and he had no padding left. He gave him an injection that helped him feel better. He was having trouble taking the heart medication. It really seemed like seeing all the doctors improved his disposition. We talked for a while.

My nephew called and we went over the upcoming performance for my book pre-launch at the summit in September. Shay said he had talked to another sound engineer, and he had talked to Tarek about coming out and playing the Santur. After the call with my nephew, he said it sounded like we had it together. I wanted his help. I always wanted his input. This man was the man I wanted to do arts with, and do business with, and have a deep loving relationship with. Even after everything that had happened when we were together, I still wanted to partner with him. He still had a brilliant mind and was an amazing sound engineer.

Even after all that happened, I didn't want to leave him. It just got worse and worse. I knew he was using drugs, no matter how he denied it. I was alone all the time. He would lock himself in his room or would be gone all night. He started a fire when he was using and burned up the desk, I made for him and the bed frame. He finally told me he accidently burned the passcode for the bitcoin investment when he burned the desk. Mine was not the only passcode burnt accidentally.

We did have a lovely conversation. He was upset that we were getting the performance together without him. He was also adamant that he hadn't taken my watch that meant so much to me. It was a very important watch that I received when I joined a mastermind group and I was, and am, very upset about it. Shay fell asleep around 3 or 4 that afternoon. Unfortunately, he did pawn the watch. That so hurt my heart.

I understood now that him falling out like that was most likely due to his heart condition and his adrenal gland failure. It stormed later that night and I went out and sat with him on the porch. Once again, he was distant. I sat in my stillness and enjoyed the storm and went inside. I went back out to the porch a short time later and he was asleep. I sat next to him for a while and went back in.

Sometime early in the wee hours of the morning, he came into my room. He touched my legs lightly and my stomach. It was a very sweet touch. He said he was going to get his money. He was loving and his touch soothed and excited me. I slept fitfully for the next few hours, waking up and falling back to sleep. I woke and went out of my room around 7. The lights were on in the house. The porch door was open. I peeked out the door and saw Shay standing there as I stated earlier.

He looked strange in that position with his upper body bent over. That's when I touched him, and the rest has been written in the beginning.

I never found someone I loved before dead unexpectedly. I cared for my father until he died, and I did find him dead in the morning, in his hospital bed in the living room. It was expected, I nursed him most of the night. Shay was shocking, although I knew for months that Shay was dying. It was so hard to kick him out. I was not being malicious. I could not afford to pay the expenses any more by myself and I also practice tough love. Addicts often seek help when no one else is supporting them. I knew I was helping him stay lost in his addiction if I kept supporting him.

I mourned my fiancé and my son often because I never got to see them again after they died except in pictures. Shay was here. I found him, I moved him, I gave him CPR. I wish I had just held him and rocked him, like I did months before when he cried. That was when he fell in love with me. I just embraced him and wouldn't let him go. He said that was a most meaningful moment in his life.

I think Shay's spirit knew he was going to die. I think he was happy. If I could have done it over, I would have embraced him again. So, he could feel that embrace that felt so loving one more time. Yet once I called 911 it was no longer my own time. Everything was then dictated by the operator, or policewomen who guarded his body and identified the parameters I could move in, in my own house.

I wanted to hold vigil for him. We are both Irish. I wanted to be next to him so he could feel another human being. I think he was still there for that. I was only allowed to go into my office, where I could see him. I talked to him. I told him I loved him. I've told him that many times now.

He would tell me he loved me often. Especially since he was out in the streets. He had softened up; he was more loving. I believe he wanted to die with me. No matter what I gave him love.

Especially when I had surgery and he wasn't there to get me and very late to pick me up last September. I knew this man was the epitome of my father. I knew that what I saw in him was how my father was. Only my father intentionally hurt me, repeatedly. Shay made it real for me. He was not hideously abusive, like my father. He was ignorantly abusive. In his addiction he could not even see how he behaved.

He took the 17k I invested in bitcoin The bitcoin quickly grew into much more than 17K, hitting highs of 80K. He didn't tell me for six months he had burned the passcode. I was glad to know what had happened. His behavior often mimicked my father. More than that he very much made the amnesic forgetfulness of the abuse in my childhood clear. At one point my father told me in a medium reading..." I am Shay, Shay is me". Only my father was worse.

Shay made all of this real to me. I was questioning my father in medium readings, and he was being completely honest with me, about the incest, about the satanic rituals, even about him planning my sacrifice. There were times with both my father and Shay that they were sweet and loving and giving. Yet it was like Shay had never been given any parental love. I know he was taken out of the home when he was young and spent time in foster care. Then he went to live with his father. He, like I, received most love from his siblings or cousins.

All that time that I was 'talking to the dead' I was living with Shay and experiencing him quickly slide down into the depth of a deep and debilitating addiction. Also, from the beginning I knew he would betray me. I knew this was a part of why he was there. He was my greatest teacher, for he was the worst petty tyrant. He reflected Daddy in true painful glory, and I knew it. The whole time I practiced Divine Openings and I never stopped going to NA meetings and I had medium readings every two weeks which brought me so much love. I leaned into recovery and my spirituality.

Shay struggled with his addiction to the bitter ends. He was out on the streets and lost just about everything. He was fighting everyone and everything and when he got here, he had 0% body fat. He looked like a street addict in the end, and I wanted to cry. He stole my watch and helped me look for it over and over. I knew. I had been in recovery for long enough.

I was learning so much from my father and seeing him grow and forgive himself. He was honest with me, and I gave him back the pain he had placed on me for so many years. I often felt like Shay mirrored my deep shame and pain or at least I saw how painful my life had been. How I had been so affected by my father and Shay brought all of this out.

It was hellish, but he, of the very few men I had relationships with, was the one that really showed me the hell I went through with Daddy. I moved through those denser emotions, the powerlessness, the pain and betrayal, the deep sadness and hurt. I truly did love you Shay. You made it all real.

75.

STUFFING STUFF

I was at my home group meeting yesterday. A home group is an NA meeting you chose to participate in and support. Currently we are one meeting of a few meetings that still meet face to face. We meet in a park. So far, the weather has permitted us to be outside in Phoenix. This could change quickly. We are shaded and the breeze has been kind to us. I love reading from our literature and hearing people share on the paragraph we just read.

We ask someone to read from the main book, which has a slightly different cover. We track what has been read by highlighting the paragraphs and often initialing the readers initials on the page. We never know what paragraph will be read. Often the paragraphs contribute to heartfelt shares from the members present.

Yesterday's paragraph was about caring for aging parents. Since many of us are 'of a certain age' caring for our parents, and attending to their dying, was a part of our experience. One sentence really struck home for many of us, "Some of our hardest moments contain the keys to healing deep and painful scars. A member shared about their painful scars and how they had stuffed them.

"I learned to stuff my feelings very young. When anything was painful with my family, I just stuffed it down. Then when I went out into the world, whatever bothered me I stuffed down again. If I was in a difficult situation at work. I would stuff it and go on. Then I fell in love and got married. After a while I was stuffing my pain about the love I felt. Then I stuffed more stuff about the marriage. Soon I was stuffing how I felt about the divorce. I just kept stuffing the stuff I couldn't deal with until there was so much stuff, I had stuffed that I was suffocating in all the stuff.

The more I stuffed the more stuff I was sensitive too. I stuffed myself until I was big from all the stuffing. My body reflected how much stuff I had stuffed inside. I stuffed the deaths in my family, so I did not have to feel them consume all the stuff I had stuffed. It got so crowded inside with all that stuff. I couldn't really communicate well if there were emotions associated with our communications because I had stuffed them."

There was a lot of great stuff shared. The pain we cause when we stuff our stuff can suffocate us. Not only that, but our outside environment can also reflect how much stuff we are stuffing. Soon every surface in our house can be filled with stuff. Stuff just to keep us comfortable. To reflect 'us' so we see ourselves in our stuff. When the truth is the real 'stuff' is stuffed way deep inside.

The most difficult aspect of recovery, and of life, is to look at the stuff we have stuffed inside. Often when we get 'clean' we wake up. Suddenly we are walking on eggshells and all that stuff comes out. In a short amount of time, we can go from anger, to fear, to pain, to rage, to judgement. Our bodies come to and whatever we have stuffed for so long is no longer staying stuffed. We can still stuff the stuff even clean. It's just harder. We must really work to keep it down. Often when we must work that hard to keep our stuff stuffed it comes out sideways. It's someone else doing it 'to us'. When we are coming up against our own stuff that we can even recognize as us. It's just been the stuff that everyone else but upon us. 'If people would just stop putting their stuff on me, I would be just fine.'

We have no idea who we are. There is just too much stuff stuffed inside. The stuff inside us is either stuff we took on from others or stuff that we responded to and then decided to stuff. Damn that's a lot of stuff. Early recovery for me was like walking around feeling like 'pigpen', in a cloud of stuff that I just could not contain anymore.

My emotions were raw and expressing themselves. I was a massive pin cushion and all the needles in the pin cushion were stuff that hurt the cushion itself. I could barely breathe without feeling stuff. Then all that stuff had a great way of making up stories in my head to explain why I had stuffed all the stuff in the first place. It was like walking on fire and I'm not talking about a Tony Robbins seminar. No, it's more like every breath felt like stuff was coming up. Every conversation seemed to trigger stuff. Alright there was a lot of stuff roaming around in my chest and tummy area too.

Do you know how hard we must work to keep that much stuff down? That takes a lot of stuffing. Drugs can do a great job of keeping our heads so zombified and our bodies so numb or artificially vibrated on whatever effect the drug has that we don't pay attention to the stuff. Eventually you must do more and the more you do the less capable you are to respond to life. The stuff we've stuffed doesn't go away; we just can't feel it anymore. Sometimes there is so much stuff we have stuffed that it just seems to attack us. We cannot get away from the stuff. Maybe we create different personae, or the drugs stop working, or all that stuff just comes out sideways and we can't keep it bottled up anymore.

Maybe we get vicious or suicidal or homicidal. That happens when we have so much stuff inside it smothering us. So how in the hell do we unstuff??

Just stop for a minute. Breathe. Imagine you're in a dark cavern and you have a lighter. Light the lighter. See how it gives you just enough light to see around you but not too much that you are inundated with a lot of stuff. Just breathe. Pay attention to the lighter. Breathe as deep as you can and notice how far down you can breathe into your chest. Now hold the lighter out a little further, you can see a little further around you. When your head starts to engage again, just listen to the sound of your breath. Maybe you try a little mantra like 'I am' or 'Bless Me', 'Thy will', 'help'. We are just doing this to keep the thoughts from overwhelming you. 'Go away" works too. We are just finding an empty place away from the stuff. We are finding space.

Now listen to your breath. Focus on the sound of your breath. When thoughts come back imagine they are clouds high above you and they smoothly float by. You do not even need to hear them and engagement with the thoughts is completely optional. You will feel freer if you just allow them to move on by. Your free from the stuffy thoughts. Back to the cavern. Now imagine a campfire right before you. It keeps those intense feelings at a distance. This space, this little practice of hearing your breath, feeling the breath in your chest, feeling where it stops, this is all the engagement you need right now. Exploring just around the campfire, feeling safe and comfortable. We must start there. The stuff gets too overwhelming. It's there, but we can explore it slowly. We do not have to let it overwhelm us all at once. Coming back to a sensate state can happen overtime. We get used to be overwhelmed and overstimulated and its necessary to keep running. Believe me the stuff will still be there until we choose what to do with it.

First, we must find peace with the one place that is truly ours. The space inside us. Let it be empty for a moment. Let it be quiet and calm. I am aware of how those stuffy thoughts want to take over. But listening to a lot of our stuff does not make us more alive, just more stuffed.

Breathe my friend. Be inside, with each breath you can reach further out from the campfire. You can always retreat when you feel the stuff around you. Say hello. This is your home. You're welcome here. Know you have an eternity to make friends with your stuff. Soon you will love yourself through it. The emotional sensory system is the best communication system in the world. We just need to listen with space and calmness and patience. It is just stuff. You will eventually integrate it and clean the house. A lot of that stuff will go away. The rest will make you whole. Welcome Home.

Trust God, Clean the House, Work with others.

76.

GRATITUDE

I am extremely grateful to have lived over half of my life in recovery. I am grateful to have lived this long. At 28, when I got clean, I was very clear I did not want to live anymore. I said often, I will take God but get me off the planet. I was done. I was miserable. I was tired. Little did I know it, but I was deeply grieved. If I had known how deep the hurt was, I do not think I would have lived. Thank God for disassociation.

In the last week I have experienced the disease of addiction from a bird's eye view. It is horrific. What was painful was seeing a man I once lived with and still love, held deeply within the grip of addiction. We lose many wonderful people to the perils of using drugs. Many die in a state of unconsciousness, many live in a state of unconsciousness. Thinking only of getting and using. I am not sure which state is worse. Addiction itself is a horrid beast, whether one is actively using or not. When an addict has stopped using and has not received any treatment or recovery, life can be horrible.

77.

THERE IS A SCROUGE ON OUR STREETS

There is a scourge on our streets. It didn't start in this century. No, drugs and drug use has been around for centuries. Yet the war on drugs has taken on a life that threatens those threatened for way to long. The war on drugs quickly became a war on people of color. Starting with President Nixon in the early 1970's when he passed the 'Comprehensive Drug Prevention and Control Act of 1970'. The 'Drug Enforcement Administration' was created under the Nixon administration to minimize interagency feuds and pool together resources to fight illicit drug production, distribution, and use.

The 'war' was then heightened by President Reagans' effort to 'stop' drugs, which quickly escalated to war created in our streets. Starting with cities like Oakland, the drug war seemed carefully planned by Government agencies who let loose a devil we still cannot contain. One still wonders how much effort was purposely done to create the horrors in low income in predominantly black neighborhoods. The Anti-Drug Abuse Act of 1986 instituted a five-year minimum penalty without parole for the possession of five grams of crack cocaine. Meanwhile, the same sentence was given for the possession of 500 grams of powder cocaine. This 100:1 disparity was criticized by some as racially biased because crack cocaine was more likely to be used by poor Americans, many of whom were African Americans.

The disparity was made painfully obvious when Obama visited the prisons, and the camera caught the multitudes of men of color in the prison yards. Prisons which today are privatized and capitalized for commerce and control. Is this what the governed meant? Was this the vision that drove the Reagans to address a scourge that was worsened by their stating it into being? Yes, I know that the President and his lovely wife may have just been a mouthpiece. The damage in our streets today is enormous. What is truly very sad is that before a war on drugs was declared by the White House, the policy towards drugs was much more therapeutic and compassionate. Many senators were experienced in their own recovery and the atmosphere was much more conducive to the therapeutic value of helping those struggling with addiction.

Drug use exploded shortly after the Reagan era. I am not an expertise on the drug trade, and I have no doubt that early scandals, especially with our south American neighbors, were escalated by the drug trade. Yet are they responsible for the rise of our prison trade. I would say Hell No! Much of the reason for the increase in the sentencing for crack cocaine was a result of the crack epidemic and the mainstream spotlight that came with it. During this time, many low-income neighborhoods suffered from increased distribution and use of crack.

In 1980, there were 500,000 incarcerated in the United States, that number rose to 2.3 million in 2008. Similarly, the incarceration rate rose from 310 per 100,000 people to 1,000 per 100,000 in the same period. Since 2008, those numbers have seen some relief. Much of the decline in recent years is a result of newer legislation that has reduced prison sentences for thousands of inmates serving for drug-related crimes.

According to statistics from the World Prison Brief, the United States has the highest prison population of any country in the world, despite not having the highest population in the world. There are 2.1 million people in prison in the United States which has a population of 325 million people, compared to 1.6 million prisoners in China, a country that has a population of 1.38 billion people.

We need to look into our hearts to find why we would lock up addicts and especially devalue people of color in our country, who are much more likely to serve longer prison sentences which leads to a greater difficulty in turning their lives around. They are also more likely to earn a living through the drug trade. How much economic value do we support in the ghettos? How have we created the hell, or at least contributed to it, by the devaluation of homes, the lack of mortgages to people of color, the poorest schools, and then the push to gentrification which often is the worst form of abuse by literally pricing out people in their own neighborhoods.

78.

GROWING THE TRADE

I grew up in New Mexico. The land of enchantment. It still is. We moved to the small town of Las Vegas when I was in second grade. My father, having just left the satanic cult and his girlfriend that he left my mother for, went in search of a job for several months. He then moved us to Las Vegas when he was hired as a librarian for Highlands University.

My mother soon became the head librarian in the towns' public library. A block down the street from our home. Our block had a church on every corner except ours. Our house was on the fourth corner. An old Victorian block house with almost no insulation. This is where I came to consciousness, and it was a place of nightmares.

We walked to elementary school with our friends. My sister would complain because we had no one to brush our hair. There was no one to pay attention. Our parents were barely hanging on to their sanity. Yet Mama created a lovely public library, and her intelligence made a name for herself.

By eighth grade, I was visiting friends in a wider circle of our small city of 10,000 souls. One friend of mine lived in a three-room house shared by her two brothers and her numerous sisters. Sam, her brother, was beautiful, literally. He had this air about him, an aura that seemed to shine. I rarely spoke to him. Yet he was my first crush. He became a heroin addict, so did his brother and at least one or more of the sisters. They were a good-looking family. Their mother worked at the state mental hospital. She raised all the kids on a small salary with the father living a few blocks away for many years. It was Sam that awakened my awareness of the heroin crisis sweeping through I-40.

My friends and I spent quite a bit of time getting stoned. We were young and would also ride our bikes or go to movies, do kid stuff. By about 13 years old, getting stoned took up more time. This was 1973. Our little town became known as 'Smack City USA'. We had more heroin addicts than all of London. This was the town I grew up in until I was sent away to a boarding school in Albuquerque in high school. That probably saved my life. There was a deeper, almost more sinister activity happening in small towns, just like Las Vegas, all over northern New Mexico.

Recently I was told that there was an effort to create a much stronger drug trade along I-40. After all this route went straight across the country. Heroin was purposely distributed to the small towns along I-40 to create a supply chain. Several small towns were targeted in northern New Mexico. This successfully built and created an empire for the 'cousins' on the other side of the Mexican border. The small towns and the heroin addiction did a great deal to spread the drug trade in the southern part of the US.

I thought Sam was truly beautiful, inside and out. I believe he died young. I know at one point he was very concerned for his life. He was sentenced to prison for drugs and feared for his life since he was once a prison guard.

New Mexico builds two economic endeavors: Community Colleges and Prisons. If you attend the community college, you may get a job as a prison guard. If you don't, you'll most likely end up in prison. The only thing sadder than the growth of prisons in this country is the drug trade that created the economic incentive to lock people up. I didn't know much of this growing up in Las Vegas. That's a joke. We also have government agencies that supply professions for the PhD's and at one time New Mexico had amassed was one of the largest nuclear arsenals on the planet.

I did know from early on, I placed myself in positions to be hurt. There were a few times I walked back to town with girlfriends after being stuck in the country with young men we didn't know well. A few of my friends were not as lucky.

Getting us out of Las Vegas probably did save our lives. It didn't stop me from 'using'. That went on through college. I consider myself lucky to get through college. It was where my mind and heart felt the most pain. Pity the young adults that have nowhere to turn. I was one.

My past weighed heavy on me and gained a magnitude which created a density that drew me down little by little. I was still very unaware of the actual abuse that took place most of my childhood. It took years to face abuse with strength.

Is it just those that suffer abuse that are pained as young adults? No in fact many lovely children, raised with love and strong parenting still battle their demons. All too often caring parents may not be aware of the pain brewing with our babies, our teenagers, our young adults. I was aware of my son's addiction and the growing pain within him. Even with that, even caring and loving for him as deeply as I could, I could not stop the rejection of self he perpetrated on himself. Ending in death. Unfortunately, this pain and obsessive thinking is so deeply internalized we may not be able to see the level of discomfort our loved ones are living in. Love is vital, so is support, care and listening.

The resulting addiction is much deeper than the use of drugs. Drugs are a symptom of internal pain, internal rejection of self, the painful reckoning, which leaves so many with a negative sense of themselves. The need for support is essential. For me, I was dying inside. At 28, I could no longer live inside my own skin. I wanted to die. It was both a dramatic gesture and a deep need to believe I could live a fulfilling life. The chances of that seemed slimmer and slimmer. My thoughts were so negative. My heart was broken.

It was my cry for a better life at a point when I truly was willing to leave this earth, that brought me to addiction recovery. This saved my life. I stared death in the face. I saw my pain and tried to find help. I was lucky enough to find it, and to find the rooms of Narcotics Anonymous. I was slow to come back from the brink.

Now thirty-three years later, I have come to see the pain and struggle of addiction in others that I love so much. Being a witness to their pain and struggle has been an eye opening and heart-breaking experience. It is not over yet.

This is a deadly disease that is killing people daily, eating people from the inside out. It is painful to see and experience the theft, and destruction that accompanies it. More painful is seeing the walking dead on the streets, barely staying alive. A community that is aware of each other, yet they live to use and use to live, they've lost values that were very dear to them. We regain our values in recovery and we come to love ourselves. We gain our spirits back. How do we overcome this huge dilemma on our streets?

It was sad to see my partner so beaten and broken, his beautiful mind overcome with the negativity and hopelessness. He died at my house after doctors confirmed a serious heart condition.

His vitality zapped, yet his last day alive he was sweet and loving and kind. He was a good man; he deserved a good life. He wanted to get into treatment. Sometimes even our best intentions are robbed from us. This book is an ode to Shay and all of my loved ones that died from the internal and external horrors of addiction, Daddy, Thorne, Ian, and Shay. So many more addicts I've known who relapsed in recovery.

79.

REPRESENTING THE WORLD IN NA

In no way do I speak as a representative of Narcotics Anonymous. NA has no representatives speaking for them. In fact, NA has 12 Traditions that guide groups just as they have the 12 Steps which guide individuals through their recovery. NA also has 12 Concepts which guide service bodies, that help fulfill the services which help carry our message that "No addict need die from the disease of addiction."

I speak from my own experience, strength, and hope. Since the topics I have raised in this book are varied and can be considered rather controversial, I only speak as a member of NA about my experience in NA and this does, by no means, speak for the whole or reflect on the whole of our worldwide fellowship.

As is stated in the beginning of our reading on "The Twelve Traditions of NA";

"We keep what we have only with vigilance, and just as freedom for the individual comes from the Twelve Steps, so freedom for the

group
 springs from our Traditions."

In particular, I honor the 11th Tradition, which states.

"Our public relations policy is based on attraction rather than promotion,
we need always maintain personal anonymity at the level of press, radio, and films."

I very much honor the wisdom of our steps, traditions, and concepts so again I reiterate that what is said here is about my experience only, in a worldwide program of recovery, that has saved millions of lives around the world. The content of this book has addressed personal lives of people I dearly loved that struggled with addiction and eventually died. Their deaths all pertained to horrors of addiction, whether they died as a direct result from this disease.

 Addiction contributed to their pain and suffering and was sometimes seen as the only escape possible from the internal degradation they struggled with. The men who are the most precious in my heart; my father, my son, my fiancé, and finally my boyfriend; were all amazing men. They were all brilliant, gifted, artistic, articulate, compassionate, personable, and tortured. I write this to say, and to hopefully make a dent in the malady of addiction in our world, bringing the message of recovery to even one still suffering addict is vital to my world.

Narcotics Anonymous exists in order that 'No addict need die from the horrors of addiction.'

I again say that statement as an opinion, so that I am not violating any of edicts that any one person be seen as a voice, or representative, of NA. Whew! I think I have made clear the extreme respect I have for a society that has done so much for the world by offering a way to recover from the disease of addiction. I also want to deeply respect all 12 step programs and any other efforts made that have helped any suffering addicts. There is no patent on how 'we' recover. I truly believe our literature when it states, "The therapeutic value of one addict helping another is beyond compare."

If even one life is changed by the content of this book, then I have done what so many of us do, help the still suffering addicts find a new way to live.

As a passage from our book, Living Clean p. 257 reads:

"The more progress we recognize in ourselves and our fellows, the more we know is possible. What first appeared to us as a way out now offers us a way in-into a life we hadn't imagined, into joy, into hope, into growth that never stops. We continue to get better. We continue to discover new ways to live, new freedom, and new paths to explore. We travel together as one in fellowship, and we pave the road as we walk it for all who may follow. No matter how far we have come, or how far we know we have to go, when we live clean, the journey continues."

In NA, we have a service structure that is in the shape of an upside-down pyramid. Recovering addicts go to meetings. The meetings are supported by a core group of people that identify themselves as 'members' of a home group. You are a member when you say you are. Anyone can join any home group. Most often members join a home group when they feel fed by the group, whether that be with support, friendship, compassion, spiritual sustenance, or a group listens a soul into existence.

Our home groups are the most vital part of our service structure. This means we value the groups that are there to create an atmosphere of recovery and are there for 'the addict who still suffers.' A home group has several functions; we collect money to pay rent to the various facilities that allow us to use their space. This is most often a church or a facility that has a mission to help communities in some way. We also purchase supplies such as coffee, cream, sometimes snacks or cakes for anniversaries when our members celebrate another year clean. We do not endorse, finance or lend the NA name to any related facility or outside enterprise, lest problems of money, property, or prestige divert us from our primary purpose (6th Tradition).

We also collect monies to buy NA literature, key tags for length of time clean, pamphlets, and meeting schedules. There are positions in home groups, such as the 'group service representative' (GSR), treasurer, and secretary. The GSR then represents the home group at Area Service meetings. We will call that Area. In those meetings we have an executive committee that makes sure the meetings run smoothly. This includes the Area Chair, Vice Chair, Treasurer, Secretary. Then we have committees that serve the greater NA services at the area level. This includes literature committee, hospitals, and institutions (H& I), where our member carries the message of NA by holding meetings in prisons, treatment centers, hospitals. H&I meetings are usually recovering addicts sharing their experience, strength and hope. We find that carrying the message of a new way to live and helping those struggling with addiction helps addicts realize that NA is a support system which allow recovering addicts to get and stay clean.

Without the support and fellowship of NA, I would have gone back to the solution of numbing my problems with drugs years ago. I have continued to learn and grow because I get fed at NA. This is a 'we' program and NA also stands for "Never Alone".

We do know that drug addiction and recidivism is greatly diminished because 12 step programs are so effective at supporting their members. If only we could really be heard by the therapeutic community to the level that they understand how long-term clean time is much more possible with the support of a community. Besides H&I we also have Public Information committee (PI) also called PR, public relations. This service group carries the message to courts, treatment centers, prisons, probation officers, judges, courthouses, and police that NA is a resource available to them. Lastly, we also have activities committees and hold dances and activities like hikes and camp outs and conventions. We find that when addicts are of service, we are more likely to grow in our recovery and stay clean.

Area meetings are also where home groups donate to NA and the monies are collected and then passed to the next level of service. This is usually known as regional service. The regional service body is made up of representatives of the various home groups and they report out to the areas, which then the GSR's take the information back to the home groups. Regional representatives are often called RCM's, Regional committee members. Regional meetings represent a larger location, most often a state in the United States where NA got it's start. This service body also has a chair and vice chair, secretary and treasurer, and regional representatives of H&I, and PR.

The next level that has developed is the Zonal Regions. These are groups that represent several regions. Our zonal region represents thirteen western states. We meet and discuss how we can serve our members. The final body of service is the world service committee (WSC). This body has representatives of regions and/or zones from all over the world. In my current service position, I am now a member of the WSC. We are called Regional Delegates since we are elected by our regions or zones, and we represent them at the world service conference every two years. NA created a world service office several decades ago that is situated in the United States. We also have a World Board of Directors that help make decisions for the body as a whole.

NA exploded on the world scene from the efforts of recovering addicts at many levels. The Office is known as NAWS, Narcotic Anonymous World Services. Many trusted servants have served in positions that grew NA in the rest of the world. Today, Narcotics Anonymous is well established throughout much of North and South America, Europe, Australia, the Middle East, New Zealand, and Russia. Groups and NA communities continue to grow and evolve throughout the Indian subcontinent, Africa, and Asia.

Currently the organization is truly a worldwide multilingual, multicultural fellowship with over 70,000 weekly meetings in 144 countries. Narcotics Anonymous books and information pamphlets are currently available in 120 languages, with translations in process for 16 languages.

There are currently 16 zones around the world. Eight of the zones are in the United States. Eight are in the rest of the world. Zones outside of the US contain much more land mass and/or countries. For example, the African Zonal Forum contains fourteen countries, or regions, in Africa. Whereas most US regions represent one state. The Asian Pacific Zone contains twenty-nine (29) countries.

This includes Afghanistan, Aotearoa, New Zealand, Australia, Bahrain, Bangladesh, Bhutan, Cambodia, China, Guam, Hawaii, Hong Kong, India, Indonesia, Iran to name just a few. Regions or zones outside the US are just starting to get seated at the World Service Conference (WSC). Many of these countries are not seated, which means that they do not have representatives at the conference yet. The representatives of the zones speak for them.

This is the most amazing thing to me. I am a Regional Delegate and represent my state at the WSC. So far, I have only had the chance to serve at a virtual conference but even that was exciting to sit with representatives around the world. There are countries around the world where NA is just on fire!!! In some of the Arab countries, NA has spread like wildfire and our memberships have gotten so big that they have their own offices and publish their own literature. Now Covid has put a damper on that. Still the excitement for NA around the world is truly awe inspiring. I was enthralled at a World Conference in 2003 when I saw a huge map of the world used to show the countries joining the conference. The map would light up when the country gained access to the convention, and you could hear recovering addicts screaming and crying.

They were so excited to be at the convention and I have been changed ever since. I was inspired to see recovery grow and I am blessed to see what has happened in the world because of our efforts. There is nothing like being at a world convention with thousands of recovering addicts and seeing how we have changed our lives and how our efforts to help the still suffering addicts, in and out of the rooms, has created a worldwide organization that has provided freedom to so many.

This phenomenon will never bring back the men I loved so dearly. My heart is broken at the loss of those I love when I see so many who learn and grow and come to find themselves and a new way to live.

I love that I can sit and cry over who I've lost and then get on a service meeting and be in a NA world service zoom meeting with people all over the world. This is a bittersweet time and the wounds of losing people to the disease of addiction pierce me deeply. Yet I know that we have given the world a gift of recovery and so many people have found a new way to live, and they scream it at the top of their lungs. I am truly blessed to live what I have lived.

In truth I have experienced the deepest heartache of watching, not one, but four people struggle desperately with drug addiction and eventually lose their lives. No matter how heartbroken I am, I am extremely grateful to be clean. It has strengthened my recovery and my self-love. It was a very painful way to understand addiction when I was lucky enough to avoid the depths of hell, I have seen others experience degradation and death, from the inability or unwillingness to stop using the drugs that were killing them. I was considered a 'high bottom' addict. Obviously from my story, the abuse I suffered created an internal malaise that robbed me of my spirit, peace and happiness for most of my early life. I know intimately the dis-ease of the horrific obsessive thoughts, and physical compulsion, including debilitating emotions, and the worse enemy of our souls, the spiritual self-centeredness, that kept me centered in the devastating lack of self-love and total distrust of others.

We are responsible for the soul between our skin. I remain grateful to know of a solution for one of the most horrid diseases on our planet today. It takes the best and the brightest. NA saved my life. Each one of us is responsible for how we choose to live this life. Those that lost their lives to addiction, in and out of the rooms of NA, have given us a gift of knowing there is a better way to live. Thank you, world, for letting me see addicts recover all over this planet. I know that death is not the end. Those I love in the beyond are also working their 'recovery'. They don't get a free pass. So deeply do I know that we evolve past death and those that lost their lives to addiction are now guiding others that couldn't find their way. The growth and love I now know from my beloveds in the beyond, strengthens my fortitude and my deepest love and compassion. No matter how, or where, we come to know ourselves, our spirits, this remains to be true...The only way out is through!

80.

IT IS DONE

I believe all of us, my father, mother, Thorne, my wonderful son, Ian; and Shay made an agreement to really live and understand the depth of abuse, betrayal, and addiction in so many of its forms. Certainly, I believe there is a reason that I have seen three dear incredible men I loved die from some aspect of addiction in less than two years. I agreed to do this. To know what this was like, to understand from my perspective of being clean so long and my understanding of the depth of addiction. This is an internal struggle with our self-centeredness, malicious thoughts, and horrific feelings, that is the depth of the disease itself.

I have gained a greater understanding how deeply compromising drug abuse is which is laid on top of the despair we already feel about ourselves. I have seen the shame and calamity up close, and I have learned. Never had I experienced the debilitation this close and personal. Shay broke my heart. He showed me clearly how everything is under suspicion, and nothing is sacred to a using addict. We have a saying in NA about addiction, an addict's primary focus is the getting and using and finding ways and means to get more. I saw that so clearly and to my own detriment. I was vulnerable, both with the household costs and with the company we created, and lastly my car being stolen as well as the watch that meant so much to me.

Still, I believe we all did this to know. To grow deeply in our souls because we agreed to. I take responsibility for my part and for choosing to love these men and my parents and I fully am willing to see it this way. I am not a victim although, I have been hurt deeply. I have become deeply myself. Deeply loving, deeply forgiving for there is nothing to forgive. For the last five years I found out I was involved in satanic rituals as a child, which included being buried in coffins, almost being a sacrifice, and probably seeing others be sacrificed. Also living through very traumatic incestual rape and abuse by my father for my first eleven years.

I recognized painfully that almost every man I had been with for a decent amount of time mirrored some part of my father. I did not have many relationships and spent 17 years celibate to address this attraction to men that had aspects of my dad. I realized even after that time, when I started practicing divine openings, that I had an extremely low frequency most of my life, basically one of dread.

Understanding how to raise my vibration has brought happiness, awareness, and joy. Even through this painful period, I am much calmer even when I felt so betrayed by Shay or Thorne or Ian and put up with their asinine or addictive behavior. I am extremely grateful to do the deep work I did with my father and seeing him become free and now work with his parents is incredible.

I have seen Thorne become this amazing being. So incredibly loving and caring. Even Ian and Shay realize how loved they are.

It is done. It is well. I love every one of these beautiful souls that taught me the depth of myself, especially Shay. So difficult was this for both of us. He is beautiful and I love him deeply, as is my true love Thorne, my incredible healed father and mother and my son that is still the light of my life.

Thank you, Shay, for what I have come through. You of all had the hardest job and were an amazing petty tyrant. I bow down to you for your willingness to show me the most painful parts of my betrayal. I know it took deep love to do this. I choose to see how this helped me grow and accept what I lived in my early life. There is much more to existence than we know. If we decide that people have just hurt us and they are bad, it may not reflect what we do for each other that allows us to reach a greater evolution. We love and you are love and will see that self-love is the greatest gift in heaven. I will be here for all of you till I can beam as bright as all of you do.

Shay died two weeks ago today. He has been a part of two medium sessions, which is phenomenal because I have experienced that there is a process with death. All three men that I loved and lost, were very dense when they died. It is a part of the process of lightening up and becoming spirit.

They learn to use vibrations to express themselves since the voice box is no longer there. Thorne wore out Star, our medium, she was exhausted for three days because his energy was so dense on the first reading she did for him. Daddy was there to receive Thorne. Thorne always says that my love was all he had known about love. No one else had really loved him. Daddy was there and stayed with him. They were inseparable. When Ian died in February, Daddy, Mama, and Thorne were there. Ian was shocked, he said he just woke up on the other side. His death was so painful. My baby, my incredible intelligent, son with a heart so big and an amazing ability to love others passed at 29 years old. Ian's memorial was incredible. The love for him was astounding. That is when he found out how deeply he was loved.

It was humiliating to be with an addict that I had fallen in love with after I had 32 years clean. I knew better. I did grill him about his drug use. He lied to me. Still, I know we all had an agreement to do this. In the last two medium readings Shay has apologized for so much. He admitted stealing my watch. He also told me he was feeling the pain he caused me a thousand-fold. He also knows that we all agreed to this journey. I do NOT feel like a victim, and I refuse to be ashamed of the most powerful journey I have ever taken. I knew Shay was dying for months. Still, I could not continue to support someone who was not contributing at all, and at the same time was killing himself by continuing to use.

The worst part was Shay marrying the girlfriend he had before he we met in June, just last month. The next day his wife's family kicked him out and his wife for a day filed for legal separation. In truth, Shay and I still talked all the time. Going to his funeral and hearing his 'legally separated' wife talk about him as if they had been married since 2018 tore my heart to bits. I told him that today. Everyone wore black at the memorial; I wore white and walked in with my two precious loving friends that never stopped holding my arms. We were beautiful and we represented Shay.

He told me last Sunday, the day before the funeral, he did not want his memorial there. I was bereft. I was his love, not she. This is out of his dead mouth, not mine. He lived with me, made love to me, and never had relations with her. However, he became her Mormon husband, and, in this way, he honored how she and her family had taken care of him years ago. She 'got' to go to her Mormon heaven. Still this week was the hardest week for me of all. Grieving that I could not meet his family properly and I was never acknowledged, hurt deeply.

I was very blunt with him on the medium reading today and he felt my pain. He has deeply felt what he did to me and how mean he was, how he hurt me in many ways, not the least was financially, however withholding his love and affection was deeply painful. He knows and I know that he is telling the truth when he says he loved me more than any other woman. He said he was so angry that he couldn't be what he wanted to be. Couldn't have what we wanted together, a deep loving partnership and business partnership that would include a great deal of music and film and writing. He was truly brilliant and my heart bursts that instead he let his addiction take him down.

He betrayed me to the point I could not deny how my father had injured me so deeply. He made that real. It was not a charade for me. Instead, it was all of us agreeing to do this, to delve into abuse, satanism, addiction to understand. Most of all I feel a tremendous love for all of them. I am stronger and I know I am worthy of love. I developed self-love years ago. I just couldn't get past not having the love of a partner, a father, a protector, a man that was there to care for me. Now I know I am worth that and anything else wouldn't be enough. Never again will I share a home and be the sole provider. I am worth so much more. I deeply love all of these amazing spirits that had their own journeys. Shay will heal. With his family members that love him deeply and the love and guidance of Thorne and Daddy and Ian. Shay is good. We're good. I am still inside.

81.

WHEN WALKING ON THE WATER ISN'T ENOUGH

The ache is too strong
Crippling loneliness bends me over
And the ground doesn't move to hold me
The night's darkness fails to yield
Enough to let me through, and
Home is a cavernous fall away

And the softness is gone
The sweet lips that melted mine
Your embrace of molten lava
Is an echo where you were

I can't stay here
Please take me with you
Even the breeze against my cheek
Creates a yearning to cry
Into buried depths

Take me home baby
Walking on water isn't enough

Without your touch
The sweetness in your eyes

When we cringe to think
The touch of another could kill
And our homes are fortresses
To keep us in

The loss of touch
Screams painfully clear

Take me home sweet Mary
Bring the stars down
To lift me up
Let me feel him brush my hair
Let me wash his feet

Feel his sweet lips on the
Arch of my neck
And his hand in mine
The soul of him
Wrapped around me

Without that walking
On water isn't enough

Sweet constellation guides me home
The birds sing from his touch
When my heart cannot break anymore
Even walking on water isn't enough

For Thorne

~ With Love

Meg Mckeon

ABOUT THE AUTHOR

 Meg is the founder and owner of ProAcct LLC, an accounting and consulting firm specializing in government cost accounting. Meg has over 25 years' experience in Accounting and Government Auditing, Business, Arts & Media (performing arts, video and feature film), Project management and Production coordination, Manufacturing and Supply chain.

Meg is also the founder and owner of 'The Champion Enthusiast Inc' a journey of discovery and recovery of the most peaceful parts of ourselves in a truly fun filled engaging manner.

Meg received her Master's degree in Accountancy from the University of New Mexico in 2007 and moved on from her position as a senior auditor at Defense Contract Audit Agency in 2013. Her experience at DCAA allowed her to work with a vast number of contractors, from very small to extremely large. She also performed 95% of the audits done at DCAA and gained expertise in business system audits (especially accounting systems), forward pricing proposals, incurred cost proposals, provisional billing rates, post award audits, and earned value management systems audits. She was known as an 'in the weeds' auditor with a knack for finding discrepancies.

Meg specializes in conducting fun, engaging, and interactive seminars for large and small government contractors, subcontractors, and commercial companies addressing how to set up their books and records for Government accounting and/or cost based pricing. Her expertise is in developing indirect rates and creating budgeted rates for upcoming years based on previous years actuals, current proposed projects, and estimated upcoming efforts. She has worked as an analyst with prime contractors to develop subcontractor's compliant cost proposals and is known for effectively training contractors, no matter what level of experience they currently possess.

Meg developed strong investigative and discernment skills and gained a deep understanding of how a well-run company, with strong internal controls and excellent administration, runs. After years of finding many deficiencies and faulty systems, as well as reviewing very well run and efficient companies, she is delighted to help companies determine how to better their process. She works with large and small companies to develop adequate business systems, policies and procedures and strong internal controls and set up their books and records correctly for specialized government. It is our privilege to serve our customers with the high standards we used as auditors.

Made in the USA
Middletown, DE
04 November 2022

13967220R00197